MORE READING CONNECTIONS
Bringing Parents, Teachers, and Librarians Together

Elizabeth Knowles

and

Martha Smith

1999
LIBRARIES UNLIMITED, INC.
and Its Division
Teacher Ideas Press
Englewood, Colorado

Copyright © 1999 Elizabeth Knowles and Martha Smith
All Rights Reserved
Printed in the United States of America

No part of this publication may be reproduced, stored in a retrieval system, or transmitted, in any form or by any means, electronic, mechanical, photocopying, recording, or otherwise, without the prior written permission of the publisher. An exception is made for individual library media specialists and teachers, who may make copies of handouts for students and project participants for use in a single school. Other portions of the book (up to 15 pages) may be copied for in-service programs or other educational programs in a single school or library. Standard citation information should appear on each page.

LIBRARIES UNLIMITED, INC.
and Its Division
Teacher Ideas Press
P.O. Box 6633
Englewood, CO 80155-6633
1-800-237-6124
www.lu.com

Library of Congress Cataloging-in-Publication Data

Knowles, Elizabeth, 1946-
    More reading connections : bringing parents, teachers, and librarians together / Elizabeth Knowles and Martha Smith.
    x, 148 p. 22x28 cm.
    Includes bibliographical references.
    ISBN 1-56308-723-5
    1. Reading--Parent participation. 2. Book clubs. 3. Children--Books and reading. I. Smith, Martha, 1946- . II. Title.
LB1050.2.K66   1999
372.41--dc20

CONTENTS

Introduction ix

Chapter 1 BOOK CLUB BEGINNINGS 1
   Starting a Book Club 1
   Planning 1
      Moderator Responsibilities in Summary 1
      Member Responsibilities in Summary 2
   Publicity 2
      Comments from Parents. 2
   Preparations 2
   Process. 3
   Acquisition of Books 3
      Library Gift Book Program 3
      Bookshare Book Fair 4
      School Book Clubs 4
      Local Civic Organizations 4

Chapter 2 CONNECTING TO THE ARTS 5
   Overview 5
   Guided Reading Questions 5
      Journal Article 6
   Annotated Journal Articles 8
   Annotated Bibliography 8
   Bibliography 9
      Primary 9
      General. 11
   Web Sites. 13

Chapter 3 IS THERE TRUTH IN HUMOR? 15
   Overview. 15
   Guided Reading Questions. 15
      Journal Article 16
   Annotated Journal Articles 20
   Annotated Bibliography 20
   Bibliography 21
      General. 21
      Primary. 23
   Web Sites. 24

v

Chapter 4   FAMILIES IN TRANSITION 25
     Overview 25
     Guided Reading Questions 25
         Journal Article 26
     Annotated Journal Articles 29
     Annotated Bibliography 29
     Bibliography 31
         Primary 31
         General 32
     Web Sites 34

Chapter 5   SOCIAL ISSUES ... TOO GRAPHIC? 35
     Overview 35
     Guided Reading Questions 35
         Journal Article 36
     Annotated Journal Articles 39
     Annotated Bibliography 39
     Bibliography 41
         Primary 41
         General 42
     Web Sites 44

Chapter 6   FOLKLORE AND MYTHOLOGY— LITERATURE OF THE FIRESIDE 45
     Overview 45
     Guided Reading Questions 45
         Folklore 45
         Myth 46
         Journal Article 47
     Annotated Journal Articles 50
     Annotated Bibliography 50
     Bibliography 52
         Myths 52
         Folklore 53
     Web Sites 55

Chapter 7   PREDICTABLE SPORTS FICTION 57
     Overview 57
     Guided Reading Questions 57
         Journal Article 58
     Annotated Journal Articles 61
     Annotated Bibliography 61

	Bibliography	62
	Primary	62
	General	63
	Web Sites	65
Chapter 8	**MANY MODERN MAGAZINES FOR KIDS**	**67**
	Overview	67
	Guided Reading Questions	67
	Journal Article	68
	Annotated Journal Articles	86
	Web Sites	86
Chapter 9	**THE FINE ART OF PICTURE BOOKS**	**87**
	Overview	87
	Guided Reading Questions	87
	Journal Article	88
	Annotated Journal Articles	91
	Annotated Bibliography	91
	Bibliography	92
	Web Sites	96
Chapter 10	**SELECTION OR CENSORSHIP?**	**97**
	Overview	97
	Guided Reading Questions	97
	Journal Article	98
	Annotated Journal Articles	100
	Annotated Bibliography	100
	Bibliography	101
	Web Sites	103
Chapter 11	**LINK TO THE INTERNET**	**105**
	Overview	105
	Guided Surfing Questions	105
	Journal Article	106
	Annotated Journal Articles	108
	Bibliography	108
	Web Sites	109
	Professional Organizations for Educators	109
	Homework/References	109
	Search Engines	110
	Internet Filters	110
	For Teachers	110

Chapter 12 — MIDDLE SCHOOL CHALLENGE ... 111
- Overview ... 111
- Guided Reading Questions ... 112
  - *Journal Article* ... 113
- Annotated Journal Articles ... 117
- Annotated Bibliography ... 118
- Bibliography ... 119
- Web Sites ... 122

Chapter 13 — IS THERE GENDER EQUITY IN CHILDREN'S LITERATURE? ... 123
- Overview ... 123
- Guided Reading Questions ... 123
  - *Journal Article* ... 124
- Annotated Journal Articles ... 126
- Annotated Bibliography ... 126
- Bibliography ... 127
  - Books for Boys ... 127
  - Books for Girls ... 131
- Web Sites ... 134

Chapter 14 — AS LONG AS WE'RE TALKING ABOUT BOOKS ... 135
- Overview ... 135
  - *Journal Article* ... 136
- Annotated Bibliography ... 138
- Web Site ... 141

Chapter 15 — CONCLUSION ... 143
- Odds and Ends ... 143
- Questionnaire ... 144
- Reference List for Teachers and Parents ... 146

INTRODUCTION

Our first book, *The Reading Connection*, included information about starting a book club and covered these topics: series, science fiction, fantasy, nonfiction, reference, read-alouds, horror, historical fiction, picture books, poetry, multicultural books, award books, biographies, and bibliotherapy. All of the topics were shared in meetings with our school's parent community. This second book includes information about starting a book club and thirteen additional new and exciting topics.

SCOPE AND PURPOSE

The purpose of this book is to interest teachers, librarians, and parents in establishing a book club for the school community. The book club members explore current children's literature and help children become lifelong readers. This book is essential in light of current trends indicating that children are reading less and less each year. Developing lifelong readers must become a home and school partnership. Topics and sample book club sessions contained herein involve literature for prekindergarten through eighth-grade students.

BOOK CLUB BEGINNINGS

The idea of a book club for parents in our school began with a parent's very real distress over what her daughter was reading from our school library. Being an affluent private school with strict entrance requirements meant we had many excellent young readers. These students tend to read by author, and some of our third-graders can easily handle young adult reading—but the topics and sophistication of some of these books upset this parent.

Therefore, we developed a program to inform parents of what is on the shelves of libraries and bookstores today. We also showed them how to steer their children toward good and appropriate selections, while encouraging and nurturing a love for reading.

The program developed as a book club, but the key to the program's success was the bibliographies and handouts we made available to the parents. They also enjoyed getting more involved in reading with their children and knowing about the variety of books available.

CHILDREN AND BOOKS

Choosing the best books for children is a difficult task. New titles, authors, and series appear in bookstores regularly. Children who read well usually come from homes where there are many books, magazines, and newspapers. Their parents make time for reading and place importance and value on reading aloud to their children from a very early age.

These parents also talk to their children, ask questions that require reflection, stimulate curiosity, and encourage their children to talk about travels and experiences. Now, television, computers, videos, and video games are taking up the time children used to spend reading. It is up to the parents to turn the television and video games off and turn their children on to reading. The best way to do this is to read to them, starting at a very early age with picture books and continuing through the middle school years.

The Association of Booksellers for Children uses the slogan, "The most important twenty minutes of your day!" to encourage reading aloud to children. They feel it is so important that pediatricians should recommend reading to children as part of a recommended routine, like dental hygiene, good nutrition, and standard inoculations. Reading aloud should be part of every school day, and every child should have books at home.

Chapter 1

Book Club Beginnings

STARTING A BOOK CLUB

A book club is only as strong and dynamic as its moderators and members. Look around at school and choose a fellow faculty member you would like to work with, one who shares your love for and commitment to reading. Once you have established your meeting format and who your members will be, split the responsibilities and launch your program.

PLANNING

Where should meetings be held? Your site should be centrally located and convenient. We selected our school library.

What is the best time for the club to meet? The time depends on your target group. Working parents might find early evening or Saturday morning convenient. If you are including teachers and students, after school might be better. Our group met first thing in the morning on a Wednesday. Your parents' association might be helpful in selecting a time.

How long should meetings last? We found that they usually lasted an hour and fifteen minutes, which was about all the time we could spare from our regular schedule.

How often should the club meet? To begin, we suggest meeting five or six times a year. A five-month schedule might include October, November, February, March, and April. A sixth-month schedule could add either September or May. We tried to avoid the beginning of school and the busy time toward the end of the school year.

Moderator Responsibilities in Summary

1. Be familiar with the books on the topic.
2. Prepare additional discussion questions.
3. Have handouts and bibliographies—included in this book—ready for club meetings.
4. Know some interesting facts about selected authors, books, and genre.
5. Include current clippings or controversial articles appropriate to present or previous topics.

6. Distribute flyers and reminders.
7. Provide necessary books.
8. Provide beverages and refreshments.
9. READ and have FUN!

Member Responsibilities in Summary

1. Take notes as you read.
2. Respond to the guided reading questions.
3. Share your feelings and experiences.
4. Read a book to a child.
5. Attend meetings and be an active participant.
6. READ and have FUN!

PUBLICITY

How do you get the word out about the book club? We picked the dates ahead of time so that they could be included in the school calendar and the information given out by the parents' association. Advertise throughout the school and introduce the program during Back to School Night or Open House, as well as at the first parents' association meeting. Send out invitations to prospective club members and suggest that they bring a friend. If the group is small at first, do not be discouraged; the word will spread and the group will grow.

Comments from Parents

"It is good to have guidelines when choosing books for the kids to read. Time is limited so you want them to read worthwhile books."

"The handouts were excellent, very informational for future use."

"It was a wonderful year of meetings."

"The meetings were informative. I also enjoyed the camaraderie of meeting other parents who were interested in reading and education. I enjoyed familiarizing myself with the quality books available to my children."

PREPARATIONS

What about the first topic? Select one of the sessions you like and are enthusiastic about. We usually started our club in October and began with "Horror for Kids." This topic was timely and generated a great deal of interest and curiosity.

How do you get books to the parents? For the first session, we set aside books in the library for the topic we had chosen, three weeks in advance. We notified the parents that they could come and check out the books they would like to read; we also offered to select some books and send them home with their son or daughter. This procedure is necessary only for the first meeting. Thereafter, books for the next session should be available at the end of each session. With this system, the books discussed that day are returned and exchanged for books on the next topic. Often, parents checked out different books on the topic just discussed, as well as books on the new topic.

What happens at the initial meeting? At the first meeting, provide name tags and have everyone introduce themselves, including the moderators. Briefly describe the club's purposes and benefits. Provide beverages and refreshments in an informal atmosphere. Push tables together or form a circle. Keep it light and fun.

PROCESS

What is the format of the meetings? The moderators should see that all members participate. After a quick update on the previous session, introduce the topic for the present session. Ask each member to comment on the books just read. Usually this is all it takes, but have some discussion questions ready in case of a lull. Draw out any members who tend to sit back. Do not allow any one member to dominate the discussion. Highlight some books in the bibliography included herein, choosing titles that are appropriate for your group. Distribute handouts at the beginning of your meeting. These might include the overview, journal article, annotated journal articles, annotated bibliography, and bibliography. Close each session with a summary of the present topic and a brief introduction to the next topic. Introduce a few books, hand out the guided reading questions, and you are on your way.

ACQUISITION OF BOOKS

How can you obtain the books needed for your book club? The following ideas were used to enhance our library and classroom collections.

Library Gift Book Program

At the beginning of the school year, send or hand out a general flyer explaining the program to all parents. Interested parents make a specified donation to the library to purchase a book(s) to mark an occasion. (A bookplate is placed in the book along with a bookmark inscribed with the name and occasion. The person honored, who is the first allowed to check out the gift book, is also given a bookmark inscribed with his or her name and the occasion as a reminder of the donated book. The funds donated cover the cost of the entire program, including preselected books and stationery.)

Possible occasions for donating books are numerous. We have even had a book donated in honor of a new family member—a puppy! Some suggestions include the following:

In Memory of

Have a Great School Year

Congratulations on a Good Year

Happy Valentine's Day—I love you! (a small red heart was affixed to the bookplate and bookmark)

To a Special Teacher

Merry Christmas

Happy Hanukkah

This is a very successful program. Solicit two or three reliable parents from the parents' association to organize and supervise the mailings and paperwork.

Bookshare Book Fair

The Bookshare Book Fair runs like any other book fair, with the exception that students and parents provide the books sold. Three weeks before the book fair, students bring in books they no longer want or have outgrown. Books are sorted by age group and checked for appropriateness. The library staff gets first pick of the books, to select any that would enhance the school's collection. At the fair, which is held in the school library, all books are sold for 50 cents each, regardless of whether they are paperback or hardcover.

We hold this function twice a year, once in the fall and once in the spring. The biggest problem we have is storage of the books prior to the book fair. Because we tended to receive a large number of books for the very young child, we invited local nursery schools to come and buy on the very last day of the book fair. Unsold books were either saved for the next book fair or donated to appropriate local charities. This worthwhile program has enhanced the library's collection and placed recycled books in the hands of many, many children.

School Book Clubs

School book clubs are another source of books and are worth the recordkeeping. They are a particularly good source of less expensive books. If you are concerned that some children are unable to purchase books, try using your bonus points for extra books. Book clubs are a good source for multiple copies of a particular book or a set of books related to one of the sessions.

Local Civic Organizations

Identify community sponsors and civic groups that might grant money or make book donations. Some organizations to consider are Kiwanis, Junior League, Rotary, public libraries, local businesses, neighborhood associations, and your school parents' association. A letter or a personal visit from the moderators may be most effective. Let the organization know that its support will be gratefully acknowledged on all handouts.

Chapter 2

Connecting to the Arts

OVERVIEW

All children should have access to books that explore different aspects of creative expression. Books on painting, dancing, theater, and cinema—where ordinary characters discover hidden talents—encourage children to explore and discover their own artistic abilities. Books from the world of performance arts might feature one or more of these viewpoints: the performer's, the originator's (composer, author), and the audience's. Connecting art, music, or dance to literature is a great way to encourage a child to dream. Children love to imitate, but first attempts at artistic creativity are often hesitant. Providing a variety of books about the arts can stimulate, inspire, and increase confidence.

GUIDED READING QUESTIONS

1. Was the information in your book presented in an interesting and accurate manner?
2. Which sensory impression was strongest?
3. Did your book invoke a mood or emotion?
4. Does your book encourage free and creative expression in children?
5. Was the subject matter of your book interesting and unique?
6. Was the book presented in an artistic style?
7. Do you think this book would entice a child to become involved in this particular art?

From *More Reading Connections*. © 1999. Knowles/Smith. Libraries Unlimited. (800) 237-6124.

JOURNAL ARTICLE

Sunday in the Library with . . .

Call on Georgia O'Keeffe and Picasso when you need help promoting art books.

You have a shelf or two of fine art books in your children's collection. They are visual treats: well-written and incredibly attractive. You have selected them with care. But to your great frustration, they are gathering dust. How do you entice (or coerce, bribe, bully) people into checking them out? That was the challenge we faced at Brown County Library in Green Bay, WI.

Our answer was to highlight the collection by inviting famous "artists" to our library for a "Meet the Artist" series. Now going into its third year, the annual four-part series for grades K–3 has proved to be very popular. A tradition has taken root.

For each hour-and-a-half program, we set up an attractive display of art books. The books, particularly artists' biographies, now circulate regularly through the year. Teachers who became aware of the materials through the series also use the collection more often.

Time-Traveling Artists

We schedule the "Meet the Artist" series for Sunday afternoons in January because Sundays attract family visits (especially in winter). We picked January because Wisconsin winters can be quite harsh and "white"—color and stimulation feed people's hunger this time of year.

Each program includes:

- a brief introduction of the featured artist by the host,
- an appearance by the artist (impersonated by a volunteer from the community), and
- an art project related to the artist's work.

Each session's 10- to 15-minute introduction includes interesting biographical details, brief comments about reproductions on display, as well as remarks about the artist's style. Then the real fun begins.

Through the magic of a time machine fashioned out of cardboard with dials and buttons, the "artist" appears. Picasso flashed on the scene, complaining that he had been snatched from a bullfight. Monet was dripping with water, explaining that he had been painting by the sea and gotten splashed. Georgia O'Keeffe was just plainly irritated by the interruption. The children enjoyed the time-machine gimmick enormously.

The actors and their characters determine the nature of their performances. Our host interviewed Vincent van Gogh with little audience participation because the local artist who played the painter was uneasy about public speaking, but enthusiastic about promoting the arts. His subdued Van Gogh read quietly from a letter from his brother.

The flamboyant friend of a staff member, however, played the charismatic sculptor Louise Nevelson by talking directly to the crowd, asking questions, and making offhand remarks. A staff member who had lost her hair

---

By Lee Walker Bock. Reprinted with permission of *School Library Journal* (December 1996), page 49. Lee Walker Bock is Children's Librarian at the Brown County Library in Green Bay, WI.

during chemotherapy agreed to play Georgia O'Keeffe. She dressed in the artist's signature black hat and head scarf, using skulls and flowers to bring back memories of her life.

With reproductions and props, we create a simple setting for each program. Van Gogh, for example, sat at a red table like the one in the famous painting of his bedroom, while Grandma Moses sat in a rocking chair.

The last half of the program involves at least one hands-on art activity that emphasizes a technique or material used by the artist: paints thickened with cornstarch (Van Gogh); structures built from scrap and found materials (Nevelson); large flowers that couldn't quite fit within the boundaries of the paper (O'Keeffe) and dot-filled stencil forms (Seurat). (*Kid's Crazy Concoction* by Jill Hansen [Williamson, 1995] is an excellent source for artist-related activities.)

Each Year a New Canvas

We were fortunate that a customer who used the children's fine art collection extensively agreed to host the series. This simplified planning considerably.

Finding volunteers to play the artists was not as easy. The first year, we contacted Evergreen Theatre, a local community theatre group, which canvassed its members for people willing to develop a role. The second year, staff identified players, mostly from among friends.

To our great delight, people now suggest artists as players for future series, and in some instances, volunteer to develop roles. Next month's series will feature Michelangelo, Diego Rivera, Frank Lloyd Wright, and Faith Ringgold, played by two parents and two teachers.

The diversity and beauty of art can inspire both children and adults. Take a look at your collection and the people in your community. Perhaps you can find a way to showcase this rich resource. And get the dust off those books. ▲

ANNOTATED JOURNAL ARTICLES

Boulanger, Susan. "Language, Imagination, Vision: Art Books for Children," *Horn Book Magazine* (May/June 1996): 295–305.

> Many art books for children are reviewed in this article. Books for the very young on lines, shapes, and colors are included, using famous works of art to illustrate these concepts. A series on paintings, books on art history, and books on famous artists and sculptors are all included.

Greenlaw, M. Jean. "Books in the Classroom," *Horn Book Magazine* (September/October 1991): 636–39.

> This article explains a connection between a literature class and the arts using a spirit of exploration. The article suggests many titles for developing various themes connecting literature and the arts.

Peck, Robin, and Barbara Rankin. "Connecting Books and the Arts," *Book Links* (September 1996): 37–41.

> Connecting reading to a theme is often a great way to capture children's interest. This article suggests the arts as a theme and recommends having groups of children explore the arts from different perspectives. An area such as dance, theater, or painting might be a focus, with each group reading several books about that topic. The article includes a list of possibilities grouped by different areas of the arts.

ANNOTATED BIBLIOGRAPHY

Auch, Mary Jane. *Bantam of the Opera.* Holiday House, 1997.

> Luigi is a bantam rooster who is bored with crowing the same old thing. His talents are not appreciated, so he wanders farther and farther away from home. One afternoon, while perched on the farmer's railing, he hears the opera *Rigoletto* for the first time, and it becomes his favorite. Unbeknownst to the farmer and his wife, Luigi goes to the city to see the opera *Rigoletto*, and does not return to the farm thereafter. When the lead tenor and his understudy come down with the chicken pox, Luigi gets his big chance—and goes on to become the most popular tenor of the Cosmopolitan Opera Company.

Catalanotto, Peter. *The Painter.* Orchard, 1995.

> Father is a painter who works in his studio throughout the day. When he is not in his studio, he plays with his little girl at breakfast, lunch, and dinner. After dinner, she is allowed in the studio. She eventually becomes a painter, too.

Gatti, Anne. *The Magic Flute.* Chronicle Books, 1997.

> Wolfgang Amadeus Mozart wrote *The Magic Flute* in 1791, the same year he died. This fairy tale was created for the popular theater.
>
> Pamina is the daughter of the evil Queen of the Night. The sorcerer, Sorastro, snatches Pamina from the Queen. The Queen meets Prince Tamino and offers her daughter in marriage if he rescues Pamina. Tamino doesn't know if he should trust the cold-eyed Queen. After three tests of courage and love, Tamino, Pamina, and Sorastro

overcome the evil Queen; good triumphs over evil, and Tamino and Pamina look forward to a happy life together.

A music compact disc comes with the book. Each page of the book corresponds with the appropriate musical selection.

Gray, Libba Moore. *My Mama Had a Dancing Heart.* Orchard, 1995.

"My Mama had a dancing heart and she shared that heart with me." A ballet dancer recalls how her mother and she would celebrate each of the seasons with various dances. For instance, in the winter they danced the snow-angel ballet and the slow-motion dance of the funny old snowmen. Mama would say, "Bless the world, it feels like a tip-tapping song-singing finger-snapping kind of day. Let's celebrate!"

Just Like Me: Self-Portraits and Stories. Harriet Rohmer, editor. Children's Book Press, 1997.

Fourteen artists from many different backgrounds are highlighted in this collection. They have all created multicultural picture books for children, published by Children's Book Press. Two pages are devoted to each artist. On one page is a self-portrait and the opposite page has a personal story. The artists express their concerns and feelings and reflect on what art means to them.

Newman, Barbara. *The Illustrated Book of Ballet Stories.* DK Publishing, 1997.

The five ballets described in this book are more than 100 years old. The featured magical tales are The Sleeping Beauty, Giselle, Coppelia, Swan Lake, and The Nutcracker. Each story is retold and illustrated with drawings and photographs. Additional illustrations and text feature the settings, lighting, dancers' positions, principal movements, and accompanying music that create the desired effect. A compact disc with eighteen musical highlights is included.

Pinkney, Andrea Davis. *Duke Ellington: The Piano Prince and His Orchestra.* Hyperion Books, 1998.

Edward Kennedy Ellington was born in 1899. He liked to be called Duke. Though his parents gave him piano lessons, he'd rather have been playing baseball. He called that kind of piano music "umpy-dump sound" and quit. Later on, he heard a different type of music—ragtime—and went back to playing the piano. Soon he was making up his own melodies, and at the age of nineteen he was playing in clubs and cabarets. He formed his own band and went to Harlem, in New York City, where jazz music ruled. In 1943, the Duke and his orchestra performed his musical suite, *Black, Brown and Beige,* at Carnegie Hall. This special suite celebrated the history of African-American peoples. Ellington was known as the King of the Keys, the Piano Prince, and the Duke. He died May 24, 1974, but his influence continues today.

BIBLIOGRAPHY

Primary

Ackerman, Karen. *Song and Dance Man.* Alfred A. Knopf, 1988.
Agee, Jon. *The Incredible Painting of Felix Clousseau.* Farrar, Straus & Giroux, 1988.
Ancona, George. *The Piñata Maker.* Harcourt Brace, 1994.

From *More Reading Connections.* © 1999. Knowles/Smith. Libraries Unlimited. (800) 237-6124.

2 ▲ CONNECTING TO THE ARTS

Brett, Jan. *Fritz and the Beautiful Horses.* Houghton Mifflin, 1981.
Brighton, Catherine. *Mozart: Scenes from the Childhood of the Great Composer.* Doubleday, 1990.
Cooney, Barbara. *Miss Rumphius.* Viking, 1982.
dePaola, Tomie. *The Art Lesson.* G. P. Putnam's Sons, 1989.
Derolf, Shane. *The Crayon Box That Talked.* Random House, 1997.
Downing, Julie. *Mozart Tonight.* Bradbury Press, 1991.
Fiarotta, Noel, and Phyllis Fiarotta. *Music Crafts for Kids: The How-To Book of Music Discovery.* Sterling, 1993.
Fox, Dan. *Go In and Out the Window: An Illustrated Songbook for Young People.* Henry Holt, 1987.
Freeman, Tony. *Photography.* Children's Press, 1983.
Gauch, Patricia Lee. *Dance Tanya.* Philomel, 1989.
Goble, Paul. *Love Flute.* Bradbury Press, 1992.
Hart, Jane. *Singing Bee! A Collection of Favorite Children's Songs.* Lothrop, Lee & Shepard, 1982.
Hausherr, Rosmarie. *What Instrument Is This?* Scholastic, 1992.
Hayes, Ann. *Meet the Orchestra.* Harcourt Brace Jovanovich, 1991.
Heller, Nicholas. *The Giant.* Greenwillow Books, 1997.
Hepworth, Cathi. *Antics! An Alphabetical Anthology.* Putnam, 1992.
Heyer, Marilee. *The Weaving of a Dream.* Viking Kestrel, 1986.
Hoffman, Mary. *Amazing Grace.* Dial Books for Young Readers, 1991.
Holabird, Katharine. *Angelina Ballerina.* Clarkson N. Potter, 1983.
Huberman, Caryn, and JoAnne Wetzel. *Onstage Backstage.* Carolrhoda Books, 1987.
Isadora, Rachel. *Lili on Stage.* G. P. Putnam's Sons, 1995.
———. *Swan Lake.* G. P. Putnam's Sons, 1991.
Kilnik, Paul. *Dancing to America.* Dutton Children's Books, 1994.
Knox, Bob. *The Great Art Adventure.* Rizzoli, 1993.
Komaiko, Leah. *Aunt Elaine Does the Dance from Spain.* Doubleday, 1992.
Krull, Kathleen. *Gonna Sing My Head Off.* Alfred A. Knopf, 1992.
Kuklin, Susan. *Going to My Ballet Class.* Bradbury Press, 1989.
Kuskin, Karla. *The Philharmonic Gets Dressed.* HarperCollins, 1982.
Locker, Thomas. *The Young Artist.* Dial Books for Young Readers, 1989.
Lowery, Linda. *Twist with a Burger Jitter with a Bug.* Houghton Mifflin, 1995.
Lyons, Mary E. *Stitching Stars: The Story Quilts of Harriet Powers.* Charles Scribner's Sons, 1993.
Macaulay, David. *Black and White.* Houghton Mifflin, 1990.
Martin, Bill. *The Maestro Plays.* Henry Holt, 1994.
Mathers, Petra. *Sophie and Lou.* HarperCollins, 1991.

Mayer, Marianna. *The Twelve Dancing Princesses*. Morrow Junior Books, 1989.

McNally, Darcie. *In a Cabin in a Wood*. Cobblehill Books, 1991.

Micklethwait, Lucy. *A Child's Book of Art*. Dorling Kindersley, 1993.

Mitchell, Barbara. *Raggin': A Story about Scott Joplin*. Carolrhoda Books, 1987.

Moss, Lloyd. *Zin! Zin! Zin! A Violin*. Simon & Schuster, 1995.

Orozco, Jose-Luis. *De Colores and Other Latin-American Folk Songs for Children*. Dutton Children's Books, 1994.

Raschka, Chris. *Charlie Parker Played Be Bop*. Orchard, 1992.

Schami, Rafik. *A Hand Full of Stars*. Dutton Children's Books, 1990.

Schroeder, Alan. *Ragtime Tumpie*. Joy Street, 1989.

Staines, Bill. *All God's Critters Got a Place in the Choir*. E. P. Dutton, 1989.

Van Allsburg, Chris. *The Z Was Zapped*. Houghton Mifflin, 1987.

Van Laan, Nancy. *Buffalo Dance*. Little, Brown, 1993.

Walter, Mildred Pitts. *Ty's One Man Band*. Simon & Schuster, 1987.

Waters, Kate, and Madeline Slovenz-Low. *Lion Dancer: Ernie Wan's Chinese New Year*. Scholastic, 1990.

Watson, Wendy. *Frog Went A-Courting*. Lothrop, Lee & Shepard, 1990.

Wilhelm, Hans. *The Bremen Town Musicians*. Scholastic, 1992.

Winter, Jeanette. *Cowboy Charlie: The Story of Charles M. Russell*. Harcourt Brace, 1995.

Yenawine, Philip. *Shapes*. Delacorte Press, 1991.

General

Ardley, Neil. *Music*. Alfred A. Knopf, 1989.

Axelrod, Alan. *Songs of the Wild West*. Simon & Schuster, 1991.

Beneduce, Ann. *A Weekend with Winslow Homer*. Rizzoli, 1993.

Blizzard, Gladys S. *Come Look with Me: Enjoying Art with Children*. Thomasson-Grant, 1990.

Bussell, Darcey. *The Young Dancer*. Dorling Kindersley, 1994.

Collier, James Lincoln. *Louis Armstrong: An American Success Story*. Macmillan, 1985.

Cummings, Pat. *Talking with Artists*. Bradbury Press, 1992.

———. *Talking with Artists, Volume Two*. Simon & Schuster, 1995.

Feiffer, Jules. *The Man in the Ceiling*. HarperCollins, 1993.

Gardiner, Stephen. *Inside Architecture*. Prentice-Hall, 1983.

Gardner, Jane Mylum. *Henry Moore: From Bones and Stones to Sketches and Sculptures*. Four Winds Press, 1993.

Greenberg, Jan, and Sandra Jordan. *The Sculptor's Eye: Looking at Contemporary American Art*. Delacorte Press, 1993.

Greene, Carol. *Johann Sebastian Bach: Great Man of Music*. Children's Press, 1992.

Hayden, Melissa. *The Nutcracker Ballet*. Andrews & McMeel, 1992.

Higginsen, Vy. *This Is My Song!* Crown, 1995.

Hollyer, Belinda. *Stories from the Classical Ballet*. Viking, 1995.

Horosko, Marian. *Sleeping Beauty: The Ballet Story*. Atheneum, 1994.

Hunt, Jonathan. *Illuminations*. Simon & Schuster, 1989.

Isaacson, Philip M. *Round Buildings, Square Buildings, and Buildings That Wiggle Like a Fish*. Alfred A. Knopf, 1988.

King, Penny, and Clare Roundhill. *Landscapes*. Crabtree, 1996.

Krull, Kathleen. *Lives of the Artists: Masterpieces, Messes (And What the Neighbors Thought)*. Harcourt Brace Jovanovich, 1995.

———. *Lives of the Musicians: Good Times, Bad Times (And What the Neighbors Thought)*. Harcourt Brace Jovanovich, 1993.

Lasker, David. *The Boy Who Loved Music*. Viking, 1979.

Lepscky, Ibi. *Pablo Picasso*. Barron's Educational Series, 1984.

Lightfoot, Marge. *Cartooning for Kids*. Greey de Pencier, 1993.

Meyer, Susan E. *Edgar Degas*. Harry A. Abrams, 1990.

Miller, Jim. *The Rolling Stone: Illustrated History of Rock and Roll*. Random House, 1976.

O'Reilly, Susie. *Batik and Tie-Dye*. Thomson Learning, 1993.

Pinkney, Andrea Davis. *Alvin Ailey*. Hyperion Books, 1993.

Probosz, Kathilyn Solomon. *Martha Graham*. Dillon, 1995.

Raboff, Ernest. *Pierre-Auguste Renoir*. J. B. Lippincott, 1987.

Rachlin, Ann. *Brahms*. Barron's Educational Series, 1993.

Richmond, Robin. *Children in Art*. Ideal Children's Books, 1992.

———. *Introducing Michelangelo*. Little, Brown, 1991.

Romei, Francesca. *Leonardo da Vinci: Artist, Inventor, and Scientist of the Renaissance*. Peter Bedrick Books, 1994.

Russell, Marion. *Along the Santa Fe Trail: Marion Russell's Own Story*. Whitman, 1993.

Salvi, Francesco. *The Impressionists: The Origins of Modern Painting*. Peter Bedrick Books, 1994.

Sills, Leslie. *Visions: Stories About Women Artists*. Whitman, 1993.

Simon, Charnan. *Evelyn Cisneros: Prima Ballerina*. Children's Press, 1990.

———. *Midori: Brilliant Violinist*. Children's Press, 1993.

Sirett, Dawn. *My First Paint Book*. Dorling Kindersley, 1994.

Skira-Venturi, Rosabianca. *A Weekend with Van Gogh*. Rizzoli, 1993.

Switzer, Ellen. *The Magic of Mozart: Mozart, the Magic Flute and the Salzburg Marionettes*. Atheneum, 1995.

Tucker, Jean S. *Come Look with Me: Discovering Photographs with Children.* Thomasson-Grant, 1994.

Turner, Robyn Montana. *Frida Kahlo.* Little, Brown, 1993.

———. *Mary Cassatt.* Little, Brown, 1992.

Venezia, Mike. *Aaron Copland.* Children's Press, 1995.

———. *Francisco Goya.* Children's Press, 1991.

Ventura, Piero. *Great Composers.* G. P. Putnam's Sons, 1989.

Walton, Sally, and Stewart Walton. *Stencil It!* Sterling, 1992.

Wolff, Virginia Euwer. *The Mozart Season.* Henry Holt, 1991.

Zhensun, Zheng, and Alice Low. *A Young Painter: The Life and Paintings of Wang Yani—China's Extraordinary Young Artist.* Scholastic, 1991.

WEB SITES

The Andy Warhol Museum Home Page
http://warhol.org/warhol/

A. Pintura, Art Detective
http://www.eduweb.com/pintura/

Art History
http://www.yahoo.com/Arts/Art_History/Artists/

The Art Institute of Chicago
http://www.artic.edu/aic/firstpage.html

Art Lessons/Games
http://www.artswire.org/kenroar/links/artgames.html

Dallas Museum of Art
http://www.unt.edu/dfw/dma/www/dma.htm

Diego Rivera Virtual Museum
http://www.diegorivera.com/diego_home_eng.html

Garden State Pops Youth Orchestra
http://www.gspyo.com/

JazClass
http://www.ozemail.com/au/~jazclass/

Jazz Central Station
http://jazzcentralstation.com/

John Philip Sousa Page
http://www.dws.org/sousa/about.htm

K-12 Resources for Music Educators
http://www.isd77.k12.mn.us/resources/staffpages/shirk/k12.music.html

Kathleen Krull
http://www.friend.ly.net/scoop/biographies/kkrull.html

Kennedy Center's Arts Edge
http://artsedge.kennedy-center.org/

Marsalis on Music Online
http://www.wnet.org:80/mom/homepage.html

Metropolitan Museum of Art
http://www.metmuseum.org/htm1file/education/kid.html

Mr. Holland's Opus Tool Kit
http://www.amc-music.com/opus/index.htm

Music Magic
http://www.geocities.com/Hollywood/Hills/5230/music2.html

Music, The Universal Language
http://www.jumpoint.com/bluesman/

Music World for Kids
http://members.aol.com/muswrld/

Musical Instruments—Illustrations and Descriptions
http://reseau.chebucto.ns.ca/Culture/SNS/instruml.html

National Gallery of Art, Washington, DC
http://www.nga.gov/

National Museum of American Art
http://www.nmaa.si.edu

Phoenix Art Museum
http://www.azcentral.com/community/phxart/home.html

Piano on the Net
http://www.artdsm.com/music.html

Web Museum
http://sunsite.unc.edu/wm/

From *More Reading Connections.* © 1999. Knowles/Smith. Libraries Unlimited. (800) 237-6124.

Chapter 3

Is There Truth in Humor?

OVERVIEW

Humor helps children contend with stress by distorting or exaggerating reality. In the context of humor, children can view things that are stressful in nonthreatening and positive ways. Humor can also provide a release of tension. When children see conflict in a humorous story, they see characters working through things, and they realize that conflicts can be resolved in different ways. Humor alleviates anxiety. Things like being afraid of the dark, separation anxiety, and strangers—when treated with humor—don't seem so bad. Humor facilitates creative thinking. It can be based on incongruity, making it necessary for children to validate the inconsistencies. It is often difficult to determine criteria for excellence in humorous children's books, because of the differences between what adults and children view as funny.

GUIDED READING QUESTIONS

1. Does the humor in the book you selected seem funny to you?
2. If you selected a picture book or an early reader's book, was it funny to you?
3. Do you think the book you read would help eliminate a child's fear or anxiety?
4. Was there any humor in your book that you think would go over a child's head?
5. Were the feelings real even though the events were not?
6. Were there any words or concepts that were funny?
7. Humor is truth. Were there any truths?

From *More Reading Connections.* © 1999. Knowles/Smith. Libraries Unlimited. (800) 237-6124.

JOURNAL ARTICLE

Fractured Fairy Tales: Spin-Offs, Spoofs, and Satires

Fee fi fo fum/Twist the tale to start the fun./Be it fractured as a spoof,/Readers' laughs will be the proof.

Fractured fairy tales, those wickedly irreverent, delightfully turned upside down, and twisted versions of classic stories that everyone loves. The fall season's bumper crop of funny take-offs prompted me to ponder and consider several points.

- What defines a fractured fairy tale?
- What makes it successful?
- What is it about previously published titles of this type that has made them last?

As I tried to pinpoint a definition for this article, I discovered that none of the standard children's literature resources cited the term. Popularization of this particular type of satire and establishment of the phrase can be traced back to the Rocky and Bullwinkle cartoon show on television in the 1960s. The animated spoofs were titled "Fractured Fairy Tales" and delighted audiences with their fun-poking and chicanery spun off from classic stories.

The word "fracture" in this sense dates back to 1946 as a show business term, meaning to delight, especially to convulse with laughter, according to the *Oxford English Dictionary Supplement*.

By Julie Cummins. Reprinted with permission of *School Library Journal* (October 1997), pages 50–51. Julie Cummins is Coordinator of Children's Services for the New York Public Library.

So let me offer some old and new examples of the types of twisted tales and fractured fables. A variety of terms such as variations, adaptations, retellings, and sequels are used to refer to these kinds of stories, but a true fractured fairy tale has a unique sensibility to it.

For instance, there are several renditions of "The Emperor's New Clothes," and while each retains the essence of the basic story, it is the illustrator's depiction of the familiar elements that creates the different humorous versions. The story line does not change[;] the plot, characters, and setting are the same.

The Principal's New Clothes (Scholastic, 1989) by Stephanie Calmenson, on the other hand, is a genuine fractured version placed in a school setting with the title indicating the twist and gist.

The basic elements of a folk or fairy tale that can be played with are: time and place of setting; characters and character traits; the problem to be solved or the conflict; development of the plot; resolution of the conflict or the conclusion.

The ways and means a folk or fairy tale can be fractured are: changes in locale, setting or time period; giving the story the flavor of a specific culture; puns and plays with names; switching the point of view; reversal of any of the standard elements.

This season of books has added an abundance of clever and entertaining methods of fracturing fairy tales to the existing body of literature. Many of the books described below are examples of "good" fracturing, in that they are well written, sustain a strong sense of story, and the humor is not adult in sensibility. Along with these titles, I've interspersed some previously published books that have contributed to the overall molding of these tales as a genre.

In Steven Kellogg's version of *The Three Little Pigs* (Morrow, 1997), Serafina's three piglets, Percy, Pete, and Prudence, have a family business making waffles. When Serafina retires to the Gulf of Pasta, the three pigs take over the wafflery and build homes nearby. Tempesto, the wolf, shows up with his mouth set for pork, growling: "Howdy, Ham. Howdy, Bacon. Howdy, Sausage. . . . Butter yourselves and hop on the griddle. I'll eat you for breakfast." The pigs outsmart the wolf, and the story ends with wolfie turned into a wolffle! The back of the jacket shows the wolf wearing a T-shirt that reads: "Thugs Need Hugs, Too."

Three books use a Western setting to rope in readers. The hootin' and hollerin' that goes on in *Little Red Cowboy Hat* (Holt, 1997) by Susan Lowell, illustrated by Randy Cecil, gives the familiar tale a southwestern spin. Little Red Cowboy Hat is off to her Grandma's with bread and cactus jelly when a wolf in a cowboy hat tries to hornswoggle her. But she and her gun-totin' Grandma use their gumption to "outwolf" the varmint.

Susan Lowell hits the trail again as she restages "The Shoemaker and the Elves" on the Western front with *The Bootmaker and the Elves* (Orchard, 1997), illustrated by Tom Curry. The story line features a poor, beleaguered bootmaker who makes ugly boots that pinch. Just when he's down to his last piece of leather, a miracle turns around his passel of bad luck. Two tiny elves appear and hammer out jim-dandy boots that have rootin', tootin' cowboys and cowgirls swaggerin' and sashayin'.

Another buckaroo rendering is Jim Harris's *Jack and the Giant: A Story Full of Beans* (Rising Moon, 1997). Jack and his ma, Annie Oakey Dokey, live in the Arizona desert. The usual sequence of cow trading, bean planting, and giant stalk growing ensue, but can Jack escape the clutches of the giant cattle rustler, Wild Bill Hiccup, *and* the giant who wants his gold-buffalo-chip-layin' bison back?

Richard Egielski flips an opposite spin by urbanizing *The Gingerbread Boy* (Harper-Collins, 1997). The gingerbread boy hops out the apartment window, slides down the fire escape, and runs through the streets of New York City and Central Park with construction workers, a policeman, and even a city rat in hot pursuit.

The most popular tale for tinkering appears to be "Cinderella." I found more fractured tales based on this story than any other. From titles published in recent years, here are three that have cracked the glass ceiling: Ellen Jackson's *Cinder Edna* (Lothrop, 1994); Frances Minters's *Cinder-Elly* (Viking, 1994), illustrated by G. Brian Karas; and Babette Cole's *Prince Cinders* (Putnam, 1992). Evidently the "rags to riches" story holds universal appeal as a tale to twist, as there are several new ones this fall. The best of the lot is Susan Meddaugh's re-creation.

She works all of the fractured angles into a comical take on this old tale with *Cinderella's Rat* (Houghton, 1997). The narrator is a rodent who is transformed by the fairy godmother into a coachboy. Life seems grand in his new shape until he is faced with having to rescue his rat of a sister, his sister rat that is. Can an inept wizard find the right spell to change her into a human? The switched ending proves that "Life is full of surprises, so you may as well get used to it."

Two examples in which the version is tailored by the adapter's recognizable personal touch are James Marshall's *Red Riding Hood* (Dial, 1987) and Lisa Campbell Ernst's *Little Red Riding Hood: A Newfangled Prairie Tale* (S & S, 1995). Marshall's madcap rendition embellishes this familiar tale with irreverent flourishes. Ernst depicts "Red" wearing a hooded sweatshirt and feisty Grandma is a muffin-baking, tractor-driving farmer. Each book is imprinted with its creator's recognizable style, and each conveys playfulness without losing the spirit of the original.

Along with folk and fairy tales, there are some related categories of children's literature that lend themselves ripe for spoofing: tall tales, fables, and cumulative stories.

Charlotte Huck in *Children's Literature in the Elementary School* (5th edition) defines tall tales: "when heroes and heroines are larger than life and perform impossible feats, all in the spirit of comic horseplay." Fractured tales take Huck's definition one step further by making the horseplay dependent on a known tale for its comic effect.

We know the tall tale of Paul Bunyan and his blue ox Babe, but Audrey Wood tells us "the rest of the story" in *The Bunyans* (Scholastic/Blue Sky, 1996), illustrated by David Shannon. Both the narrative and pictures add a contemporary staging to the tallness of this original tale (e.g., Mr. and Mrs. Bunyan on the golf course).

There are two wonderful illustrations of the sequel/continuation approach. A golden example from the new tales this year is Diane Stanley's *Rumpelstiltskin's Daughter* (Morrow, 1997). The miller's daughter marries Rumpelstiltskin because she likes his ideas on parenting and has a weakness for short men. Their daughter repeats the original scenario and becomes prime minister for the kingdom. Stanley's comical, exaggerated illustrations and rollicking spoof spin 24-karat fun.

In Jon Scieszka's *The Frog Prince Continued* (Viking, 1991), the Princess and the Frog Prince are *not* living happily ever after. She can't stand his froggy habits, such as hopping on the furniture and occasionally flicking his tongue at a fly. (That's genuine tongue-in-cheek!) The Prince decides to change back to a frog and sets off to find a witch to help him. In the end, true love triumphs.

The following three titles are delightful examples of the "switch and bait" technique, so to speak, as they either switch the point of view or roles of the characters. *The True Story of the Three Little Pigs* (Viking, 1989) by Jon Scieszka, illustrated by Lane Smith, in which readers hear the wolf's version about the bum rap he got, has become a classic. Text and illustrations are completely in sync to project a "wise guy" sensibility.

Eugene Trivizas's *The Three Little Wolves and the Big Bad Pig* (McElderry, 1993) concisely conveys the twist of this reverse retelling. When the big bad pig tries to get into the first house, the three little wolves chime: "No, no, no. . . . By the hair on our chinny-chin-chins, we will not let you in, not for all the tea leaves in our china teapot." The subtleties in the kind of house building, wording in the phrasing, and harmonious ending reflect a modernized spin.

So why does there appear to be a proliferation of this type of tale among picture books? Just as movies often look to the solid storytelling of established novels for entertaining plots, this body of folklore and fairy-tale literature offers a natural waterfall of material for authors and illustrators in which to splash, play, and create refreshing fun.

And why are these tales so popular? Perhaps it is because we need and welcome a little levity in our lives. Folk and fairy tales are so well-known and familiar that they readily serve as grist for the humor mill, where we can poke fun and laugh. They provide the calcium for our funny bones. Well-done fractured folk and fairy tales also help children to laugh at themselves. The humor doesn't rely on sly, adult references for them to "get the joke." It's adding another layer to an already good story, a layer that spawns giggles and grins. Who can resist a golden goose that lays a golden egg and says, "The yolk's on you, Jack"?

Teachers have discovered fractured tales as an enjoyable classroom device to demonstrate writing-language-plot development that also leads back to appreciation of the original story.

A successful fractured fairy tale is one that doesn't belittle the original source in its approach, that is written with young people as its intended audience, and that follows the same criteria of good writing for children's books in general. It's one thing to "skewer" a story by punching holes in it and another, to "baste" the original to give it a new flavor. Just as there are picture books published for the commercial adult market, there are fractured fairy tales whose appeal is sophisticated, wise-cracking adult punditry that may leave children bewildered or uncomfortable. These books miss the mark.

After analyzing these stories as a genre, I would offer this definition: a fractured fairy tale is: a classic folk or fairy tale rewritten with tongue-in-cheek or as a spoof using twists and spins on the story's features; text and visual references poke fun at the original, resulting in a witty, clever, and entertaining tale.

You could say, fractured fairy tales are the comic relief of children's literature. So, hooray for chuckles and giggles and kudos to Boris and Natasha. Once upon a time, favorite fairy tales got twisted and tangled, and everyone laughed happily ever after. ▲

ANNOTATED JOURNAL ARTICLES

Hassler, Patricia Jana. "Roald Dahl's *Matilda*," *Book Links* (July 1996): 17–19.
    This is a comprehensive summary of the story, *Matilda,* and ideas for discussion, activities, and research connected with the story. The article also contains an annotated bibliography of books about family life, school stories, and writing.

Howe, James. "Mirth & Mayhem: Humor and Mystery in Children's Books," *Voices from the Middle* (September 1995): 4–9.
    The popular author of the Bunnicula books and the Sebastian Barth mysteries shares some of his personal feelings about mixing mirth and mayhem. It is nature's way of saying, "Lighten up." It's only a game. The events are not real, but the feelings are. Some words and concepts are inherently funny. Take the road less traveled if it takes you to a good joke. Humor and mysteries are not only about playing, but also about playing games.

ANNOTATED BIBLIOGRAPHY

Clement, Rod. *Grandpa's Teeth.* HarperCollins, 1997.
    Help! Grandpa's teeth have disappeared from a glass of water by his bed. The police are called and pictures of the missing teeth are posted all over town. Anyone who is not smiling is under suspicion. Soon the whole town is smiling . . . so much so that tourists are afraid to get out of their cars. The townspeople are beginning to suffer from the loss of business and the constant strain of smiling. After an emergency town meeting, the people chip in money and Grandpa gets new teeth. Grandpa loves his new teeth and smiles all the time. Even his old dog, Gump, smiles at the end for the first time ever. The illustrations are as humorous as the story.

Clements, Andrew. *Double Trouble in Walla Walla.* Millbrook Press, 1997.
    "It was an ordinary Monday morning in Walla Walla—until Lulu raised her hand in class." It seems she has an itty-bitty problem with her homework. A word warp infects Lulu; her teacher, Mrs. Bell; and Mr. Thomas, the principal. Everything they say is duplicated. Mrs. Carter, the school nurse, immediately recognizes the problem and comes up with a solution—or does she?

King-Smith, Dick. *A Mouse Called Wolf.* Crown, 1977.
    When it came time for Mary mouse to give a name to her youngest mouse, she decided to give him two names, because he was the runt. She named him Wolfgang Amadeus mouse. His brothers and sisters nicknamed him Wolf. Everyone left the family hole next to Mrs. Honeybee's piano, except for Wolf and Mary. Twice a day Wolf listened to the sometimes sad, sometimes cheery music of Mrs. Honeybee. One day Mrs. Honeybee heard the clear, beautiful voice of Wolf. From then on, she bribed and coaxed Wolf with chocolate to come out of his hole and eventually sing with her accompaniment. True to his name, Wolfgang Amadeus composes his own "Swallow Sonata." Wolf is a resourceful, clever mouse who develops an endearing relationship with the widowed Mrs. Honeybee.

Palatini, Margie. *Piggie Pie!* Clarion Books, 1995.
> Gritch the witch woke up grouchy and hungry. She wanted something special, piggie pie. She had all the ingredients except eight plump pigs. She opened the Yellow Pages and found Old MacDonald's farm. Gritch circled overhead and saw the little porkers but when she landed, there were no pigs. After questioning the ducks, cows, chickens, and even Old MacDonald, she met up with Mr. Wolf. He had been chasing three little pigs for days. Both had each other in mind for lunch, when Gritch asked the wolf home.

Stanley, Diane. *Rumpelstiltskin's Daughter.* Morrow Junior Books, 1997.
> This starts out the same as the traditional tale except that in this version the miller's daughter decides she would rather marry Rumpelstiltskin than the king. So the two escape out the window of the palace and go to live far away on a farm. Sixteen years later, Rumpelstiltskin sends his daughter to town shopping, to exchange the spun gold for coins. News of this reaches the king and reminds him of the miller's daughter who spun straw into gold many years ago.
>
> Rumpelstiltskin's daughter is brought to the king and placed in a room full of straw. She knows the king will never be satisfied until all the straw in the kingdom has been turned into gold. She thinks about all the poor farms and hungry children and concocts her own plan to reverse her fortune as well as the fortunes of the people of the kingdom.

Vande Velde, Vivian. *Tales from the Brothers Grimm and the Sisters Weird.* Harcourt Brace, 1995.
> Directions inside the front cover of the book tell how to fracture a fairy tale—make the hero a villain or the villain a hero, and tell what really happened. "Straw into Gold" is a parody of the Rumpelstiltszkin tale. "Frog" is a humorous story of a frog waiting to be turned back into a prince: this time not by a kiss, but instead by eating from a princess's plate and sleeping on her pillow—with an unusual ending. "Beast and Beauty" is similar to the regular tale but with some funny parts.

BIBLIOGRAPHY

General

Avi. *Who Was That Masked Man, Anyway?* Orchard, 1992.

Bechard, Margaret. *My Sister, My Science Report.* Viking, 1990.

Blume, Judy. *Freckle Juice.* Macmillan, 1971.

———. *Fudge-A-Mania.* Dutton Children's Books, 1990.

———. *Superfudge.* Dell, 1980.

Bunting, Eve. *Our Sixth-Grade Sugar Babies.* HarperCollins, 1990.

Butterworth, Oliver. *The Enormous Egg.* Little, Brown, 1956.

Byars, Betsy. *The Cybil War.* Viking, 1981.

22 / 3 ▲ IS THERE TRUTH IN HUMOR?

Carris, Joan. *When the Boys Ran the House*. J. B. Lippincott, 1982.
Cleary, Beverly. *Ramona and Her Father*. William Morrow, 1977.
———. *Runaway Ralph*. William Morrow, 1970.
Clifford, Eth. *Harvey's Horrible Snake Disaster*. Houghton Mifflin, 1984.
Dahl, Roald. *Danny: The Champion of the World*. Alfred A. Knopf, 1975.
———. *Matilda*. Viking, 1988.
Fitzgerald, John. *The Great Brain Does It Again*. Dial Press, 1975.
Hurwitz, Johanna. *Class Clown*. William Morrow, 1987.
Hutchins, Pat. *Rats*. Greenwillow Books, 1989.
King-Smith, Dick. *Sophie's Snail*. Delacorte Press, 1988.
Korman, Gordon. *The Twinkle Squad*. Scholastic, 1966.
Lawson, Robert. *Ben and Me*. Little, Brown, 1939.
———. *Mr. Revere and I*. Little, Brown, 1953.
Lowry, Lois. *Anastasia Krupnik*. Houghton Mifflin, 1979.
———. *Anastasia on Her Own*. Houghton Mifflin, 1985.
———. *See You Around, Sam!* Houghton Mifflin, 1996.
———. *Switcharound*. Houghton Mifflin, 1985.
MacLachlan, Patricia. *Arthur, for the Very First Time*. Harper & Row, 1980.
Mahy, Margaret. *The Blood and Thunder Adventure on Hurricane Peak*. Macmillan, 1989.
Manes, Stephen. *Be a Perfect Person in Just Three Days!* Houghton Mifflin, 1982.
McCloskey, Robert. *Homer Price*. Viking, 1943.
McKenna, Colleen O'Shaughnessy. *Mother Murphy*. Scholastic, 1992.
Nabb, Magdalen. *Josie Smith*. Macmillan, 1990.
Naylor, Phyllis Reynolds. *Beetles, Lightly Toasted*. Macmillan, 1987.
———. *The Boys Start the War*. Delacorte Press, 1993.
———. *The Girls Get Even*. Delacorte Press, 1993.
Park, Barbara. *Beanpole*. Alfred A. Knopf, 1983.
———. *Junie B. Jones and the Stupid Smelly Bus*. Random House, 1992.
———. *The Kid in the Red Jacket*. Bullseye Books, 1987.
Peck, Robert Newton. *Soup*. Alfred A. Knopf, 1974.
———. *Soup on Fire*. Delacorte Press, 1987.
———. *Soup on Ice*. Alfred A. Knopf, 1985.
Perl, Lila. *Hey, Remember Fat Glenda?* Ticknor & Fields, 1981.
Pinkwater, Daniel. *The Snarkout Boys and the Avocado of Death*. Lothrop, Lee & Shepard, 1982.
Pryor, Bonnie. *Vinegar Pancakes and Vanishing Cream*. William Morrow, 1987.

Raskin, Ellen. *The Tattooed Potato and Other Clues*. Dutton Children's Books, 1975.

Robertson, Keith. *Henry Reed, Inc.* Viking, 1958.

Robinson, Barbara. *The Best Christmas Pageant Ever*. Harper & Row, 1972.

Rockwell, Thomas. *How to Eat Fried Worms*. Franklin Watts, 1973.

Rodgers, Mary. *Freaky Friday*. Harper & Row, 1972.

Sachar, Louis. *Wayside School Is Falling Down*. Lothrop, Lee & Shepard, 1989.

Schwartz, Amy. *Bea and Mr. Jones*. Bradbury Press, 1982.

Silverstein, Shel. *Falling Up*. HarperCollins, 1996.

Smith, Robert K. *Chocolate Fever*. Putnam, 1989.

Woodruff, Elvira. *The Secret Funeral of Slim Jim the Snake*. Holiday House, 1993.

Primary

Allard, Harry. *Miss Nelson Is Missing*. Houghton Mifflin, 1977.

———. *The Stupids Step Out*. Houghton Mifflin, 1977.

Atwater, Richard, and Florence Atwater. *Mr. Popper's Penguins*. Little, Brown, 1938.

Barrett, Judi. *Animals Should Definitely Not Wear Clothing*. Atheneum, 1969.

———. *Cloudy with a Chance of Meatballs*. Atheneum, 1978.

Buehner, Caralyn. *Fanny's Dream*. Dial Books for Young Readers, 1996.

Byars, Betsy. *Ant Plays Bear*. Viking, 1997.

Chetwin, Remy. *Box and Cox*. Macmillan, 1990.

dePaola, Tomie. *Bill and Pete*. Putnam, 1978.

———. *Strega Nona*. Simon & Schuster, 1975.

Etra, Jonathan, and Stephanie Spinner. *Aliens for Lunch*. Random House, 1991.

Fleischman, Sid. *The Ghost in the Noonday Sun*. Greenwillow Books, 1989.

———. *McBroom Tells the Truth*. Little, Brown, 1981.

Harvey, Jayne. *Great-Uncle Dracula*. Random House, 1992.

Heide, Florence Parry. *The Shrinking of Treehorn*. Holiday House, 1971.

Kellogg, Steven. *A Rose for Pinkerton*. Dial Press, 1981.

Lear, Edward. *The Pelican Chorus*. HarperCollins, 1995.

Lobel, Arnold. *Mouse Tales*. Harper & Row, 1972.

Mahy, Margaret. *The Boy Who Was Followed Home*. Franklin Watts, 1975.

Marshall, Edward. *Space Case*. Dial Press, 1980.

Marshall, James. *The Cut-Ups Carry On*. Viking, 1992.

Meddaugh, Susan. *Martha Speaks*. Houghton Mifflin, 1992.

Noble, Trinka Hakes. *Jimmy's Boa Bounces Back*. Dial Books for Young Readers, 1984.

24 / 3 ▲ IS THERE TRUTH IN HUMOR?

Parish, Peggy. *Teach Us, Amelia Bedelia*. Greenwillow Books, 1977.

Peet, Bill. *Big Bad Bruce*. Houghton Mifflin, 1977.

Prelutsky, Jack. *The Random House Book of Poetry for Children*. Random House, 1983.

Scieszka, Jon. *The Stinky Cheese Man: and Other Fairly Stupid Tales*. Viking, 1992.

Sendak, Maurice. *Chicken Soup with Rice*. Harper & Row, 1962.

Seuss, Dr. *And To Think That I Saw It on Mulberry Street*. Random House, 1937.

―――. *If I Ran the Circus*. Random House, 1956.

Slobodkina, Esphyr. *Caps for Sale*. Harper & Row, 1947.

Spier, Peter. *Oh, Were They Ever Happy*. Doubleday, 1978.

Stadler, John. *The Cats of Mrs. Calamari*. Orchard, 1997.

Stanley, Diane. *Saving Sweetness*. Putnam, 1996.

Teban, Maurice. *Eight Ate: A Feast of Homonym Riddles*. Clarion Books, 1982.

Wood, Audrey. *King Bidgood's in the Bathtub*. Harcourt, Brace, 1985.

WEB SITES

Dav Pilkey
http://www.pilkey.com

Dr. Seuss
http://www.seussville.com

Jon Scieszka
http://www.friend.ly.net/scoop/biographies/jscieszka.html

Margaret Mahy
http://www.friend.ly.net/scoop/biographies/mmahy.html

Roald Dahl Index
http://www.tridel.com.ph/user/bula/dahl/index.htm

Shel Silverstein
http://falcon.jmu.edu/~ramseyil/silverstein.htm
http://www.geocities.com/SunsetStrip/Club/6166/ss/ssbook.html

Sid Fleischman
http://www.bdd.com/bin/forums/teachers/flei.html

Chapter 4

Families in Transition

OVERVIEW

The family stories of today include single-parent families, divorced and remarried (blended) families, adoptive and foster families, and extended families. Sibling rivalry is a common theme in family stories, and children usually love to hear stories about when their parents were children. Many books about families explore grandparents and other relatives making up an extended family.

Earlier family-life stories tended to portray families without moments of anger or hurt, emphasizing only happy or adventurous moments. Today the balance has tilted in the other direction, and it is very difficult to find a family story with well-adjusted children and happily married parents. Another, newer subset of family stories is about families in transition. In most of these stories, children deal with changes, confusion, anger, hurt, and disruption resulting from divorce.

GUIDED READING QUESTIONS

1. What kind of family is described in your book?
2. Are the characters realistic?
3. Is sibling rivalry evident?
4. Does your book tell a family story of well-adjusted children and happily married parents?
5. Does the book present a conflict or problem? If so, what is the problem?
6. Do you agree with the portrayal of adult family members in your book?
7. If grandparents are included in your book, are they treated with respect?

From *More Reading Connections*. © 1999. Knowles/Smith. Libraries Unlimited. (800) 237-6124.

All in the Family: Parents in Teen Fiction

The family is still alive and functioning and worth the effort to build and maintain.

Parents pose a problem in young adult fiction. Peruse the book reviews of the past few years and notice how many of the parental figures mentioned fall into one of two categories—ineffectual or antagonistic.

Many of the teenage characters don't even seem to have parents, or if they do, the parents are only minimally involved in their children's lives. Parents may remain so far in the background that they have little or no role in or impact on the stories. They often come across as self-absorbed caricatures who foot the bills and ask only to be left alone in return.

Terms like "cardboard stereotype" come up regularly in referring to parents in reviews, but even more frequent are terms such as, "abusive stepfather" and "alcoholic mother." These parents *are* the problem for their teenage offspring, and typically the teens either find their own solution, or resolve their situation with the help of a friend or caring relative.

Carl Staggers, in Alden R. Carter's *Up Country* (Putnam, 1989), is used to dealing with his mother's drinking binges, but when she is arrested for a hit-and-run accident and sent to a treatment center to dry out, he is shipped off to live with an aunt and uncle he hardly knows, leaving behind a basement full of stolen stereos. He finally builds a new life for himself in this rural setting, but not until his past catches up with him and family wisdom saves him.

By Joyce Burner. Reprinted with permission of *School Library Journal* (November 1989), pages 42–43. Joyce Burner is formerly a librarian at the Spring Hill Middle School, Spring Hill, KS.

Susan Beth Pfeffer's "Sebastian Sisters" series *(Evvie at Sixteen* [1988], *Thea at Sixteen* [1988], *Claire at Sixteen* [1989], *Sybil at Sixteen* [1989], all Bantam) features a father who is charming and endearing, but who is also a blatant manipulator and con-artist. He moves his four daughters and adoring wife from town to town as his schemes succeed and fail, having somehow secured the loyalty of all despite his questionable character. The mother is a true romantic, blinded to her husband's faults by love. The family ties are strong, however, and the girls display remarkable maturity and devotion.

An interesting variation on this theme shows up in Amy Ehrlich's *Where It Stops, Nobody Knows* (Dial, 1988). Nina and her mother have spent their lives moving from town to town. Finally the truth comes out—Nina's mother kidnapped newborn Nina from the hospital nursery, and the FBI is on their trail. Likewise, in Robert Hawks's *This Stranger, My Father* (Houghton, 1988), Patty's father is on the run, having escaped from prison after being convicted for selling secrets to the Soviets. During the 20 years he'd spent underground, Patty was born and her mother died; but then he is discovered and arrested. Escaping again, he and Patty become fugitives in a perilous cross-country chase with federal agents in pursuit. With both Nina and Patty's parents, the personal integrity of each comes seriously into question. Yet both characters are developed as loving and caring, trying to cope with the present situation.

A mother who does manage to salvage something positive from her mistakes is featured in Bruce Brooks's *No Kidding* (Harper, 1989). Set in a 21st century where most of the population is both sterile and alcoholic, the novel centers around Sam, a 14-year-old who has the legal power to decide who will get custody of his younger brother—his mother or his brother's foster family. This mother seems hopelessly self-centered until the end of the story, when she intentionally manipulates events to insure that the boy will remain with his stable foster family.

Should popular teen fiction merely reflect the problems which readers may face—or should it point them to a higher sense of personal morality? Do we assume that traditional family values are wrong because they have been so undermined by society? Teens need not only to find themselves and their concerns in the fiction they read, but also to see functioning families dealing with these issues effectively.

Fortunately, a number of excellent YA titles are available that portray strong families. Norma Johnston's "Carlisle Chronicles" *(The Carlisle's Hope, To Jess, With Love and Memories, Carlisles All,* all Bantam, 1986), offer great characters, interesting plots, and sharp dialogue. Jess, 15, is the central character who holds fast to family traditions despite uncertainties caused by her father's foreign service post, uncovered family secrets, or a beloved aunt's death.

Five Summers (Clarion, 1983) by JoAnn Bren Guernsey and Alden R. Carter's *Growing Season* (Coward, 1984) share rural settings. Guernsey takes Mandy through *Five Summers* of her life from age 12 to 16, as she copes with her own physical and emotional maturing, her mother's recurring bouts with cancer, and the intrusion of her domineering grandmother. In *Growing Season,* his family's move from the city to a dairy farm interrupts Rick's senior year and threatens his plans to become an architect. The oldest of six, he must learn to put others before himself. Both Mandy and Rick have strong, warm relationships with their parents that ultimately see them through.

Sib, 16, is a world-class cellist who enjoys a warm, relaxed relationship with her father, but knows nothing of the mother who deserted her as an infant. Bruce Brooks's *Midnight Hour Encores* (Harper, 1986) follows Sib and her father, Taxi, as they travel to San Francisco to meet her mother. Taxi is remarkably selfless as he introduces Sib to her past and steps aside to let her choose between her now-affluent mother and himself. The integrity of her decision reveals the solid values he has instilled in her.

Crises that arise at school often require solutions by the students involved to build self-esteem and assertiveness, but their successes may depend on the home foundation laid in childhood. Betsy Byars's *The Burning Questions of Bingo Brown* (Viking, 1988) is a lighthearted look at the musings of a newly adolescent boy puzzling over relationships, girls, and other problems that shake the junior-high earth. His parents, well drawn and amusing, lend him warm, subtle support when his teacher has a motorcycle accident that is possibly a suicide attempt.

Nick Swansen is a learning-disabled high schooler trying to find his niche in a fast-paced and prejudiced world. *Probably Still Nick Swansen* (Holt, 1988) by Virginia Wolff offers rare insight into the world of students with special needs as it affects their self-image. Nick's parents are wise and discerning as they encourage him to become all he can, yet provide the shelter his fragile ego requires.

A strong sense of family is frequently intergenerational. In Berlie Doherty's *Granny Was a Buffer Girl* (Orchard, 1988), a young woman's parents and grandparents gather the night before she leaves for a year's study abroad and all share the stories of their lives. A beautifully painted family chronicle emerges.

Rob starts out as a stereotypically rebellious teenager in Sue Ellen Bridgers's *Permanent Connections* (Harper, 1987). Sullen and contemptuous, involved in drugs and drinking, he is the cause of many parental arguments.

His life changes drastically when he is sent, protesting all the way, to help out his eccentric relatives for several months on a small mountain farmstead. He unexpectedly falls in love and manages to get himself arrested. Throughout his ordeal, he comes to value the family—quirks and all—and realizes that his actions have profound effects on those around him. By not limiting herself to Rob's point of view but getting into the head of each character, Bridgers does an excellent job of drawing adult characters as they separately try to cope with their unhappy offspring. Rob's and his girlfriend's parents are able to lay aside their own anger and confusion and effectively help their teenagers grow up.

In Julie Reece Deaver's *Say Goodnight, Gracie* (Harper, 1988), Morgan's parents and her psychiatrist aunt gently encourage her, giving her the time and freedom to heal when her best and lifelong friend is killed in an accident.

In *Phoenix Rising* (Atheneum, 1989), Cynthia Grant portrays a family in the aftermath of the oldest daughter's death from cancer, shifting from the younger daughter's viewpoint to the older daughter's diary of her final year. Jessie comes very close to an emotional breakdown before she is able to accept the reality of her loss, largely due to the steadfast love of her mother, who sets aside her own grief and encourages Jessie. Their father is caught up in his own anger over Helen's death and focuses on arguing with his son. By the end of the book, all have at least begun to find healing, and it is apparent that this family will survive and endure.

Family life needn't be dreary or humdrum, as illustrated in Joanne Greenberg's *Simple Gifts* (Holt, 1987), the hilarious tale of a close, eccentric family living on a tumbledown Colorado ranch. It's a story that's absurdly funny, and warm as this family pulls together for survival.

Simon Irving fights the very corporation his father heads in Gordon Korman's *Son of Interflux* (Scholastic, 1986). He anonymously leads his school in a battle over land the company wants to take over, and earns his father's respect in the end. This father can truly leave his work at the office, and the love and admiration he has for his son are evident.

A touch of fantasy marks *Hangin' Out with Cici* (Viking, 1977) by Francine Pascal. Victoria is a self-centered, spoiled, rebellious brat who finds herself transported back in time to meet her mother as a teenager. Despite the Disneyesque overtones, Pascal subtly relays the message that parents are often only trying in their own awkward way to save their children from repeating their mistakes.

Realistic fiction belongs in the YA collection, so teens will know they aren't alone in their experiences, but they also need literature that offers a positive model to emulate and reinforces the concept that the family is still alive, functioning, and worth the effort to build and maintain. Kids who come from solid homes need to have that foundation reinforced, and those whose family life is rocky or even nonexistent need to have the idea planted in their minds so that they can succeed with their own children. ▲

ANNOTATED JOURNAL ARTICLES

Lodge, Sally. "Books on Parental Love Prove an Easy Sell," *Publishers Weekly* (April 20, 1998): 25–26.

> This article highlights children's books about parental love. Some books tell of the transition children go through from complete dependence on parents to gradual independence. All of the books tell of the unconditional love that parents provide. Many of the books use animal characters. Impressive sales figures for some of the more popular titles are listed.

McDermott, Cynthia, and Suzanne Gemmell. "Fathers and Sons," *Book Links* (September 1996): 42–46.

> Family situations in which the father takes an active role or the father is a single parent are discussed at length. A teacher doing research noted that boys read better when they are read to by their fathers. The authors suggest a reading celebration where males are invited to the classroom to read to the kids: police officers, firefighters, doctors, mayor, dads, other male teachers, principals, etc.

Vossler, Jane M. "A Tangle of Emotions," *Middle School Journal* (May 1996): 49–52.

> The author begins by stating that middle school readers often stick to one type of book and are reluctant to change. She suggests that teachers need to put different types of books in readers' hands and encourage them to give the book a try. The article reviews realistic fiction books that portray strong, well-developed characters who are struggling with the types of concerns and emotions that most middle school students deal with on a regular basis. Many excellent titles are mentioned.

ANNOTATED BIBLIOGRAPHY

Crew, Linda. *Children of the River.* Delacorte Press, 1989.

> Sundara's parents shelter her from the war and spirit her away from Phnom Penh to her aunt and uncle's fishing village. Two weeks later Sundara, age thirteen, flees Cambodia with her aunt, uncle, grandmother, and cousins to escape the Khmer Rouge army.
>
> Three weeks at sea and the responsibility for a small baby leave Sundara struggling with guilt. She cannot go home to her land and people. Four years later, she must adjust to her new life in Oregon. Jonathan, the star football player, begins to interview Sundara for an international project. Sundara knows that she should follow Cambodian customs and not even talk to a boy. After many hardships and sorrows, Sundara finds peace with her aunt and uncle, and hopes that she will be reunited with her younger sister and Jonathan, her love.

Henkes, Kevin. *Protecting Marie.* Greenwillow Books, 1995.

> This is the story of a girl who always wanted a dog. Her father gives her a puppy, but then takes it away after it ruins the house. Fanny is devastated by this and never really trusts her father again. He is an older man and is going through some problems with his career as an artist. Eventually he gets Fanny another dog and she lives in fear of her father taking the dog away again. It turns out that the dog, Dinner, is helpful to her father's career.

From *More Reading Connections.* © 1999. Knowles/Smith. Libraries Unlimited. (800) 237-6124.

Meddaugh, Susan. *Hog-eye.* Houghton Mifflin, 1995.

    Little pig explains to her family what happened when she didn't go to school that day. She missed her school bus and boarded one that left her beside an unfamiliar road. To her parent's horror, she followed the path through the dark woods. When the wolf grabbed her, she was scared but cool. The wolf asked little pig to read his mother's recipe for pig soup. The wolf couldn't read, so little pig sent the wolf to collect nearly impossible ingredients while little pig tried to get away. The final ingredient was Green Threeleaf (poison ivy). Mr. Wolf was outsmarted. Little pig fixed him with her hog-eye, a magic stare that made him itch everywhere. She said if wolf let her go she would release her spell. Mr. Wolf learns never to trust a pig.

Nolan, Han. *Dancing on the Edge.* Harcourt Brace, 1997.

    Miracle McCloy was named "Miracle" by her grandmother, Gigi, because she was born "out of the body of a dead woman." Sissy, Miracle's mother, was killed in an accident. Miracle lives with Dane, her father, and Gigi, who practices the occult and communicates with spirits. Dane was a child prodigy and wrote his first book at a young age. When Sissy died at the age of seventeen, Dane never wrote another book and became a recluse in the McCloy home.

    When Miracle is around twelve years old, Gigi teaches her to become an apprentice. On the night of Miracle's first séance, Sissy communicates through a Ouija board. "Dane's gone, N-O-W." Gigi explains Dane's strange disappearance—he's melted. From that moment on, Miracle tries to bring Dane back. Miracle's actions become bizarre as her surroundings frighten her and bring her closer to the edge. In a test to find out if she is real, Miracle sets herself on fire.

    After her medical recovery, Aunt Casey arranges for Miracle's transfer to The Cedars. Dr. DeAngelis, a young psychiatrist, works with Miracle and her search for the truth and love that make her feel real. A powerful National Book Award winner.

Peck, Jan. *The Giant Carrot.* Dial Books for Young Readers, 1998.

    The Giant Carrot was adapted from the Russian folktale, "The Turnip." One morning Papa Joe decides to plant a carrot seed. Mama Bess and Brother Abel decide to help. Each has a different idea of what to do with the carrot. Along comes Sweet Little Isabelle, who dances and sings to the carrot to make it grow. Tall Papa Joe, Wide Mama Bess, and Strong Brother Abel all take care of the plant and the carrot top grows a little each time. But when Sweet Little Isabelle sings and dances, it grows and grows. Soon it is time to pull the carrot from the ground. It takes all three pulling and Isabelle singing and dancing before the huge carrot pops out of the ground. The last page has a recipe for Little Isabelle's Carrot Puddin'.

Wood, June Rae. *When Pigs Fly.* Putnam & Grosset, 1995.

    Buddy's father loses his job and moves the family to a farm that he inherited from Aunt June. Everything about the move upsets Buddy. She has to take the bus to school with her neighbor, Dallas the ragpicker, and has a falling out with her longtime friend. In contrast, her sister, who has Down's syndrome, loves the move and demonstrates to the whole family that she is growing up and a hero. Buddy adjusts and finds a new friend in Dallas.

From *More Reading Connections.* © 1999. Knowles/Smith. Libraries Unlimited. (800) 237-6124.

BIBLIOGRAPHY

Primary

Ackerman, Karen. *Song and Dance Man*. Alfred A. Knopf, 1988.

Alexander, Martha. *Nobody Asked Me If I Wanted a Baby Sister*. Dial Press, 1971.

Aliki. *Jack and Jake*. Greenwillow Books, 1986.

Bunting, Eve. *Night Tree*. Harcourt Brace, 1991.

———. *A Perfect Father's Day*. Houghton Mifflin, 1991.

———. *The Wednesday Surprise*. Clarion Books, 1989.

Cooney, Barbara. *Miss Rumphius*. Viking, 1982.

dePaola, Tomie. *Nana Upstairs and Nana Downstairs*. Putnam, 1973.

———. *Watch Out for the Chicken Feet in Your Soup*. Simon & Schuster, 1974.

Ehrlich, Amy. *Parents in the Pigpen, Pigs in the Tub*. Dial Books for Young Readers, 1993.

Flournoy, Valerie. *The Patchwork Quilt*. Dial Books for Young Readers, 1985.

Garland, Sherry. *The Lotus Seed*. Harcourt Brace, 1993.

Gray, Libba Moore. *My Mama Had a Dancing Heart*. Orchard, 1995.

Greenfield, Eliose. *Grandpa's Face*. Putnam, 1988.

Hest, Amy. *The Mommy Exchange*. Macmillan, 1988.

Howard, Elizabeth F. *Aunt Flossie's Hats (and Crab Cakes Later)*. Houghton Mifflin, 1991.

Isadora, Rachel. *At the Crossroads*. Greenwillow Books, 1991.

Johnson, Angela. *Julius*. Orchard, 1993.

Johnston, Tony. *Yonder*. Dial Books for Young Readers, 1988.

Keats, Ezra Jack. *Peter's Chair*. HarperCollins, 1967.

Lasky, Kathryn. *Sea Swan*. Macmillan, 1988.

Levinson, Riki. *Our Home Is the Sea*. E. P. Dutton, 1988.

Lyon, George Ella. *Come a Tide*. Orchard, 1990.

McCully, Emily Arnold. *My Real Family*. Harcourt Brace, 1994.

McPhail, David. *Sisters*. Harcourt Brace, 1984.

Polacco, Patricia. *Babushka's Doll*. Simon & Schuster, 1990.

———. *The Bee Tree*. Philomel, 1993.

———. *Just Plain Fancy*. Bantam Books, 1990.

———. *The Keeping Quilt*. Simon & Schuster, 1994.

———. *My Ol' Man*. Philomel, 1995.

———. *My Rotten Redheaded Older Brother*. Simon & Schuster, 1994.

———. *Thundercake*. Philomel, 1990.

From *More Reading Connections*. © 1999. Knowles/Smith. Libraries Unlimited. (800) 237-6124.

Rosenberg, Liz. *Monster Mama*. Philomel, 1990.

Rylant, Cynthia. *The Relatives Came*. Bradbury Press, 1985.

———. *When I Was Young in the Mountains*. E. P. Dutton, 1982.

Samuels, Barbara. *What's So Great About Cindy Snappleby?* Orchard, 1992.

Schwartz, Amy. *Oma and Bobo*. Bradbury Press, 1987.

Shelby, Anne. *Homeplace*. Orchard, 1995.

Shulevitz, Uri. *The Treasure*. Farrar, Straus & Giroux, 1979.

Spinelli, Eileen. *Thanksgiving at the Tappletons*. HarperCollins, 1982.

Viorst, Judith. *Alexander and the Terrible, Horrible, No Good, Very Bad Day*. Macmillan, 1972.

———. *I'll Fix Anthony*. Harper & Row, 1969.

Wild, Margaret. *Our Granny*. Ticknor & Fields, 1994.

Wilder, Laura Ingalls. *Dance at Grandpa's*. HarperCollins, 1994.

Winthrop, Elizabeth. *Sloppy Kisses*. Puffin Books, 1983.

Wishinsky, Freida. *Oonga Boonga*. Little, Brown, 1990.

Wood, Audrey. *Weird Parents*. Dial Books for Young Readers, 1990.

Zolotow, Charlotte. *Something Is Going to Happen*. Harper & Row, 1988.

General

Adler, C. S. *One Sister Too Many*. Macmillan, 1989.

Alcott, Louisa May. *Little Women*. Putnam, 1947.

Armstrong, William H. *Sounder*. Harper & Row, 1969.

Beatty, Patricia. *Be Ever Hopeful Hannalee*. Morrow Junior Books, 1988.

Blume, Judy. *Fudge-A-Mania*. Dutton Children's Books, 1990.

———. *Superfudge*. Dell, 1980.

———. *Tales of a Fourth Grade Nothing*. Dell, 1972.

Brink, Carol. *Caddie Woodlawn*. Macmillan, 1973.

Byars, Betsy. *Goodbye, Chicken Little*. Scholastic, 1979.

———. *Wanted . . . Mud Blossom*. Delacorte Press, 1991.

Cameron, Ann. *The Stories Julian Tells*. Pantheon Books, 1981.

Cleary, Beverly. *Dear Mr. Henshaw*. Morrow Junior Books, 1983.

———. *Ramona the Brave*. Morrow Junior Books, 1975.

———. *Ramona the Pest*. Morrow Junior Books, 1968.

Cleaver, Vera. *Belle Pruitt*. J. B. Lippincott, 1988.

Curtis, Christopher Paul. *The Watsons Go to Birmingham—1963*. Delacorte Press, 1995.

Delton, Judy. *Angel's Mother's Boyfriend*. Houghton Mifflin, 1986.

Estes, Eleanor. *The Moffats*. Harcourt Brace, 1941.

Fleischman, Paul. *The Borning Room*. HarperCollins, 1991.

Hamilton, Virginia. *M. C. Higgins, the Great*. Macmillan, 1974.

Heide, Florence Parry. *Sami and the Time of the Troubles*. Houghton Mifflin, 1992.

Hermes, Patricia. *Someone to Count On*. Little, Brown, 1993.

Hest, Amy. *Travel Tips from Harry: A Guide to Family Vacations in the Sun*. Morrow Junior Books, 1989.

Hinton, S. E. *That Was Then, This Is Now*. Laurel-Leaf, 1971.

Hurwitz, Johanna. *E Is for Elisa*. Morrow Junior Books, 1991.

———. *A Llama in the Family*. Morrow Junior Books, 1994.

Hutchins, Pat. *Rats!* Greenwillow Books, 1989.

L'Engle, Madeleine. *Meet the Austins*. Vanguard, 1981.

Levitin, Sonia. *Annie's Promise*. Macmillan, 1993.

Lowry, Lois. *Anastasia Again!* Dell, 1981.

———. *Attaboy, Sam!* Houghton Mifflin, 1992.

MacLachlan, Patricia. *Cassie Binegar*. Harper & Row, 1982.

Martin, Ann M. *Ten Kids, No Pets*. Holiday House, 1988.

McKenna, Colleen O'Shaughnessy. *Too Many Murphys*. Scholastic, 1988.

Mills, Claudia. *Dynamite Dinah*. Macmillan, 1990.

Mowat, Farley. *Owls in the Family*. Bantam Books, 1961.

Myers, Walter Dean. *Somewhere in the Darkness*. Scholastic, 1992.

Nabb, Magdalen. *Josie Smith*. Macmillan, 1990.

Naylor, Phyllis Reynolds. *Maudie in the Middle*. Macmillan, 1988.

———. *A String of Chances*. Atheneum, 1984.

Paterson, Katherine. *Come Sing, Jimmy Jo*. Lodestar, 1985.

Rabe, Bernice. *Margaret's Moves*. E. P. Dutton, 1987.

Robinson, Nancy K. *Angela and the Broken Heart*. Scholastic, 1991.

Shreve, Susan. *The Formerly Great Alexander Family*. Tambourine Books, 1995.

Smith, Janice Lee. *The Monster in the Third Dresser Drawer and Other Stories About Adam Joshua*. Harper & Row, 1981.

Smith, Robert Kimmel. *The War with Grandpa*. Dell, 1984.

Taylor, Sydney. *All-of-a-Kind Family*. Follett, 1951.

Voigt, Cynthia. *Dicey's Song*. Atheneum, 1982.

———. *Homecoming*. Fawcett, 1981.

Wilder, Laura Ingalls. *Little House in the Big Woods*. Harper & Row, 1932.

WEB SITES

Betsy Byars
http://www.bdd.com/bin/forums/teachers/byar.html

Beverly Cleary
http://www.teleport.com/~krp/cleary.html

Family
http://www.family.com

Family Games!
http://www.familygames.com

Family Internet Directory Online
http://www.clark.net/pub/soh/fido.htm

Family Internet Home Page
http://www.familyinternet.com

Family Planet
http://family.starwave.com/contents.html

Father Net
http://www.cyfc.umn.edu/Fathernet/

Linda Crew
http://www.bdd.com/bin/forums/teachers/crew.html

Lois Lenski
http://www.uncg.edu/lib/speccoll/lenski/

Louisa May Alcott
http://www.coppersky.com/louisa/

Parent Soup
http://www.parentsoup.com

Parent Time
http://pathfinder.com/@vp8bqwqa7mzroutd/ParentTime/welcome/welcom.html

Parents Place
http://www.parentsplace.com

Patricia MacLachlan
http://www.bdd.com/bin/forums/teachers/macl.html

Patricia Polacco
http://www.patriciapolacco.com

Robert Kimmel Smith
http://www.bdd.com/bin/forums/teachers/smit.html

Zilpha Keatley Snyder
http://www.bdd.com/bin/forums/teachers/snyd.html

Chapter 5

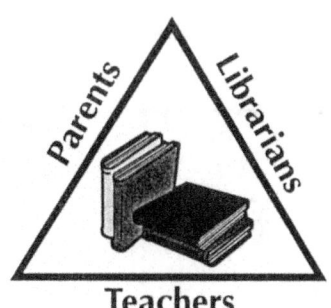

Social Issues . . . Too Graphic?

OVERVIEW

People in all times and all places must cope with social issues like homelessness, poverty, divorce, disabilities, abuse, and the like. Children do not escape these problems, but literature gives them a way to view these aspects of life. It shows them characters who face, survive, and overcome these issues.

Psychologist David Elkind, in his book *The Hurried Child*, says that we might be overburdening our children with so many books depicting the ills of society. They need a chance to be *children* before they tackle these subjects. They need a chance to deal with the problems of children before they hear about the woes of society.

The success of books of this nature depends on the author's ability to provide an emotional frame of reference so children in general can relate. Once thought to be unsuitable, these topics have now invaded picture books as well. The attainment of a level of understanding and the overall treatment of a topic makes literature on social issues an important aspect of life in the twenty-first century.

GUIDED READING QUESTIONS

1. Read two books, preferably on different levels, treating the same social issue. Compare and contrast how the issue is treated.
2. Is the treatment of this social issue appropriate for this age level?
3. Does the story have a happy ending? Is the ending realistic?
4. Would the book be appropriate for an introduction to the issue? Would it prompt discussion? Would it foster understanding?

From *More Reading Connections*. © 1999. Knowles/Smith. Libraries Unlimited. (800) 237-6124.

JOURNAL ARTICLE

Kissing the Genie: The Use of Ritual in Children's Literature

These books ... show readers that others, like themselves, experience hurt and frustration and yet find a way to survive.

Rituals are as old as time, often associated with family functions such as weddings and funerals. They are patterns of behavior employed to put children to sleep or to start a new school year. Rituals can have group meaning or be singularly personal. It is the ritual of the private, inner world that comforts us most and guards against our deepest hurt. For children, rituals bring direction to parts of their lives over which they have little or no control. They can act as shields and safeguards, insurance and security. As childhood is a constant state of testing limitation and freedom, youngsters often look for the "comfort zone" in their existence. When none is found, rituals can be used to enact a self-made social order.

In many psychological novels for children, a pattern unites several characters' experiences. Rituals are used by children as a tool for bargaining, a mode for self-punishment, and a shield from extreme abuse. Ultimately, they are used as a protective device during a crisis to assure youngsters that peace will be restored to their lives. Once stability is established, the need for ritual diminishes.

What is the purpose of these novels that so graphically depict children's psychological struggles with the adult world? They bring to life events that occur in readers' lives. Without sugar-coating honest experience, they cover societal issues from a personal point of view. Children's ability to read about others experiencing pain, finding coping mechanisms, and emerging with a new sense of self is the most valuable quality of these books because they show readers that others, like themselves, experience hurt and frustration and yet find a way to survive. These stories act out the process of maturation and the induction into an adult world. In the classic home/away/home pattern of timeless storytelling, these novels follow children as they experience a devastating loss or debilitating crisis, and yet somehow manage to thrive.

In several examples from children's literature, the rituals involve the character's bargaining with a typically undefined higher power. Mia, in Suzanne Freeman's *The Cuckoo's Child* (Greenwillow, 1996), wishes only for the safe return of her parents, presumed lost at sea. She frequently contracts with herself to try and control a situation hopelessly out of her reach. At one point, she forsakes all sweets in an attempt to bring back her parents. When she is tempted by a piece of candy, a warning flashes through her mind: "Stop now if you want your mom and dad back." This self-conscious denial of

---

By Kate O'Dell Madison. Reprinted with permission of *School Library Journal* (February 1997), pages 36–37. Kate O'Dell Madison is a Youth Services Librarian at the Tempe Public Library, AZ.

pleasure is Mia's attempt to gain control of a situation over which she has no control. Kevin Henkes's *Protecting Marie* (Greenwillow, 1995) features Fanny, an adolescent girl bargaining with the fates to help her understand her father's actions after he gets rid of her dog and spends the night of his 60th birthday away from home. One of her rituals involves game playing to win her father's return that night: "If any of my father's initials are on the license plate of the next car we pass, he'll be home, she told herself." Both examples illustrate children using a simple ritual to regain a sense of right with the world.

Children also inflict unconscious self-punishment if they blame themselves for the crisis they are in. In *The Cuckoo's Child,* Mia's long-awaited return to the United States is paid for with the price of her parents' lives; Mia's mistakenly placed guilt consumes her. The internal pressure she places on herself manifests itself in physical effects. She no longer sleeps through the night, and she practices a bizarre, yet extremely personal, ritual of touching the individual numbers on the kitchen clock face. But this alone does not sustain her. "Touching the numbers was routine now, too simple. I had to do more, always more." She expands her ritual to include opening and closing doors, kissing the Mr. Clean bottle three times, and illuminating the bones of her hands with a flashlight. Mia continues her sleep only after performing these rituals. The acts convince her that she has control. "When morning came back and the light showed in the window, it was because I'd been good, doing everything I had to do."

In *Protecting Marie,* Fanny's inability to sleep affects her so deeply that she struggles through the night for rest, eventually coming up with a name for her difficulty: internity, "the dismal, endless time of night when one cannot fall asleep." Fanny's nighttime rituals show her in a vain attempt to control her body. During the day, her anxiety is further expressed in the "tightness" that engulfs her stomach.

But self-punishment can go even further than mild disruption of routine. Not recognizing the futility of physical pain as remedy to her problem, Mia not only jumps off a water tower to bring back her parents but also scours herself with steaming hot water after breaking the "no sweets" rule. "I would never cheat again, never try to change the rules." Mia creates these "rules" to follow some sort of order in her chaotic life. She believes that "the more you wanted something, the more likely it was that you would have to give it up." And if you don't give it up, you pay for it in some way.

Two examples of using ritual as a shield from abuse are found in Carolyn Conlan's *What Jamie Saw* (Front Street, 1996) and Cynthia Voigt's *When She Hollers* (Scholastic, 1994). Magic has great appeal for Jamie, a preadolescent boy living in the upheaval of his mother's dysfunctional life. When Jamie and his family flee his mother's abusive boyfriend, he takes his set of magic tricks with him and repeatedly uses them not only as entertainment but also as protection. When the violent man finds the family, Jamie calls on his magic for the greatest trick imaginable: protecting the family, "It was . . . as if all those hours of practice had been for this one moment." While the boy cannot control a grown man in his actions, he can use the power he has in his performing to attempt to control the situation. Jamie is the exception to the rule of most of these characters; after the crisis passes, he does not give up his ritual. He continues to perform magic tricks. It is a talent that will sustain him as his journey through an unstable adolescence continues.

When She Hollers demonstrates the daily hell of an adolescent being molested by her stepfather. Trish's life is made up of dozens of small, intricate rituals involving the clothes she wears, the lipstick she puts on, and the knife she carries in her boot as protection from her abuser. When faced with confrontation, she cannot will herself to use it on him, but still it acts as a comfort and defense.

In most of these novels, characters face a crisis and use ritual to gain mastery of their wildly spinning worlds. Once they start to gain control again, they can give up the ritual, or go home in the classic sense of the journey. Trish surrenders the knife when she finds an older authority figure to defend her. When Mia can learn to trust her aunt and sisters and face a life without her parents, her need for so much self-control diminishes. When Fanny admits to her father that she is afraid of him and he the same to her, both of them get to know one another under new identities.

Many children display mild symptoms of obsessive-compulsive neurosis in daily life when faced with stress. To deal with it, they often create these rituals out of overanxious concern in what is a natural reaction. In these novels, readers are given an honest portrayal of how some children respond to difficult times. These characters are so vivid with such strong inner monologues that it is impossible to doubt their stories or the authenticity of their anguish. At one point in *Protecting Marie,* Fanny wonders at the pure pain inflicted on children by the adults who control them. "It occurred to Fanny that children, as they grow older, probably forget how awful it is to experience that powerlessness." What these novels provide is a voice to tell children that not everyone forgets. Their experiences are real, and true, and universal. Suzanne Freeman, in an ongoing Internet listserv discussion of *The Cuckoo's Child,* said that, "The rituals that Mia follows weren't part of my original plan, but they worked themselves into the story and they felt powerful, so they stayed and eventually became an integral part of the book." These rituals may not be intentional but rather the natural results of how some children, and adults, react to difficult times.

When children are very young, they may need a special blanket or toy to comfort them, and as they mature these protective devices take different and more elaborate form. The use of ritual exists in the commonplace and the extreme to assist them in their crises. How expressive and truly honest literature can be when readers know they aren't the only ones kissing a picture of a bald genie in an effort to exert their own destiny. ▲

ANNOTATED JOURNAL ARTICLES

Hawkes, Gail. "Problem Novels in the Classroom," *Book Report* (March/April 1996): 20–21.

    A teacher shows how she used young adult problem novels in a high school psychology class. She required that the students select a novel from a list and then write a paper about how the author treated the social issue. The papers revealed a high level of understanding, and during oral presentations about their findings, many students highly recommended their novels to classmates. The article includes the list of 31 problem novels.

Lanes, Selma G. "Civil People, Uncivil Times," *Horn Book Magazine* (September/October 1996): 555–58.

    The author questions the kind of books published today, which seem to accept a level of social unrest and violence to go along with what children see on television, both in the news and in other programming. We are becoming numbed by the over-exposure, because it seems that violence is no longer taken seriously. The author reminds us of the most exalted roles for children's literature: to expand our horizons, to influence our moral outlook, to examine all the wonderful possibilities that life can bring us, and to show us what kind of people we should endeavor to be.

Zvirin, Stephanie. "Disabled Kids: Learning, Feeling, and Behaving," *Book Links* (May 1996): 15–20.

    This annotated bibliography of books will lead children away from harmful stereotypes and labels and promote understanding instead. These books are excellent choices for discussion and a variety of genres is represented, including stories about disabled kids as well as stories told by the disabled. It complements a previous article in *Book Links*: "Disabled Kids: Choices and Challenges" (January 1994).

ANNOTATED BIBLIOGRAPHY

Calhoun, Mary. *Flood.* Morrow Junior Books, 1997.

    Sarajean cannot believe that her beloved river, the Mississippi, might overflow its banks. The levee is piled high with sandbags and it is time for Mom and Dad to sandbag around their home. They move some of the furniture to Uncle Perry's home inland and tie the john boat to the front porch. Grandma refuses to leave. If the river keeps rising, they will move to the second floor. Sarajean feels safe. That night, the levee breaks and her family flees in the john boat to Uncle Perry's. Sarajean reassures Grandma that they will not lose their home: "Because home means us. Home is when we're all together." *Flood* is dedicated to the victims and workers in the Midwest floods of 1993.

Martinez, Victor. *Parrot in the Oven: Mi Vida.* HarperCollins, 1996.

    Manuel Hernandez is trying to find out what it means to be a *vato firme*, a guy to respect, during a year with his family in the projects. His father loses his job and spends most of his time and what little money there is at Rico's pool hall. Nardo,

Manny's older brother, always has a different job but manages to stay out of serious trouble. His older sister, Magda, is the only one working a steady job. His mother cannot complain about Magda's behavior for fear she will move out. The mother tries to keep the family together by spending most of her time cleaning. Incidents in the novel are told from Manny's perspective and they lead up to his joining a gang. Manny learns that gangs are not the answer while he demonstrates the person he should be, a man to respect.

Mochizuki, Ken. *Passage to Freedom: The Sugihara Story.* Lee & Low, 1997.

In 1940, five-year-old Hiroki Sugihara and his family lived in a small town in Lithuania. Hiroki's father was a Japanese diplomat. One morning hundreds of Polish-Jewish refugees appeared outside their home, asking for help. They wanted visas, which would give them official written permission to travel to another country. Without the visas, the Nazis would soon catch up to them. Hiroki's father asked permission from the Japanese government to write the visas. He was denied permission three times. The entire family agreed that something had to be done regardless of their personal danger. For the next month, Chiune Sugihara wrote visas early in the morning until late at night. Hiroki's father insisted that he would be the only one involved, so that no one else would get in trouble. He continued to write the visas until it was time for him to leave Lithuania. The years after Lithuania were difficult ones for Hiroki and his family. This was a story about one brave person who made a difference. It was believed that Chiune Sugihara saved as many as 10,000 Jewish refugees. In 1985, he was chosen to receive the "Righteous Among Nations" Award from the famous Holocaust Memorial, Yad Vashem, in Israel. He was the first and only Asian ever to receive this award.

Sisulu, Elinor Batezat. *The Day Gogo Went to Vote: South Africa, April 1994.* Little, Brown, 1996.

Gogo was Thembi's great-grandmother. Gogo called Thembi her tail because she followed her everywhere. One day, Thembi's parents were very excited. There could be an election for a new government in South Africa. On April 26, 1994, there would be a special voting time for the old and very sick. Everyone was shocked when Gogo announced that she was going to vote. Gogo was very old and never went out of the yard. She refused to listen to her family, who thought she was too infirm to vote. Gogo told Thembi, "Black people in South Africa have fought for many years for the right to vote. This is the first time we have a chance to vote for our own leaders, and it might be my last. That is why I must vote, no matter how many miles I have to walk, no matter how long I have to stand in line!"

Taylor, Mildred. *The Well.* Dial Books for Young Readers, 1995.

The Logan family has more than 200 acres of land and the sweetest well water around that part of Mississippi. When there is a drought and all the creeks and wells dry up, the neighbors, black and white, line up to get barrels of the Logan's water. Even Mr. Simms, the meanest man in town, sends his teenage son, Charlie, to get water. This creates a problem for David Logan and his proud older brother, Hammer. Hammer does not like Charlie Simms's lack of respect for Mama, and the way he demands water because he is white. This leads to a confrontation between the boys, even though

Hammer knows he could be hung for hitting a white boy. To save Hammer, Mama whips and humiliates David and Hammer in front of the Simms family. The Logan family troubles do not end there. The well, which was the equalizer when water was scarce, becomes the target of a cowardly act: it is poisoned with dead animals. David and Hammer know who did this terrible crime but will the townspeople believe two black boys?

Wersba, Barbara. *Whistle Me Home.* Henry Holt, 1977.

Noli thinks she has found her soul mate in T.J. He is sensitive, gentle, and kind. T.J. likes Noli to dress like him and tries to get her to stop drinking vodka secretly. When Noli's parents leave for the weekend, she plans the perfect evening. When T.J. does not respond to her advances, she says, "You're gay, aren't you?" Sadly, Noli learns that T.J. has been in therapy for a year. He loves Noli and hasn't been using her. Three months later, Noli runs into T.J. and his new male friend. She doesn't hate him now, and maybe in the future they will be friends.

BIBLIOGRAPHY

Primary

Applebaum, Diana. *Giants in the Land.* Houghton Mifflin, 1993.

Baker, Jeannie. *Window.* Greenwillow Books, 1991.

Bradbury, Marie. *More Than Anything Else.* Orchard, 1995.

Bunting, Eve. *The Day Before Christmas.* Clarion Books, 1992.

———. *Fly Away Home.* Clarion Books, 1991.

———. *Smoky Night.* Harcourt Brace, 1994.

———. *Train to Somewhere.* Clarion Books, 1996.

Carrick, Carol. *What a Wimp!* Clarion Books, 1982.

Cherry, Lynne. *A River Ran Wild.* Harcourt Brace Jovanovich, 1992.

dePaola, Tomie. *Nana Upstairs and Nana Downstairs.* Putnam, 1973.

———. *Now One Foot, Now the Other.* G. P. Putnam's Sons, 1981.

———. *Oliver Button Is a Sissy.* Harcourt Brace Jovanovich, 1979.

Dolphin, Laurie. *Neve Shalom-Wahat Al-Salam: Oasis of Peace.* Scholastic, 1992.

Flournoy, Valerie. *The Patchwork Quilt.* Dial Books for Young Readers, 1985.

Garland, Sherry. *I Never Knew Your Name.* World Publications, 1994.

———. *The Lotus Seed.* Harcourt Brace, 1993.

Heide, Florence Parry. *The Day of Ahmed's Secret.* Lothrop, Lee & Shepard, 1990.

———. *Sami and the Time of Troubles.* Clarion Books, 1992.

Hendershot, Judith. *In Coal Country.* Alfred A. Knopf, 1987.

Henkes, Kevin. *Chester's Way*. Greenwillow Books, 1988.
Leighton, Maxinne Rhea. *An Ellis Island Christmas*. Viking, 1992.
Sendak, Maurice. *We Are All in the Dumps with Jack and Guy*. HarperCollins, 1993.
Van Allsburg, Chris. *Just a Dream*. Houghton Mifflin, 1990.

General

Adler, C. S. *Split Sisters*. Macmillan, 1986.
Anderson, Rachel. *The Bus People*. Henry Holt, 1989.
Armstrong, Jennifer. *Steal Away*. Scholastic, 1992.
Avi. *The Barn*. Orchard, 1994.
Bauer, Marion Dane. *On My Honor*. Clarion Books, 1986.
———. *A Question of Trust*. Scholastic, 1994.
Blume, Judy. *Blubber*. Bradbury Press, 1973.
Brooks, Bruce. *Everywhere*. Harper & Row, 1990.
Bunting, Eve. *Sharing Susan*. HarperCollins, 1991.
———. *A Sudden Silence*. Harcourt Brace Jovanovich, 1988.
Butterworth, Oliver. *A Visit to the Big House*. Houghton Mifflin, 1993.
Byars, Betsy. *Cracker Jackson*. Viking Kestrel, 1985.
———. *Good-bye Chicken Little*. Harper & Row, 1979.
———. *The Pinballs*. Harper & Row, 1977.
Cadnum, Michael. *Taking It*. Viking, 1995.
Choi, Sook Nyul. *Echoes of the White Giraffe*. Houghton Mifflin, 1993.
———. *Year of the Impossible Goodbyes*. Houghton Mifflin, 1991.
Cleary, Beverly. *Dear Mr. Henshaw*. Dell, 1983.
———. *Ramona and Her Father*. William Morrow, 1977.
———. *Strider*. Avon Books, 1991.
Coman, Carolyn. *What Jamie Saw*. Front Street, 1995.
Cooney, Caroline B. *Whatever Happened to Janie?* Delacorte Press, 1993.
Creech, Sharon. *Walk Two Moons*. HarperCollins, 1994.
Doherty, Berlie. *Street Child*. Orchard, 1993.
Duffey, Betsy. *Coaster*. Viking, 1994.
Ellis, Sarah. *Pick-Up Sticks*. Margaret K. McElderry, 1992.
Fox, Paula. *The Moonlight Man*. Bradbury Press, 1986.
———. *One-Eyed Cat*. Bradbury Press, 1984.

From *More Reading Connections*. © 1999. Knowles/Smith. Libraries Unlimited. (800) 237-6124.

Franco, Marjorie. *So Who Hasn't Got Problems?* Houghton Mifflin, 1979.

Freedman, Russell. *Kids at Work: Lewis Hine and the Crusade Against Child Labor.* Clarion Books, 1994.

Gardiner, John Reynolds. *Stone Fox.* Thomas Y. Crowell, 1980.

Greene, Constance. *Beat the Turtle Drum.* Viking, 1976.

Hamilton, Virginia. *Plain City.* Blue Sky Press, 1993.

Klass, Sheila Solomon. *Kool Ada.* Scholastic, 1991.

Lasky, Kathryn. *Memoirs of a Bookbat.* Harcourt Brace, 1994.

Lowry, Lois. *A Summer to Die.* Houghton Mifflin, 1997.

Martin, Ann M. *With You and Without You.* Holiday House, 1986.

Mazer, Norma Fox. *After the Rain.* Morrow Junior Books, 1987.

Mikaelsen, Ben. *Sparrow Hawk Red.* Hyperion Books, 1993.

Moeri, Louise. *Downwind.* E. P. Dutton, 1984.

Myers, Walter Dean. *Scorpions.* Harper & Row, 1988.

———. *Somewhere in the Darkness.* Scholastic, 1992.

Park, Barbara. *The Kid in the Red Jacket.* Alfred A. Knopf, 1987.

Paterson, Katherine. *The Great Gilly Hopkins.* Thomas Y. Crowell, 1978.

———. *Park's Quest.* Lodestar, 1981.

Peck, Robert Newton. *Arly.* Walker, 1989.

Rylant, Cynthia. *A Fine White Dust.* Bradbury Press, 1986.

Smith, Doris Buchanan. *A Taste of Blackberries.* Scholastic, 1973.

Spinelli, Jerry. *Maniac Magee.* Little, Brown, 1990.

Staples, Suzanne Fisher. *Shabanu: Daughter of the Wind.* Alfred A. Knopf, 1989.

Taylor, Theodore. *The Bomb.* Harcourt Brace, 1995.

———. *Sweet Friday Island.* Harcourt Brace, 1994.

Temple, Frances. *Grab Hands and Run.* Orchard, 1993.

Voigt, Cynthia. *Dicey's Song.* Atheneum, 1982.

———. *Homecoming.* Atheneum, 1981.

———. *Izzy, Willy-Nilly.* Atheneum, 1986.

Wallace, Bill. *The Christmas Spurs.* Holiday House, 1990.

5 ▲ SOCIAL ISSUES... TOO GRAPHIC?

WEB SITES

Ability Online Support Network
http://www.ablelink.org

The Body Home Page
http://www.thebody.com

Children's Care Hospital & School
http://www.cchs.org/kids.html

Christopher Paul Curtis
http://www.bdd.com/bin/forums/teachers/curt.html

Convomania
http://www.mania.apple.com

Deaf CyberKids
http://dww.deafworldweb.org/kids

Eve Bunting
http://www.friend.ly.net/scoop/biographies/ebunting.html

Family Village
http://familyvillage.wisc.edu

Graham Salisbury
http://www.bdd.com/bin/forums/teachers/sals.html

A Guide to Children's Literature and Disability
http://www.kidsource.com/NICHCY/literature.html

How You Can Help
http://www.educational.net/charity.htm

Kazumi Yumoto
http://www.bdd.com/bin/forums/teachers/yumo.html

Kids' Home at the National Cancer Institute
http://icic.nci.nig.gov/occdocs/KidsHome.html

Mildred Taylor
http://falcon.jmu.edu/~ramseyil/taylor.htm

Virginia Hamilton
http://www.virginiahamilton.com

Walter Dean Myers
http://www.bdd.com/bin/forums/teachers/myer.html

Chapter 6

Folklore and Mythology—Literature of the Fireside

OVERVIEW

Ever since human beings realized they were unique, in that they could think and talk, they have tried to explain themselves and their world. People created stories that helped their primitive minds understand the world. The storytellers told these tales again and again around the fires of the early tribes, by the hearths of humble cottages, before the great fire in the king's hall; they told them as they sat in the grass huts of the jungle, the hogans of the southern plains, and the igloos of the northern tundra. Their children told them and their children's children, until the stories were as smooth and polished as the roundest stones in a stream. And so people created their myths and their folklore, their legends and epics—the literature of the fireside, the poetry of the people, and the memory of humankind.

C. Huck, S. Hepler, J. Hickman, & B. Kiefer, *Children's Literature in the Elementary School* (Brown and Benchmark, 1997).

GUIDED READING QUESTIONS

Folklore

1. What type of folktale did you read?
    a. Did it answer the question *why* (*pourquoi*)?
    b. Did it have animals that talk and act like humans?
    c. Did the folktale contain magic (e.g., fairy tales)?
    d. Was this a realistic tale? One that could have happened?

From *More Reading Connections*. © 1999. Knowles/Smith. Libraries Unlimited. (800) 237-6124.

2. Did your folktale include sounds, language, or customs from the country of its origin?
3. Did the illustrations reflect the culture of the country?
4. Were any words repeated over and over?
5. Compare several versions of the same folktale: are they different or similar?
6. Read a fairy tale you remember from your childhood. Is it as you remembered? Were there any surprises?

Myth

1. Did your story explain any phenomena? If so, what?
2. Compare myths of two different cultures. How are they alike and/or different?
3. Read a Greek myth. Do you see any evidence of pride or hubris in the main character? Did you notice the disastrous results of pride?

Multicultural Publishing: The Folktale Flood

Discerning fantasy from reality is not a problem
when the tale is from one's own heritage,
but that is not necessarily so when the culture is unfamiliar.

The past decade has seen a welcome increase in the numbers of children's books about non-European cultures. Publishers have responded to our nation's increasing diversity and the call for a more inclusive curriculum. The whole language movement, with its emphasis upon trade books in the classroom, has also contributed to the rise of multicultural publishing.

The wealth of materials about diverse cultures has not been evenly distributed, however. Picture books and folktales for the youngest readers dominate. Those seeking chapter books and stories for older readers, as well as contemporary fiction for any age group, often come up empty-handed. For many regions of the world, including Africa, much of Asia, and Latin America, folktales far outnumber books of any other genre. The same situation exists for Native Americans. Young readers wanting books about the indigenous people of Oceania have little else from which to choose.

Scholastic editor Phoebe Yeh has pointed out that folktales dominate because they are "the 'safest' way to publish multiculturally."[1] In comparison to other genres, they require very little research, although Betsy Hearne, in her excellent *SLJ* two-part article, "Reducing Cultural Chaos in Picture Books," has observed that often authors and publishers do not even engage in that minimal amount of research.[2] Given adequate source notes, people tend to take the authenticity of a folktale for granted, while authenticity must constantly be proven for a contemporary story, particularly if it has been written by someone outside that culture. Even though the choice of folktales published may say as much about issues in our society today as about traditional themes (witness the explosion of tales from Native American and African roots with environmental messages), restricting ourselves to this genre allows us to sidestep contemporary conflicts and problems. It is far easier to offer a legend from South Africa, for example, than to portray children enduring the consequences of apartheid.

Folktales offer other advantages to publishers and book creators, not the least of which are ready-made characters and plots. Personifications of the struggle between good and evil, noble heroes and cruel villains would seem forced and unrealistic in an original tale, but are part of traditions the world over.

Other advantages are economic. Tales "collected" by the author or that appear in older anthologies belong to the public domain. Writers and publishers can copyright an adaptation without paying fees or royalties; furthermore, a wholly different version of the same

---

By Lyn Miller-Lachmann. Reprinted with permission of *School Library Journal* (February 1994), pages 35–36. Lyn Miller-Lachmann is Editor-in-Chief of *MultiCultural Review*.

tale may be published later and copyrighted by that reteller or illustrator. For this and other reasons, publishers have come to see folktales as showcases for the work of distinguished artists.

These adaptations have been a major presence on lists of award-winning and distinguished books. In the past 10 years, they have won many Caldecott medals and honor citations. Specialists in multicultural literature must (and do) acknowledge the place of folktale retellings as among the best of what is available. For instance, in 1992, the first children's book award of the African Studies Association went to David Wisniewski's *Sundiata: Lion King of Mali* (Clarion, 1992). Tony Fairman's *Bury My Bones but Keep My Words* (Holt, 1992), a folklore collection for older readers, also received almost universal praise.

So what's the problem? Aren't myths and folktales, in the words of Donna Norton, "the great stories on which whole cultures have been founded, the threads that weave the past with the present and the themes and values that continue to be important to the people"?[3] However, when they are virtually the only materials available, children receive an incomplete and distorted picture.

Most folktales are set in rural or village communities untouched by the radical changes of the 20th century—the commercialization of agriculture, industrialization, urbanization, and, in the case of many indigenous groups, dispossession, and even genocide. Niki Daly's original picture book *Not So Fast, Songololo* (McElderry, 1985) presents a very different portrait of life in South Africa from that revealed in folktales from the region. Malusi, known as Songololo, and his grandmother travel to the city from their village on the outskirts, and they shop in a discount department store much like one found in the U. S. While the social and political context remains unstated in this book for young children, its portrayal of urban life in South Africa today is authentic. Even an original story set in a rural area, such as Karen Lynn Williams's *Galimoro* (Lothrop, 1990), offers insight into a changing culture. Here, Kondi, a boy in Malawi, searches for wire to build a toy car; once he is done, he imagines building an ambulance, an airplane, or a helicopter. (In reality, he can also find plastic or metal toys at the village marketplace, though homemade toys are still common in rural areas of southern Africa.)

In addition to overemphasizing the rural, folktales tend to highlight what is exotic in a culture. Too many books set in Africa, both folklore and concept books such as Hannah Heritage Bozylinsky's *Lah Salama* (Philomel, 1993), show children romping with wild animals. Other examples of exotica that appear frequently are oversized masks, elaborate and colorful costumes, face painting and scarification, and rocks or other natural features that have supernatural powers. While any or all such things may have a place within a culture, and within its folklore, they reinforce the sense of cultural difference without pointing out commonalities and the ways in which cultures change over time.

All folktales have an element of fantasy. European Americans do not eat children or force poor young women to spin straw into gold under penalty of death, but these practices are part of European folk tradition. Even beginning readers know to suspend disbelief when presented with such tales, which are designed, nonetheless, to entertain and/or to teach. Discerning fantasy from reality is not a problem when the tale is from one's own heritage, but that is not necessarily so when the culture is unfamiliar. Michael Afolayan, professor of African literature at Obafemi Awolowo University in Nigeria, in discussing the highly regarded *Mufaro's Beautiful Daughters* (Lothrop, 1987), gives examples of "elements of fantasy that form part of the oral tradition but are not characteristic of everyday life in Africa."[4] Among those elements are the "competition call" made by the region's most beautiful women to the king seeking a wife and the tameness of otherwise wild animals in the presence of the good characters.[5] Nonfiction, historical fiction, and contemporary fiction all have a place in helping children to distinguish what is fantasy and what is real.

In the absence of other materials, folktales may be interpreted according to our own cultural concerns and agendas. Verna Aardema's retelling of a Rwandan tale in *Sebgugugu the Glutton* (Eerdmans, 1993) uses Zulu terms inappropriately, but even more serious is the potential for misinterpretation. The tale warns of gluttony, of taking more than one needs, in the tradition of much of the region's didactic folklore. We in the West, however, may read it as an example of the "noble savage" stereotype, in which humankind lives in harmony and interdependence with nature. The reality is much more complex, as the cattle Sebgugugu seeks are the measure of a person's worth in traditional societies of southern Africa, and to seek more cattle (or to engage in enterprise of any kind) is encouraged rather than forbidden. Offering another perspective through accurate nonfiction and authentic fiction written for the same age group will prevent tales from being read out of context and their meaning from being distorted.

For many cultures, no such alternative perspectives exist. Thus, our multicultural books do a better job of highlighting differences, spiritual roots, fantasies, and ancient ways of life—all necessary but not the complete picture—than showing what we have in common and the way people around the world live today. South Africa is an exception, as there are several outstanding novels for intermediate readers, including Beverly Naidoo's *Journey to Jo'burg* (HarperCollins, 1986) and Sheila Gordon's *The Middle of Somewhere* (Orchard, 1990). Both of these books portray young black heroines living in a country marked by poverty, injustice, conflict, and yet, hope for the future. The South Africa of these two titles bears little resemblance to the villages featured in the published folktales from the region, and while the authors describe a different way of life from that experienced by most youngsters in the U. S., there are many commonalities: poverty, loneliness, separation from one or both parents, and dreams for the future. Yet for the rest of Africa, there is little nonfiction or contemporary fiction for intermediate readers. And the growing number of folktale collections aimed at this group does little to remedy the situation.

As those committed to increasing children's awareness of other cultures, we must be aware of the contributions of folktales but also of their limitations. Above all, we must strive to find other works that offer more contemporary perspectives in order to place the traditional tales we study in their proper context.

References

1. Yeh, Phoebe. "Multicultural Publishing: The Best and the Worst of Times." *Journal of Youth Services in Libraries.* (6:2) Winter 1993, p. 157.

2. Hearne, Betsy. "Cite the Source: Reducing Cultural Chaos in Picture Books, Part One." *School Library Journal.* (39:2) July 1993, p. 24.

3. Norton, Donna. "Teaching Multicultural Literature in the Reading Curriculum." *The Reading Teacher.* (44:1) September 1990, p. 28.

4. Afolayan, Michael, Patricia Kuntz, and Brenda Naze. "Sub-Saharan Africa." In *Our Family, Our Friends, Our World: An Annotated Guide to Significant Multicultural Books for Children and Teenagers.* Lyn Miller-Lachmann. New Providence, NJ: R. R. Bowker, 1992. p. 429.

5. Ibid.: p. 428, 429. ▲

ANNOTATED JOURNAL ARTICLES

Hurst, Carol Otis. "Mythology for the Masses," *Teaching K-8* (March 1996): 82.
    This is a review of three books on the Trojan War. It focuses on one, *Dateline: Troy* (Candlewick, 1996), by Paul Fleischman. It provides a fairly detailed summary and a list of seven possible extension activities.

Ingrassia, Michele, Karen Springen, and Pat Wingert. "What If the Wolf Tried Conflict Mediation?" *Newsweek* (January 31, 1994): 62–63.
    Golden Books rewrote some of the classic fairy tales to put a nonviolent twist on tradition. *The Three Little Pigs, Little Red Riding Hood,* and *Chicken Little* were the ones changed. Some psychologists feel that a safe scare through a fairy tale is fine and even necessary, although they stress that parents should be there to explain and discuss. Others say there is no reason to expose the youngest to these scary stories, as they will experience many scary things later on in life. The article deals with all the pros and cons of this issue.

ANNOTATED BIBLIOGRAPHY

Ben-Ezer, Ehud. *Hosni the Dreamer: An Arabian Tale.* Farrar, Straus & Giroux, 1997.
    Hosni, a shepherd, works for a sheik. The other shepherds think Hosni is strange. He keeps to himself and tells the sheep his dreams of a faraway city. When the sheik decides to sell some of his camels in the city, he takes Hosni and several of the other shepherds with him. After the camels are sold, the sheik gives each shepherd a *dinar* and the rest of the day to explore the city. Hosni does not spend his money on food or treats, but buys a verse from an old man. The old man slowly says, "Don't cross the water until you know its depth." The old man does not speak again. When the sheik and the other shepherds learn that Hosni spent his money on a verse, they burst out laughing. Hosni wisely listens to the verse and changes his life and fortune forever.

Climo, Shirley. *Atalanta's Race.* Clarion Books, 1995.
    When Atalanta is born, her father, King Iasus, is disappointed that she is a girl. He casts her away on a mountainside. A she-bear hears the baby whimpering and places Atalanta alongside her cubs for the winter. A hunter stumbles upon the cave and baby. He raises Atalanta and teaches her how to hunt and take care of herself. After winning many awards for her athletic ability, she is summoned to King Iasus, where she learns of her biological father and her earlier fate. Princess Atalanta decides to stay and the king urges her to choose a husband and marry. Atalanta decides that she will challenge prospective suitors to a footrace and that "he who loses will lose his head."
    Melanion, a young Greek warrior, is regarded as a hero and an athlete. Atalanta pleads with Melanion to withdraw from the race. With the help of Aphrodite, Melanion wins and marries Atalanta. However, the couple never offer appropriate thanks to Aphrodite and are turned into a lion and lioness. Atalanta's famous race was about the length of a present-day 1,500-meter run.

Hamilton, Virginia. *Her Stories: African American Folk Tales, Fairy Tales, True Tales.* Blue Sky Press, 1995.

There is one full-page illustration, by Leo and Diane Dillon, per story. The book represents a broad range of folk tales, fairy tales, and stories of legendary women. The last three stories give true accounts of events in African history. "Catskinella" is a Cinderella story; "Lonna and the Cat Woman" tells about a her-vampire; and "Miz Hattie Gets Some Company" puts a twist on the idea of where and how cats originated. Each story has endnotes with additional information and explanations from the author.

Levine, Gail. *Ella Enchanted.* HarperCollins, 1997.

This is a type of Cinderella story, though it is not really clear that this is the case until near the end of the book. Ella is visited by a fairy as a baby and given a gift of obedience, which turns out to be a curse. Ella must obey every command said to her; she cannot refuse. Ella becomes friends with Prince Char at a young age. Ella's mother dies when Ella is still young and her father sends her off to finishing school. The two daughters of an acquaintance go along, but the older girl discovers Ella's curse and makes Ella her personal slave. Ella runs away from school and makes her way home. Then her romance with Prince Char culminates with a true "Cinderella" ending.

Mayer, Mariana, reteller. *Pegasus.* Morrow Junior Books, 1997.

This is the story of Pegasus and Bellerophon and their struggle to defeat the monster, Chimera, so that Bellerophon can marry the king's daughter. The Greek tale is delightfully illustrated.

Napoli, Donna Jo. *Zel.* Dutton Children's Books, 1996.

This is a young adult version of the fairy tale of Rapunzel, told in alternating chapters from the points of view of Zel, Mother, and Konrad, the young noble. Zel is an innocent 13-year-old girl who was locked in a tower by her mother. Mother is a barren woman who gave up her soul to acquire Zel. Zel's real name is Rapunzel, a type of lettuce. Her birth mother craved Rapunzel so much that she bewitched her husband into trading the newborn baby for some lettuce.

Mother happily raises Zel but cannot share her, so she locks Zel in the tower. Konrad, after a brief encounter with Zel, searches for two years to find her. Once again, he succeeds, but not before Mother blinds Konrad and has Zel carried off by the trees. After another two years and Zel gives birth to twins, Konrad finds Zel. Zel's tears run into Konrad's eyes and he is able to see. They are happy at long last.

Philip, Neil. *The Illustrated Book of Myths.* Dorling Kindersley, 1995.

This is a well-illustrated anthology of myths. It begins with an introduction describing myths in general. There are maps of the eastern and western hemispheres indicating where various kinds of myths originated. The book begins with 12 creation myths representing different cultures. It continues to explore myths in the following categories: Fertility and Cultivation, Gods and People, Gods and Animals, Visions of the End, and Gods and Pantheons. There is also a "Who's Who in Mythology" at the end of the book, with pronunciations of the names, cultures represented, and many character descriptions.

From *More Reading Connections.* © 1999. Knowles/Smith. Libraries Unlimited. (800) 237-6124.

Yep, Laurence. *Tree of Dreams—Ten Tales from the Garden of Night*. Bridge Water Books, 1995.

    There is a full-page illustration at the beginning of each story. These stories about dreams come from Brazil, Japan, India, China, Greece, and Senegal. In the first tale, a man and his wife befriend a family of badgers and then the badgers help the man during his dream. In another story, a boy accidentally kills his father's fighting cricket and then dreams that his soul has entered the cricket's body.

BIBLIOGRAPHY

Myths

Aliki. *The Gods and Goddesses of Olympus*. HarperCollins, 1994.

Bellingham, David. *An Introduction to Greek Mythology*. Chartwell Books, 1989.

Caselli, Giovanni. *Gods, Men and Monsters*. Schocken Books, 1992.

Craft, Marie. *Cupid and Psyche*. Morrow Junior Books, 1996.

D'Aulaire, Ingri, and Edgar D'Aulaire. *Book of Greek Myths*. Doubleday, 1962.

Evslin, Bernard. *The Dolphin Rider and Other Greek Myths*. Scholastic, 1976.

———. *Heroes and Monsters of Greek Myths*. Scholastic, 1967.

Fisher, Leonard Everett. *The Olympians: Great Gods and Goddesses of Ancient Greece*. Holiday House, 1984.

———. *Theseus and Minotaur*. Holiday House, 1988.

Fleischman, Paul. *Dateline: Troy*. Candlewick Press, 1996.

Goddesses, Heroes and Shamans: The Young People's Guide to World Mythology. Kingfisher, 1994.

Hamilton, Virginia. *In the Beginning: Creation Stories from Around the World*. Harcourt Brace Jovanovich, 1988.

Harris, Geraldine. *Gods and Pharaohs from Egyptian Mythology*. Schocken Books, 1982.

Hodges, Margaret. *The Arrow and the Lamp*. Little, Brown, 1989.

Hutton, Warwick. *The Trojan Horse*. Margaret K. McElderry, 1992.

Low, Alice. *The Macmillan Book of Greek Gods and Heroes*. Macmillan, 1985.

McCaughrean, Geraldine. *Greek Myths*. Margaret K. McElderry, 1993.

Osborne, Mary Pope. *Favorite Greek Myths*. Scholastic, 1989.

Osborne, Will, and Mary Pope Osborne. *The Deadly Power of Medusa*. Scholastic, 1988.

———. *Jason and the Argonauts*. Scholastic, 1988.

Philip, Neil. *The Illustrated Book of Myths*. Dorling Kindersley, 1995.

Richardson, I. M. *Prometheus and the Story of Fire*. Troll, 1983.

Simon, Jamie, and Scott Simon. *Why Dolphins Call: A Story of Dionysus*. Silver Press, 1991.

———. *Why Spiders Spin: A Story of Arachne*. Silver Press, 1991.

From *More Reading Connections*. © 1999. Knowles/Smith. Libraries Unlimited. (800) 237-6124.

Vautier, Ghislaine. *The Shining Stars: Greek Legends of the Zodiac*. Cambridge University Press, 1989.

———. *The Way of the Stars*. Cambridge University Press, 1989.

Yolen, Jane. *Wings*. Harcourt Brace Jovanovich, 1991.

Folklore

Aardema, Verna. *Borreguita and the Coyote*. Alfred A. Knopf, 1991.

———. *Traveling to Tondo: A Tale of the Nkundo of Zaire*. Alfred A. Knopf, 1991.

Andersen, Hans Christian. *The Nightingale*. Doubleday, 1989.

Brett, Jan. *Beauty and the Beast*. Clarion Books, 1989.

———. *Town Mouse Country Mouse*. G. P. Putnam's Sons, 1994.

Brusca, Maria Cristina, and Tona Wilson. *When Jaguars Ate the Moon*. Henry Holt, 1995.

Bucknall, Caroline. *The Three Little Pigs*. Dial Books for Young Readers, 1987.

Campbell, Katie. *The Steadfast Tin Soldier*. Unicorn, 1990.

Cecil, Laura. *The Frog Princess*. Greenwillow Books, 1994.

Climo, Shirley. *The Egyptian Cinderella*. Thomas Y. Crowell, 1989.

dePaola, Tomie. *The Legend of the Bluebonnet*. G. P. Putnam's Sons, 1983.

Duncan, Lois. *The Magic of Spider Woman*. Scholastic, 1996.

Ehrlich, Amy. *Rapunzel*. Dial Books for Young Readers, 1989.

Galdone, Paul. *Adopted by the Eagles: A Plains Indian Story of Friendship and Treachery*. Bradbury Press, 1994.

———. *Buffalo Woman*. Bradbury Press, 1984.

———. *Iktomi and the Boulder*. Orchard, 1988.

———. *Iktomi and the Buffalo Skull*. Orchard, 1991.

———. *Love Flute*. Bradbury Press, 1982.

———. *The Three Billy Goats Gruff*. Clarion Books, 1973.

Grifalconi, Ann. *The Village of Round and Square Houses*. Little, Brown, 1986.

Hong, Lily Toy. *How the Ox Star Fell from Heaven*. Whitman, 1991.

Hyman, Trina Schart. *The Sleeping Beauty*. Little, Brown, 1977.

Isadora, Rachel. *The Firebird*. G. P. Putnam's Sons, 1994.

Karlin, Barbara. *Cinderella*. Little, Brown, 1989.

Kimmel, Eric A. *Anansi and the Talking Melon*. Holiday House, 1994.

Kirstein, Lincoln. *Puss in Boots*. Little, Brown, 1992.

Lacapa, Michael. *The Flute Player*. Northland, 1990.

Langley, Jonathan. *Rumpelstiltskin*. HarperCollins, 1991.

Lesser, Rika. *Hansel and Gretel.* Dodd, Mead, 1984.

Lester, Julius. *How Many Spots Does a Leopard Have?* Scholastic, 1989.

Lewis, Patrick. *The Tsar and the Amazing Cow.* Dial Books for Young Readers, 1988.

———. *Coyote: A Trickster Tale from the American Southwest.* Harcourt Brace, 1994.

Marshall, James. *Goldilocks and the Three Bears.* Dial Books for Young Readers, 1988.

Mayer, Marianna. *The Sleeping Beauty.* Macmillan, 1984.

———. *The Twelve Dancing Princesses.* Morrow Junior Books, 1989.

McDermott, Gerald. *Arrow to the Sun.* Viking, 1974.

Mollel, Tololwa M. *Rhinos for Lunch and Elephants for Supper!* Clarion Books, 1991.

Montresor, Beni. *Little Red Riding Hood.* Doubleday, 1991.

Moser, Barry. *The Tinderbox.* Little, Brown, 1990.

Ormerod, Jan. *The Frog Prince.* Lothrop, Lee & Shepard, 1990.

Oughton, Jerrie. *How the Stars Fell into the Sky: A Navajo Legend.* Houghton Mifflin, 1992.

Page, P. K. *The Traveling Musicians of Bremen.* Little, Brown, 1991.

Perrault, Charles. *Puss in Boots.* Farrar, Straus & Giroux, 1990.

Plume, Ilse. *The Shoemaker and the Elves.* Harcourt Brace Jovanovich, 1991.

Poole, Josephine. *Snow White.* Alfred A. Knopf, 1992.

Rogasky, Barbara. *The Water of Life.* Holiday House, 1986.

Rounds, Glen. *Three Little Pigs and the Big Bad Wolf.* Holiday House, 1992.

Sherman, Josepha. *Vassilisa the Wise.* Harcourt Brace Jovanovich, 1988.

Snyder, Dianne. *The Boy of the Three-Year Nap.* Houghton Mifflin, 1988.

Steptoe, John. *The Story of Jumping Mouse.* Lothrop, Lee & Shepard, 1984.

Stevens, Janet. *Coyote Steals the Blanket.* Holiday House, 1993.

Thorne, Ian. *Monster Tales of Native Americans.* Crestwood House, 1978.

Trivizas, Eugene. *The Three Little Wolves and the Big Bad Pig.* Margaret K. McElderry, 1993.

Van Laan, Nancy. *Buffalo Dance.* Little, Brown, 1993.

Wells, Ruth. *The Farmer and the Poor God.* Simon & Schuster, 1996.

Wilhelm, Hans. *The Bremen Town Musicians.* Scholastic, 1992.

Wood, Audrey. *The Rainbow Bridge.* Harcourt Brace Jovanovich, 1995.

Yep, Laurence. *The Man Who Tricked a Ghost.* Bridgewater Books, 1993.

Yolen, Jane. *The Emperor and the Kite.* Philomel, 1988.

Young, Ed. *Donkey Trouble.* Atheneum, 1995.

———. *Lon Po Po.* Philomel, 1989.

Zelinsky, Paul O. *Rapunzel.* Dutton Children's Books, 1997.

———. *Rumpelstiltskin.* E. P. Dutton, 1986.

WEB SITES

Creation Stories and Traditional Wisdom
http://www.ozemail.com.au/~reed/global/mythstor.html

The Encyclopedia Mythica
http://www.pantheon.org/mythica/

Folktales from Around the World—Aaron Shepard Books
http://www.aaronshep.com

Gerald McDermott
http://www.friend.ly.net/scoop/biographies/gmcdermott.html

Hans Christian Andersen
http://terminate.com/hc

Home Page of Korean Folktales
http://www.csun.edu/~hcedu004

Japanese Folktales
http://www.artsunimelb.edu.au/fcf/ucr/student/1996/a.lin/index.html

The Literature Nook Presents . . . Mythology on the Web
http://members.tripod.com/adm/popup/roadmap.shtml

Mayan Folktales
http://www.folkart.com/~latitude/folktale/folktale.htm

Mythos—Zeus Speaks
http://www.onlineclass.com/Mythos/mythos.html

Myths and Folklore
http://www.acs.ucalgary.ca/~dkbrown/storfolk.html

Robin McKinley
http://ofb.net/~damien/mckinley

Tales of Wonder
http://darsie.ucdavis.edu/tales

From *More Reading Connections*. © 1999. Knowles/Smith. Libraries Unlimited. (800) 237-6124.

Chapter 7

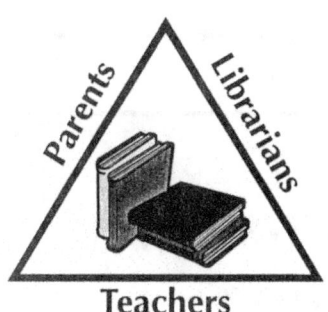

Predictable Sports Fiction

OVERVIEW

Interest in sports stories reflects the great interest felt by many children who either participate in or are fans of both individual and team sports. Fiction, biography, and informational books extend and enrich a child's personal experiences. However, it is difficult to find well-written sports stories. Usually the characters are flat or one-dimensional; one often encounters stilted dialogue, predictable plots, and pages of boring, blow-by-blow description of actual game play. Nevertheless, children often select these books because many are so personally involved on teams or as fans. It is still difficult to find female athletes in formula sports fiction. Most stories dwell on the same topics: hard work, overcoming pain, facing defeat, and good/bad sportsmanship. A new addition to sports fiction has been girls on traditional boys' teams. This used to be unheard of but is now treated without much comment or protest.

GUIDED READING QUESTIONS

1. Did you select a sports fiction book based on a sport your children play or have played?
2. Did you find the story to be well written?
3. Were there many pages of boring description of detailed game play?
4. Did you read a book with a female athlete?
5. Did your book have a traditional boys' team with a girl team player?
6. How were the coaches and parents depicted in your book?
7. Did the story deal with the traditional topics of sportsmanship, defeat, and pain?

From *More Reading Connections.* © 1999. Knowles/Smith. Libraries Unlimited. (800) 237-6124.

Slam Dunks and Strikeouts: The Status of Sports Fiction

Sports fans have even more diversions than other young people . . .

It's getting better, but it still has a ways to go. For years, sports fiction was mired in stereotypes and formulaic writing. A typical plot line was: A young boy tries out for the team. He makes it (barely). He overcomes problems on the field (dealt with at length) and off the field (mentioned in passing). He finally gets his chance in the BIG game. He is the hero. The protagonist was male, white, and part of a middle- or upper-class family, as were his friends and teammates. Adults and girls appeared in the story, but only in the background.

Is combining sports action with a tight story line, fleshed-out characters, and a realistic and interesting plot beyond the reach of most of the authors in this area? Are distinguished children's authors not sports fans, or are athletic enthusiasts not especially articulate? Could it be that young readers are so hungry for material that they'll read anything in spite of the quality? Maybe it's just that I, as a librarian and a sports junkie, am asking for too much!

In many instances, authors and publishers seem to be going for the quick sell rather than making a genuine effort to put out top-quality literature in this genre. Following the enormous popularity of juvenile series such as the "Babysitters Club" (Scholastic) and the various "Sweet Valley" lines (Bantam), it's not surprising that sports series are hitting the market in large numbers. Likewise, it's no shock that quality in this prepackaged format is sorely lacking. Publishers have recently put out series that follow particular teams, with the same kids participating in different sports; and sports/mysteries, which end up being not very successful examples of either genre. Some series feature different authors writing entries about the same children, which detracts from character development and destroys continuity from title to title.

All of the trends are not negative, though. In surveying the juvenile sports fiction of the past few years, I find that there have been some small but positive steps forward. An increase in the ethnic diversity of all characters, the inclusion of more girls as protagonists, and the tendency to look at sports in the context of larger social issues can be seen in recent offerings. Gary Soto's *Taking Sides* (HBJ, 1991) looks at the various conflicts Lincoln Mendoza faces after he and his mother move from a San Francisco barrio to an affluent, predominantly white suburb. As a starting basketball player on his new school's team, Lincoln faces an internal dilemma when a game is to be played against his former school and friends. Soto, whose *Baseball in April and Other Stories* (HBJ, 1990) was an ALA Best Book for Young Adults, skillfully draws from his own Hispanic heritage in his writings.

Alfred Slote, who has written a number of better-than-average sports novels, combines baseball with a bit of mystery in *Finding Buck*

By Tom Hurlburt. Reprinted with permission of *School Library Journal* (July 1992), pages 30–31. Tom Hurlburt is Children's Librarian at the La Crosse Public Library, WI.

McHenry (HarperCollins, 1991). After being cut from his Little League team, Jason convinces himself that his school janitor, Mack Henry, is really Buck McHenry, a former standout in the old Negro Leagues. Included are recollections of some of the Negro League players' brilliant athletic achievements, many of which were accomplished under adverse conditions. This book will provide readers with a glimpse of an aspect of professional baseball—the pre-Jackie Robinson days of segregated leagues—that is often overlooked in the literature.

Walter Dean Myers's *Me, Mop, and the Moondance Kid* (Delacorte, 1988) centers around two African-American brothers, J.J. and Moondance, and a girl, Mop, who grew up together in an orphanage. After the boys are adopted, Mop hopes to attract the eyes of [pro]spective parents who coach her friends' Little League team by playing catcher for them. The interaction between this atypical cast of characters allows this book to stand above many others of its genre.

While not brand new, and aimed at slightly older audiences, Bruce Brooks's *The Moves Make the Man* (HarperCollins, 1984) is such a compelling read that it begs to be mentioned. The story is told through the witty narrative of protagonist Jerome Foxworthy. An outstanding basketball player, a scholar, and the product of a single-parent home, Jerome is the first and only black to integrate a large North Carolina junior high school. The precarious friendship he forms with an emotionally troubled, white athlete provides the story line for this gripping book.

As Renée Steinberg noted in her article, "Striking Out Stereotypes: Girls in Sports Fiction" *(SLJ,* June, 1990, p. 62), there is a severe imbalance in what's available in regard to male and female protagonists throughout the genre. Since women have been involved in, and continue to enter, organized sports competition at astonishing rates, it is more important than ever that this gap be bridged. While not so long ago a lot of young women longed to make the cheerleading or dance squads in school, they are now more likely to strive to be a member of a sports team instead. A female athlete is not a rarity, and hopefully sports fiction will soon reflect this reality.

For younger, transitional readers, or possibly for use as a high/low title, Alison Herzig's *The Boonsville Bombers* (Viking, 1991) features a girl, Emma, who yearns to play on her older brother's baseball team. A lucky quirk of fate allows her to entice the boys to make a place for her on their roster. No major lessons are learned here, and character development is somewhat slight, but this title will still be enjoyable reading for sports-minded youngsters, especially girls.

Another likable female protagonist is Shirley Temple Wong in Betty Lord's *In the Year of the Boar and Jackie Robinson* (HarperCollins, 1984). The Chinese girl is full of happiness and hope as she begins a new life in America in 1947. After a friendless beginning at P.S. 8 in Brooklyn, Shirley starts to feel at home and part of the American dream when she finds herself playing right field on a stickball team and becoming an avid fan of the Brooklyn Dodgers. While not as strong in on-field action, the well-written narrative does reflect the role sports play in American culture.

No matter what the genre of writing, it's a challenging task for authors to incorporate larger social issues into a work of fiction while maintaining an interesting plot and not sounding didactic. It's especially difficult when the book's major focus is a form of entertainment such as sports. While authors who attempt this tricky mix often doom themselves to failure, the result of a successful effort is both interesting and enlightening.

Margot Marek's *Matt's Crusade* (Four Winds, 1988) looks at a boy wrestling with the decision of whether or not to join an antinuclear protest, knowing it could cost him his cherished spot on his school's football team. Pulled in many directions as the townspeople take sides over the possibility of nuclear weapons being deployed at a local military base, Matt has to decide whether to take a stand or follow the easier path of complacency. Although not without its flaws, this title has much more substance than most of this type.

Prolific author Matt Christopher's protagonist Scott Kramer in *Tackle Without a Team* (Little, 1989) gets kicked off his football squad after marijuana is found in his gym bag. The story takes a mysterious twist since the incriminating drugs were actually planted by someone out to get him. Typical of Christopher's work, description of on-field action is plentiful, but this time larger issues such as jealousy, revenge, and drugs, all familiar to the intended readers, are also examined.

The inclusion of multiethnic and female characters, and the interweaving of lessons of maturity and social issues into plots are welcome developments in juvenile publishing. But when it comes right down to it, most children who read this type of literature are looking for descriptive play-by-play and plenty of it.

Robert Kimmel Smith's *Bobby Baseball* (Delacorte, 1989) is sure to please the sports junkie in training. Bobby Ellis, playing on a team coached by his father, begins to realize a fact that most young athletes eventually come to understand: that dreams of stardom and fame are often not realized. Exciting and accurate game descriptions and a hefty dose of baseball trivia combine with excellent character development, including a female second (baseperson?), to produce a winning effort.

Thomas Dygard aims for slightly older audiences than Matt Christopher, but delivers the same sort of nonstop action. *The Rookie Arrives* (Morrow, 1988) features a talented but cocky third baseman who foresees himself going right from high school to the Major Leagues. Deciding against college, he signs with the Kansas City Royals, and quickly finds out that the level of competition is drastically better than anything he has faced. The player gets his comeuppance and readers are treated to some riveting baseball action.

John Tunis's "Baseball Diamond" series has been reprinted in paperback (HBJ), allowing a new generation to follow the exploits of Bones Hathaway, Spike Russell, Jacko Klein, and many others. Originally written in the early 1940s, Tunis's books provide gripping baseball action and superb character development. Readers will feel a bond with the ballplayers that transcends the playing field as they read through the series. Bruce Brooks provides insightful introductions to each of the titles in the new editions.

Hopefully the quality and content of sports fiction for children will continue to improve, and at an accelerated rate. Those interested in sports need entertaining and well-written books to draw them in. An educated guess says that sports fans have even more diversions than other young people to keep them from reading. Speaking from experience, I know that a child's day can easily be consumed by playing sports and watching them on television. I was able to fill my days with such activity even before ESPN. This is a two-way street though—as parents, librarians, and teachers, we can draw upon this passion to encourage sports-minded youngsters to explore the world of fiction by introducing them to quality examples in this genre and we can also push other material that just might capture their interest.

Promoting books where athletics play a part, but not necessarily the central theme might propel fans into other areas of literature. Jerry Spinelli's Newbery Medal winner, *Maniac Magee* (Little, 1990), has substantial doses of running and baseball woven into its outstanding story line. Likewise, while no one would think of Gary Paulsen as a sports fiction writer—hunting, dog sledding, and sailing might not be baseball, basketball, and football—but they are sports that are found in *Tracker* (1984), *Dogsong,* (1985, both Bradbury), and *Voyage of the Frog* (Orchard, 1989), respectively. Try suggesting these titles to youngsters ready to embark on a third reading of all of Matt Christopher's titles. ▲

ANNOTATED JOURNAL ARTICLES

Niblett, Kathleen. "Can a Book Change Your Life?" *Reading Teacher* (March 1996): 498.
    This is a letter written to Carl Lewis by a teenager after she read his book, *Inside Track*, for a "Letters about Literature" contest. Kathleen had dropped out of school, drifting without direction. Her grandfather had died and a triathlon was coming up and she wanted to win the triathlon in his memory. The article tells how hard she worked and how she often remembered things that Lewis had written in his book.

Tallman, Eve. "Books and Beyond for the Athletic Adventurer," *Library Journal* (June 1, 1997): 67–70.
    This article tells about books, videos, magazines, and Web sites that all have to do with "extreme" sports. These action sports include rock climbing, surfing, backpacking, mountain biking, and snowboarding. The article is intended for librarians who are thinking of including books about these new sports in their collections. Each of the books is annotated and there is a very complete list of magazines and videos.

ANNOTATED BIBLIOGRAPHY

Carter, Alden R. *Bull Catcher*. Scholastic, 1997.
    Neil Larsen, nicknamed Bull, starts to think about baseball in November, even though the season doesn't start until April. His best friend, Jeff, plays shortstop and Bull is the catcher. They played together in middle school, but this book is divided into their four years at Shiply High School. The highlight of every year is the game with Caledonia. Three years in a row they have lost the final game of the season. Senior year will be different. It is dedicated to Billy, who died in a tragic car crash. Bull wants to win this championship and final game, but decides that would be enough, for "it was never quite the same after Billy died."

Crutcher, Chris. *The Crazy Horse Electric Game*. Greenwillow Books, 1987.
    Willie feels he can do almost anything. He is better at sports than any other kid his age. He is not particularly thankful for his gifts and would have been cocky if it weren't for his father. The highlight of his young life is his pitching win in the Crazy Horse Electric game. In the fall, Willie's recklessness changes his life forever. It is the last water skiing outing for the season. Willie's father and girlfriend are in the boat and while Willie is skiing, he crouches down and "cracks the whip." In the process, he falls and the ski hits him in the head. Willie's father panics and Willie is underwater too long. As a result, he has severe disabilities with walking and talking. He has to think about each word before he struggles to say it. Willie uses a cane and walks with a lurch and jerk. Willie's world as he knew it starts to unravel. His girlfriend and friends are too careful and on guard.
    One night, Willie overhears his mother and father arguing about him. Willie figures that if he doesn't get out of Coho, Montana, he would rather be dead. Early one morning, Willie runs away and takes the Greyhound bus to California. He ends up in Oakland, California, crippled physically and mentally. During the next year and a half, Willie gradually changes from a sheltered Montana cowboy kid to being

From *More Reading Connections*. © 1999. Knowles/Smith. Libraries Unlimited. (800) 237-6124.

able to survive in a tough city. Life becomes valuable because of what he has and has lost. He learns this through the street people he comes in contact with and the School of One More Last Chance.

Jackson, Alison. *Blowing Bubbles with the Enemy.* Dutton Children's Books, 1993.
This book demonstrates why it is difficult to write a sports story for girls. Bobby Lorimer, new to the middle school, decides to try out for the boys' team. The deck is stacked against her and she fails to win a spot on the team. A letter from the editor is published in the school newspaper. The girls' basketball team challenges the boys' basketball team to a game in six weeks. The girls rally around Bobby and they do their best to play organized ball. Ultimately, the girls lose the big game but win the respect of the boys. The story line is predictable and dated.

Martin, Bill, and Michael Sampson. *Swish.* Henry Holt, 1997.
The final seconds of a girls' championship basketball game are told in rhythmic text and action-filled illustrations. With less than one minute left, the Blue Jays are ahead of the Cardinals by two points. Cindi of the Cards is on the three-point line. The basketball is spinning, falling, swirling—and with a swish the Cardinals win.

Powell, Randy. *Dean Duffy.* Farrar, Straus & Giroux, 1995.
Dean, a recent high school graduate, spends the summer helping his parents remodel a huge house into a bed and breakfast. At one time, Dean was a very promising baseball player who thought he would receive a scholarship to play college baseball. He had a long slump and the scholarship never happened. The story follows him as he tries to decide what to do about a family friend's offer of a baseball college scholarship, after his long layoff from playing.

Spinelli, Jerry. *Crash.* Alfred A. Knopf, 1996.
The story of John Coogan, nicknamed Crash as a small child, and his denial of friendship with neighbor and schoolmate, Penn Webb. Crash is a football player in seventh grade; Penn runs track, is a nerd, and is the only male cheerleader. When Crash's grandfather has a stroke, it causes Crash to do some reflecting on his life and priorities.

BIBLIOGRAPHY

Primary

Allard, Harry. *Miss Nelson Has a Field Day.* Houghton Mifflin, 1985.

Christopher, Matt. *The Dog That Stole Home.* Little, Brown, 1983.

———. *Zero's Slider.* Little, Brown, 1994.

Hooks, William H. *Mr. Baseball.* Bantam Books, 1991.

Kessler, Leonard. *Here Comes the Strikeout.* Harper & Row, 1965.

———. *Old Turtle's Baseball Stories.* Greenwillow Books, 1982.

———. *Old Turtle's Soccer Team.* Greenwillow Books, 1982.

From *More Reading Connections.* © 1999. Knowles/Smith. Libraries Unlimited. (800) 237-6124.

Marzollo, Claudio. *Kenny and the Little Knickers*. Scholastic, 1992.

Marzollo, Jean. *The Pizza Pie Slugger*. Random House, 1989.

———. *Soccer Sam*. Random House, 1987.

McCully, Emily. *Grandmas at Bat*. Harper & Row, 1993.

Oechsli, Kelly. *Mice at Bat*. Harper & Row, 1986.

Parish, Peggy. *Play Ball, Amelia Bedelia*. Harper & Row, 1972.

Shannon, David. *George Radbourn Saved Baseball*. Blue Sky Press, 1994.

Standler, John. *Hooray for Snail*. Harper & Row, 1984.

Teague, Mark. *The Field Beyond the Outfield*. Scholastic, 1992.

Tyron, Leslie. *Albert's Ballgame*. Atheneum, 1996.

General

Avi. *S.O.R. Losers*. Macmillan, 1984.

Bennett, James W. *The Squared Circle*. Scholastic, 1995.

Brown, Susan M. *You're Dead*. Atheneum, 1995.

Butterworth, W. E. *Fast and Smart*. W. W. Norton, 1970.

———. *Grand Prix Driver*. Grosset & Dunlap, 1969.

Christopher, Matt. *Dirt Bike Runaway*. Little, Brown, 1983.

———. *The Lucky Baseball Bat*. Little, Brown, 1991.

———. *Red-Hot Hightops*. Little, Brown, 1987.

———. *Tackle Without a Team*. Little, Brown, 1989.

Cohen, Barbara. *Thank You, Jackie Robinson*. Lothrop, Lee & Shepard, 1974.

Cooper, Ilene. *Choosing Sides*. Morrow Junior Books, 1990.

Cottonwood, Joe. *The Adventures of Boone Barnaby*. Scholastic, 1990.

Dadey, Debbie, and Marcia T. Jones. *Leprechauns Don't Play Basketball*. Scholastic, 1992.

Decker, Duan. *Fast Man on a Pivot*. William Morrow, 1951.

———. *Rebel in Right Field*. William Morrow, 1961.

Deuker, Carl. *On the Devil's Court*. Little, Brown, 1988.

Duffey, Betsy. *Lucky in Left Field*. Simon & Schuster, 1992.

Dygard, Thomas J. *Forward Pass*. William Morrow, 1989.

———. *Infield Hit*. Morrow Junior Books, 1995.

———. *Running Wild*. William Morrow, 1996.

———. *Soccer Duel*. William Morrow, 1981.

Freeman, Mark. *Rookies: Big-League Break*. Ballantine Books, 1989.

———. *Rookies: Play Ball!* Ballantine Books, 1989.

From *More Reading Connections*. © 1999. Knowles/Smith. Libraries Unlimited. (800) 237-6124.

64 / 7 ▲ PREDICTABLE SPORTS FICTION

Gibbs, Davis. *Major-League Melissa*. Bantam Books, 1991.
Giff, Patricia Reilly. *Left-Handed Shortstop*. Delacorte Press, 1980.
Gilson, Jamie. *Soccer Circus*. Lothrop, Lee & Shepard, 1993.
Glenn, Mel. *Play-by-Play*. Clarion Books, 1986.
———. *Squeeze Play*. Clarion Books, 1989.
Herzig, Alison Gragin. *The Boonsville Bombers*. Viking, 1991.
Heymsfield, Carla. *Coaching Ms. Parker*. Macmillan, 1992.
Hughes, Dean. *Nutty Can't Miss*. Macmillan, 1987.
———. *Pressure Play*. Alfred A. Knopf, 1991.
———. *Team Picture*. Atheneum, 1996.
Hurwitz, Johanna. *Baseball Fever*. William Morrow, 1981.
Klass, David. *Danger Zone*. Scholastic, 1996.
Kline, Suzy. *Herbie Jones and the Monster Ball*. Putnam, 1988.
———. *Orp Goes to the Hoop*. Putnam, 1991.
Konigsburg, E. L. *About the B'nai Bagels*. Atheneum, 1969.
Krone, Julie, and Nancy Ann Richardson. *Riding for My Life*. Little, Brown, 1995.
Lee, Marie G. *Necessary Roughness*. HarperCollins, 1996.
Lord, Bette Bao. *In the Year of the Boar and Jackie Robinson*. Harper & Row, 1984.
Lynch, Chris. *Slot Machine*. HarperCollins, 1995.
Manes, Stephen. *An Almost Perfect Game*. Scholastic, 1995.
Marshall, Kirk. *Hoops: Half-Court Hero*. Ballantine Books, 1989.
———. *Hoops: Pressure Play*. Ballantine Books, 1989.
Myers, Walter Dean. *Slam!* Scholastic, 1996.
Nichols, Paul. *Blitz: Champions*. Ballantine Books, 1989.
———. *Blitz: Team Spirit*. Ballantine Books, 1989.
Park, Barbara. *Skinnybones*. Alfred A. Knopf, 1982.
Slote, Alfred. *Finding Buck McHenry*. Harper & Row, 1991.
———. *Rabbit Ears*. Harper & Row, 1982.
Smith, Robert K. *Bobby Baseball*. Delacorte Press, 1989.
Soto, Gary. *Taking Sides*. Harcourt Brace Jovanovich, 1991.
Spinelli, Jerry. *Crash*. Alfred A. Knopf, 1996.
———. *There's a Girl in My Hammerlock*. Simon & Schuster, 1991.
Tunis, John R. *The Kid from Tomkinsville*. Harcourt Brace Jovanovich, 1990.
Voigt, Cynthia. *Tell Me If Lovers Are Losers*. Atheneum, 1982.
Walker, Paul Robert. *The Sluggers Club: A Sports Mystery*. Harcourt Brace Jovanovich, 1993.

From *More Reading Connections*. © 1999. Knowles/Smith. Libraries Unlimited. (800) 237-6124.

Wallace, Rich. *Wrestling Sturbridge*. Alfred A. Knopf, 1996.

Weaver, Will. *Farm Team*. HarperCollins, 1995.

———. *Striking Out*. HarperCollins, 1993.

Zirpoli, Jane. *Root in the Outfield*. Houghton Mifflin, 1988.

WEB SITES

American Youth Soccer Organization
http://www.ayso.org

Athletes in Gold
http://home.earthlink.net/~athngold/

Bigleaguers
http://www.bigleaguers.com

Black Baseball's Negro League
http://www.blackbaseball.com/

Blackbelt Magazine
http://www.blackbeltmag.com

In-Line Skater
http://www.xcscx.com/skater

International Gymnast Magazine Online
http://www.intlgymnast.com

International Tennis Federation
http://www.itftennis.com/

Judo Information Site
http://www.rain.org/~ssa/judo.htm

Little League
http://www.littleleague.org/justkids/index.html

Major League Baseball
http://www.majorleaguebaseball.com/

Major League Soccer
http://www.mlsnet.com/index.html

Matt Christopher
http://www.ipl.org/youth/AskAuthor/Christopher.html

National Baseball Hall of Fame
http://www.baseballhalloffame.org/index.html

NBA (National Basketball Association)
http://www.nba.com

NFL (National Football League)
http://www.nfl.com

NHL (National Hockey League)
http://www.nhl.com

Special Olympics
http://www.specialolympics.org

Sports Illustrated for Kids
http://www.sikids.com

Sports Science @ the Exploratorium
http://www.exploratorium.edu/sports/index.html

Tennis Worldwide
http://www.tennisw.com/

United States Fencing Association
http://www.usfa.org/

United States Olympic Committee
http://www.olympic-usa.org

USA Gymnastics Online
http://www.usa-gymnastics.org/index-text.html

WebSwim
http://www.webswim.com/

WNBA (Women's National Basketball Association)
http://www.wnba.com

Women Athlete Profiles
http://www.feminist.org/other/olympic/wap.html

Young Equestrian Magazine
http://www.halcyon.com/2001/y.e.index.html

Chapter 8

Many Modern Magazines for Kids

OVERVIEW

There are tens of thousands of magazines and periodicals published around the world, and each of them is unique in some way. Magazines vary in subject matter and approach, but even magazines that focus on the same subject and have the same reader profile differ from each other. It is important that parents and teachers be aware of the magazines that are available at the local bookstore. Some of the articles and topics can be surprisingly mature. Few magazines advertise the age group they target, in hopes of appealing to a wider audience.

GUIDED READING QUESTIONS

1. Does the magazine clearly show what age group it targets?
2. What is the general focus of the magazine?
3. Does it include book reviews and tips on studying or other school-related topics?
4. Are there articles or columns that surprise you?
5. What is the focus of the advertisements?

From *More Reading Connections.* © 1999. Knowles/Smith. Libraries Unlimited. (800) 237-6124.

JOURNAL ARTICLE

Periodicals Information Directory

Descriptive copy for the listed periodicals in this directory was excerpted from evaluations in *Magazines for Young People*, or was written by the publishers themselves. All information not enclosed by quotation marks is paraphrased from the full evaluations or represents the statements of the periodicals' publishers, who have paid for their entries in this directory. The latest edition used for this compilation is *Magazines for Young People* (R. R. Bowker, 2nd ed., 1997, $38), which is compiled by Bill Katz and Linda Sternberg Katz. The volume contains critical evaluations of periodicals under 100 subject headings, assessing them for their value to various types of library collections.

. . . A guide to the acronyms used for the abstracts and index services that list the content of most magazines is included.

———

Reprinted with permission from *School Library Journal* (May 1997), pages 35–50.

Abstracts and Indexes

AbRG	Abridged Readers Guide	HistAb	Historical Abstracts
AcAB	Academic Abstracts	HSSA	Health and Safety Science Abstracts
AcI	Academic Index	HumI	Humanities Index
AmerH	America: History and Life	INfTr	InfoTrac
API	Alternative Press Index	Ineg	Index to Periodicals by and about Blacks
ArtI	Art Index	Liblit	Library Literature
AquaSci	Aquatic Sciences and Fisheries Abstracts	LISA	Library & Science Abstracts
BiblGeo	Bibliography and Index of Geology	MAS	Magazine Article Summaries
BioAb	Biological Abstracts	MgI	Magazine Index
BioAg	Biological and Agricultural Index	MLA	MLA International Biography of Books & Articles on the Modern Languages and Literature
BioI	Biography Index		
BoRvI	Book Review Index	MRD	Media Review Digest
CanI	Canadian Periodical Index	MusicI	Music Index
ChemAb	Chemical Abstracts	PAIS	PAIS International in Print
CIJE	Current Index to Journals in Education	PolAb	Pollution Abstracts
CMG	Children's Magazine Guide	RelAb	Religious and Theological Abstracts
CurrCont	Current Contents	RG	Readers' Guide to Periodical Literature
EdI	Education Index	RIO	Religious Index One: Periodicals
EnvperB	Environmental Periodicals Biography	SCI	Science Citation Index
ERIC	Educational Resources Information Center	SocWAb	Social Work Research and Abstracts
ExAcI	Expanded Academic Index	WomAB	Women Studies Abstracts
ExchAb	Exceptional Child Education Abstracts		
GSI	General Science Index		

Antiques

ORNAMENT. 1974. 4 Issues $23.97 Int'l. Library rate. $20.70; $24.30 Int'l. Ornament, P.O. Box 2349, San Marcos, CA 92079. Illus. Adv. Circ.: 41,000. Back Issues available. ISSN 0148-3897. (760) 599-0222. E-mail: Ornament@cts.com. Indexed: Art Index; Artbibliographies Modern; British Archaeological Abstracts; Design and Applied Arts Index UK.

Ornament is the oldest English language publication on personal adornment in existence. Covering contemporary, ancient and ethnic [this is a] valuable resource, providing an in-depth guide to the finest special events, news and publication reviews exclusive to the stimulating world of personal adornment.

Arts

SchoolArts. 1901. q. 9 issues $24.50; foreign $30.50. Davis Publications, Inc., 50 Portland Street, Worcester, MA 01608. (508) 754-7201. Illus. Adv. Circ.: 24,000. Back Issues available. ISSN 0036-6463.

SchoolArts is the leading art education magazine, offering K-12 teachers a wealth of classroom-tested resources and ready-to-use lesson ideas in every issue. Each theme-oriented issue presents an inside look at art education and lets you look inside classrooms from around the country. Proven lessons and ready-to-use resources make *SchoolArts* an essential tool for creating meaningful art experiences with students.

Arab/Muslim World

Aramco World (1044-1891). 1949. Bi-m. Free. Ed.: Robert Arndt. Aramco Services Company, Box 2106, Houston, TX 77252-2106. Illus. Index. Circ.: 175,000. Sample. Vol. ends: Nov/Dec.
Aud: GA, Ac, I-IS

Aramco World, the prime U.S. source for nonpolitical information about the Arab and Muslim worlds—particularly the Middle East—covers the history, culture, geography, natural history and economics of those areas, emphasizing cultural connections with the West. It is accessible, attractive and widely used as supplementary reading: about 45% of its U.S. subscribers are educators or libraries. Multiple subscriptions, back issues and bulk quantities are available.

Aljumuah/Authentic source of Islam. P.O. Box 5387, Madison, WI 53705. Toll Free: 1-888-425-5868; Phone: (608) 277-1855; Fax: (608) 277-0323. Editor: Hassen A. Laidi. Monthly. 12 Issues/yr. $30 institutional/individuals. Circ. 12,000. Free Sample copy available. ISSN #109237772.

Educational, Informational, Objective. *Aljumuah* Magazine is an indispensable reference for people anyone [sic] interested in the beliefs and practices of Muslims. Scholarly written articles are drawn from original authentic texts of Islam and cover the way religion applies to contemporary situations. *Aljumuah* is the only major Islamic magazine in the United States that presents topics such as prayer, fasting, pilgrimage and Islamic Holiday celebration in detail. It is also an educational tool for children.

Astronomy

Sky & Telescope. 1941. m. $37.95. Sky Publishing Corporation, 49 Bay State Rd., Cambridge, MA 02138. illus. index. adv. Circ: 113,000. Sample. Vol. ends: June, Dec. Microform: UMI.
Aud: EIH, HS, GA

Since 1941, *Sky & Telescope* has been the best source of astronomy news and information in the universe. Each monthly issue brings you the latest astronomical discoveries, expertly written feature articles, reviews of telescopes and accessories, spectacular astrophotography and a detailed calendar of celestial happenings for all levels of skygazers. From reports on the discoveries made by the Hubble Space Telescope, to special coverage of Comets Hale-Bopp and Hyakutake, *Sky & Telescope* is on the cutting edge of astronomical discovery. The essential Magazine of Astronomy.

Skywatch. 1997. a. $3.95. Sky Publishing Corporation, P.O. Box 9111, Belmont, MA 02178. illus. Circ.: 75,000. For subscription information 800-253-0245. Outside the U.S. and Canada call 1-617-864-7360. Email: Order @skypub.com Web Site: http://www.skypub.com/.

Skywatch is an annual publication which offers beginner and advanced amateurs alike an observing handbook, buyer's guide, and "how to" manual in one convenient, user-friendly package. It features exciting, colorful coverage of celestial and space highlights throughout the year and answers the most common questions asked by newcomers to astronomy. A useful reference year-round, it is particularly well suited to introducing youngsters to the joys of stargazing and the wonders of the latest piloted and robotic missions. From the publisher of *Sky & Telescope*.

Books and Book Reviews

KLIATT. 1967. 6/yr. $39 (Canada $41). Eds: Claire Rosser, Paula Rohrlick, Jean Palmer. 33 Bay State Road, Wellesley, MA 02181, (781) 237-7577. Index. adv. Circ.: 2,300. Sample. Vol. ends: Nov. Microform: UMI. Indexes: Media Review Digest. Book Review Index. Books reviewed/yr.: 1600. 200-word signed reviews.
Aud: ETH, HS, GA

"Any librarian serving YAs or desiring to enhance the adult audio or general book collection will thrive" on *KLIATT*'s "perceptive, cogent assessments in lucid prose," says *Library Journal*. *KLIATT* reviews over 1200 paperbacks (and hardcover YA fiction), 300 audiobooks, and dozens of educational CD-ROMs annually. Each bimonthly issue includes a feature article.

The FIVE OWLS. 1986. (A Selection Guide/Review of Children's Books). 5/yr. Bi-m. $35/1 yr.; $60/2 yrs.; $85/3 yrs. The FIVE OWLS, 2004 Sheridan Avenue S., Minneapolis, MN 55405; Tel: 612-644-7377. Fax: 612-377-4816. Illus. index. adv. Vol. ends: May/June.
Aud: GA, SA

The FIVE OWLS celebrates the real treasures among children's books. It encourages literacy and reading among young people by advocating intelligent, beautiful and worthwhile children's books. A lively mix of book reviews, engaging articles about reading, interviews with leading authors and illustrators, thematic booklists. A trusted selection tool for educators, librarians, parents and anyone involved with children's literature. For a free sample issue, send $1.00 for postage.

The Horn Book Magazine. 1924. Bi-monthly. $50.00. The Horn Book, Inc., 11 Beacon Street, Suite 1000, Boston, MA 02108. 617-227-1555; 800-325-1170. Email: Info@hbook.comhttp://www.hbook.com index. adv. ISSN 0018-5078. Circ: 21,000.

The Horn Book Magazine combines an extensive book review section of the best new available for children and young adults with provocative and informative articles, columns, and interviews covering all aspects of children's literature. Annual themed issues cover timely topics in the field of children's books. Professional reading that is also a pleasure.

Voya. 1978. Bi-m. $38.50/yr. Vol. Ends: February. Scarecrow Press, 4720 Boston Way, Lanham, MD, 20706. 1-888-486-9297. ISSN 0160-4201.
Aud: JH, HS, GA

Voice of Youth Advocates is only about materials and services for teens, saving valuable time for librarians serving this group. It includes concise reviews of fiction, science fiction, fantasy, horror, and professional books as well as CD-ROMs and Web sites. Each issue also features annotated booklists and articles written by and for librarians who serve young adults.

Bulletin of the Center for Children's Books. 1945. M. (Sept.-July; 11/yr.). $40 ($35 ind.). University of Illinois Press, 1325 S. Oak St., Champaign, IL 61820. (217) 333-8935. puboff@alexia.lis.uiuc.edu. Index monthly. Adv. Vol. ends July. Microfilm: UMI. Website: http://edfu.lis.uiuc.edu/puboff/bccb.
Aud: SA, GA, EJH

Thousands of new books for youth are published each year, but you are able to purchase only a fraction of those new titles. How do you find the books you need? Turn to the *Bulletin of the Center for Children's Books* for help in making informed selection decisions. Each issue is devoted entirely to the review of current books for children and youth and provides concise summaries and critical evaluations.

Careers

Careers & Colleges. 1981. 4/yr. $10; discounts available for volume orders. E.M. Guild Inc., 989 Avenue of the Americas, New York, NY 10018. 212-563-4688; fax: 212-967-2531. Circ: 500,000. Call 800-964-0763.
Aud: SA

"This is a unique title among the teen magazines because it is developed solely to provide information on careers, employment, and (higher) education.... Feature articles include topics such as financial aid... job hunting (tips), and choosing the right college.... Each issue has profiles of careers with educational requirements, salary ranges, and sources for further information included.... A beneficial title for libraries whose teenage patrons are college and career-bound."—*Magazines for Libraries,* 7th ed.

Children

The Lion and the Unicorn: a Critical Journal of Children's Literature. 1977. 3x/yr. $58.00/yr. The Johns Hopkins University Press, P.O. Box 19966, Baltimore, MD 21211-0966. Illus. ISSN 0147-2593.
Aud: GA, EC, EJH, AC

Edited by Louis Smith and Jack Zipes, this theme- and genre-centered journal of international scope is committed to a serious, ongoing discussion of literature for children. Forthcoming topics include: * The Sports Craze and Childrens' Culture * Violence and Children's Literature * Beyond the Book: Children and Technology and more. Each volume now features one general issue, two thematic issues, and an expanded book review section.

YouthLine USA. 1997. weekly. $29.00. S&S Plus, Inc., PO Box 1597, Lakewood, NJ 08701. Circulation: 20,000. Web Site: www.YouthlineUSA.com, Email: Saki@YouthlineUSA.com.

YOUTHLINE USA is the new weekly newspaper for kids. In many respects, it is similar to an adult newspaper covering the same news items that are in the general media at the time. In addition, it has sports news and feature articles, including Author of the week, Animal of the week, and much more. Kids absolutely love it and anxiously await its arrival each week.

Babybug. The listening and looking magazine for infants and toddlers ages 6 months to two years. 1995. 9/yr. $32.97. Editor-in-Chief: Mariane Carus. Editor: Paul Morrow. Carus Publishing Co., 315 Fifth Street, Peru, IL 61354. Illus. Vol. ends: Nov.
Aud: Ages 6 months to 2 years

Before you walked, you crawled. And before you were a reader, you were a listener and a looker. Now there's *BABYBUG* for babies who love to be read to and parents who love to read to them. Each 24-page issue is filled with simple stories, rhymes, and activities, all beautifully illustrated. The youngest member of the Cricket Magazine Group is made of sturdy cardboard pages (6 1/4" x 7") with rounded corners and no staples. *BABYBUG* is the perfect way to start a child on a lifelong love of books and reading. A removable parenting section written by child development expert Dr. Sally Nurss offers suggestions for further activities related to the content of each issue.

Click. 1998. Bi-monthly. $24/year. Editor-in-chief: Mariane Carus. Carus Publishing Co., 315 Fifth Street, Peru, IL 61354.
Aud: Ages 3 to 7

NEW from the *Cricket* Magazine Group. CLICK introduces science and other nonfiction topics to children ages 3 to 7. Designed to help young readers discover the world around them, *CLICK* features fun characters like Click the mouse, photo essays, and engaging stories that answer children's questions about how and why things happen. Each issue includes a removable Parent's Companion section which includes book reviews, an article on child development, and a guide to using the articles in the magazine.

Cricket. 1973. m. $32.97. Editor-in-Chief: Marianne Carus. Editor: Debby Vetter. Carus Corporation, 315 Fifth Street, Peru, IL 61354. Illus. Vol. ends: Aug. Microfilm: UMI. Indexed: CMG.
Aud: 9-14

The only truly literary magazine for children ages 9-14. The editorial board includes Virginia Hamilton, Nancy Larrick, Clifton Fadiman, Lloyd Alexander, and others. International known writers and artists are contributors of never-before-published stories, poems, and articles which make up the major portion of each issue. Also included are some reprinted materials, craft ideas, puzzles, tongue twisters, and letters to *Cricket*. There is a section devoted to contributions from young readers. The excellent format is complemented by artistically pleasing and stunning full-color illustrations. Highly recommended to storytellers as a source for new and exciting literature to share with children.

Ladybug: The Magazine for Young Children. 1990. m. $32.97. Editor-in-Chief: Marianne Carus. Editor: Paula Morrow. Carus Corporation, 315 Fifth Street, Peru, IL 61354. Illus. Vol. ends: Aug. Indexed: CMG.
Aud: 2 to 6 years

Ladybug is a charming collection of the best stories, poems, songs, games and adventures for young children ages 2 to 6. Each page is beautifully illustrated by the best children's artists around the world and is guaranteed to delight parents and children alike. In fact, the very nature of the magazine promotes parent-child interaction. Each issue includes a removable 8-page insert for parents, offering articles on child development, suggestions for further activities, reviews for recommended children's books, and a profile of an author or artists featured in the issue. *School Library Journal* said: "This is a stimulating publication that is highly recommended for home and public libraries."

Spider: The Magazine for Children. 1994. m. $32.97. Editor-in-Chief: Marianne Carus. Editor: Laura Tillotson Walske. Carus Publishing Co., 315 Fifth Street, Peru, IL 61354. Illus. Vol. ends: Dec. Indexed: CMG.
Aud: 6 to 9 years

Designed for independent young readers ages 6 to 9, SPIDER features easy-to-read adventures, realistic stories, fairy and folk tales, and articles on science, nature, and the world. The beloved characters, Kate and Toady, appear each month as well as *Spider*'s own cast of bug characters who have hilarious adventures and help explain the more difficult words. Also included are jokes, games, puzzles, and foreign language activities, plus a 4-page insert with a hands-on educational project. Illustrated with bright, detailed drawings and paintings by world-renowned children's artists.

Muse. Bi-m. $24.00. Editor-in-Chief: Marianne Carus. Editor: Diane Lutz. Carus Publishing Co., 315 Fifth Street, Peru, IL 61354. Illus. Vol. ends: Dec.
Aud: 8 to 14 years

Kids interested in everything in the universe will love *MUSE,* a new nonfiction magazine from the publishers of *Cricket* and *Smithsonian* magazines. *MUSE* introduces children ages 8 to 14 to the world of knowledge with articles on the sciences and the arts that are written by the experts. In 52-full color pages, *MUSE* also offers highlights of the Smithsonian, contests, and book and media reviews.

Cicada. 1998. Bi-monthly. $32.97. Editor-in-Chief: Marianne Carus. Carus Publishing Co., 315 Fifth Street, Peru, IL 61354.
Aud: Teenagers and young adults, 14+

New from the *Cricket* Magazine Group, *CICADA* is published for teenagers and young adults who value quality literature. Each issue of *CICADA* is filled with intelligent, vivid, and exciting reading by adults authors and by teens themselves. Those familiar with *CRICKET* (and *CRICKET's* devotion to excellent literature) will see [that] *CICADA* is the next logical step up—a storehouse of fiction and poetry that focuses on the issues and attitudes teens encounter as they become adults. *CICADA* is a literary magazine about, for, and by teenagers and young adults. *CICADA* offers something for every reading interest.

Stone Soup. 1973. 6/yr. $32. Ed.: Gerry Mandel & William Rubel. Children's Art Foundation, P.O. Box 83, Santa Cruz, CA 95063. Illus. Circ: 20,000. Vol. ends: July/August issue. Call 1-800-447-4569. Visit our Web Site at www.stonesoup.com.
Aud: EIH

"Absolutely essential for a basic collection," says Bowker's *Magazines for Libraries*. Now celebrating its 25th year, *Stone Soup* is the ultimate magazine for 8- to 13-year-olds who love to read, write, and draw. It's the only literary magazine made up entirely of the creative work of young people. Budding writers and artists are inspired and encouraged to create and submit their own work. Each issue of *Stone Soup* is filled with thought-provoking writing in a wide range of forms and styles, personal narratives, descriptive essays, family histories, science fiction, mystery, humor, poetry, book reviews—all from the unique perspective of the young author. Beautiful color illustrations by young artists complement the stories, and a letters section and photos of the authors and illustrators are also included. "This is a thoughtfully conceived magazine that offers quality literature and creative encouragement to aspiring authors and artists."—*Magazines for School Libraries*.

Owl Magazine. 1976. 9/yr. $16.95. Owl, 25 Boxwood Lane, Buffalo, NY 14225. Subscription telephone: 1-800-551-6957. Circulation: 100,000+.
Aud: ages 8 and up

OWL is an award winning "discovery" magazine for kids. Filled with entertaining features, facts, puzzles, games, contests and fun in science, nature and technology. Includes regular features such as the popular Might Mites adventure comic strip, exciting science discoveries with Dr. Zed, vibrant pullout poster, and much more. Honored by the Educational Press of Americas and Parents' Choice Foundation.

ChickaDEE Magazine. 1979. 9/yr. $16.95. c/o OWL, 25 Boxwood Lane, Buffalo, NY 14225. Subscription Telephone: 1-800-551-6957. Circulation: 100,000+.
Aud: ages 6 to 9

ChickaDEE is designed especially for beginning readers. Its award-winning hands-on approach introduces children to the world of science, nature, and animals. Each issue includes puzzles, stories, games, easy-to do science experiments, crafts and much more. Honored by the Educational Press of America and Parents' Choice Foundation.

Chirp Magazine. 1997. 9/yr. $16.95. c/o OWL, 25 Boxwood Lane, Buffalo, NY 14225. Subscription Telephone: 1-800-551-6957. Circ.: 40,000.
Aud: ages 3 to 6

NEW! *CHIRP Magazine* for preschoolers designed to get kids looking, pointing, and giggling while preparing them for their reading years. Each issue is filled with games, stories, crafts, rhymes that will teach preschoolers about animals, nature, letters, numbers, and more. It's the "see and do" magazine that has already received rave reviews from parents, early educators, and children.

Highlights for Children. 1946. Published monthly (index in December issue). Single issues (Current or back copies) $3.95. Subscription prices: 1-year (12 issues) $2.47 per issue and 3-year (36 issues) $1.94 per issue. Add shipping and handling, $10 per year for Canada not including GST/HST and $10 per year other foreign. ISSN 0018-165X.

Highlights for Children. A monthly children's magazine which contains Hidden Pictures, "What's Wrong?" pages, puzzles, jokes, riddles and games; appealing stories and articles—all colorfully illustrated; craft projects children can do on their own. All materials are geared toward developing, thinking and reading skills. Content appeals to interest of children from ages 2–12.

SESAME STREET Magazine and SESAME STREET PARENTS. 10/yr. $19.97 for both. Children's Television Workshop, One Lincoln Plaza, New York, NY 10023. Circ: 1,100,000.

Big Bird and his delightful TV gang bring dozens of playful surprises ten times a year. Puzzles, activities, games, A-B-C's, 1-2-3's. It's the entertaining education that Sesame Street does best. The Award-winning *Sesame Street Magazine* is designed for preschoolers. *Sesame Street Parents,* which accompanies every issue of *SSM,* keep parents informed on a wide variety of issues. Practical, useful articles cover stages of child development, education and health questions, parent-child activities, book reviews, and tips from parents. Ages 2 and up.

KID CITY Magazine. 10/yr. $19.90. Children's Television Workshop, One Lincoln Plaza, New York, NY 10023. Circ: 250,000.

KID CITY—The perfect magazine for graduates of *Sesame Street, KID CITY Magazine* is created for the beginning reader. Each issue is full of puzzles, stories, jokes and activities that are both entertaining and educational; all developed to spark the imagination, develop creativity, enhance self-esteem and make learning fun. From the educational experts at Children's Television Workshop. Ages 6 and Up.

Contact Kids. 10/yr. $17.97. Children's Television Workshop, One Lincoln Plaza, New York, NY 10023. Circ: 300,000.

Contact Kids—Award winning articles about nature, science and technology written in a lively style that is sure to entertain the young adult reader. *Contact Kids Magazine* delivers ten big issues each year packed with projects, puzzles, experiments and colorful feature stories. PLUS . . . TECH ZONE, an 8-page section about technology in kids' lives—from video game tips & reviews to high tech news. It's an involving fun way to learn and helps young minds develop confidence in solving math problems. From the educational experts at Children's Television Workshop. Ages 9 and up.

Caboodle: the interactive kid's magazine. 1996. 4/yr. Subscriptions: Basic $59.95/Network $129.95/Five-Pack $149.95. Orders: Caboodle Interactive, P.O. 61417, Denver, CO 80206. 1-800-903-9111. Email Caboodleus@aol.com.

Caboodle, the next step in children's publishing, is the first CD-ROM-based magazine for digikids from 7 to 12. Each colorful, noisy issue provides hours of learning fun with interactive, narrated features and stories, videos, crafts, puzzles, games, music clips, reviews and more. Content is drawn from elementary school curricula and is teacher-tested and approved. PC/Mac compatible. Free tech support. Preview at http://www.caboodle.com.

Culture

FACES, Places, People, Cultures. 1984. 9/yr. $26.95. Ed: Elizabeth Crooker. Cobblestone Publishing Company, 30 Grove Street, Peterborough, NH 03458. Illus. Sample. Circ: 13,000 Indexed: CMG.
Aud: 8-14 yrs

Now in full color! "A treasure-trove of important facts and insights into the panorama of human experience." (Robert D. San Souci, author) With each issue of *FACES* young readers gain a better understanding of other parts of the world with their many cultural differences as well as similarities. *FACES* offers a balance of articles and activities, as well as folktales and legends, photos and illustrations, to introduce each theme. A must to encourage global curiosity and respect for different ways of life!

Education

CREATIVE CLASSROOM Magazine. 6/yr. $19.97. Children's Television Workshop, One Lincoln Plaza, New York, NY 10023. Circ: 175,000.
Aud: SA

CREATIVE CLASSROOM is Children's Television Workshop's magazine for elementary school teachers. In a lively and concise format, *CREATIVE CLASSROOM* provides useful hands-on activities within the curriculum—and beyond. In addition to articles in core subjects areas and innovative approaches to covering the basics, it offers book reviews, interactive reproducible, exciting literature, and current news about the teaching profession.

Environment

E: The Environmental Magazine. 1990. $20/yr (6 issues), $36/2 yrs., $50/3 yrs. Subscription address: P.O. Box 2047, Marion, OH 43305-2047. 64-72 pp. per issue, full-color on recycled paper. Indexed: Reader's Guide to Periodical Literature, Ebsco's Magazine Article Summaries, Environmental Periodicals Bibliography, Alternative Press Index, InfoTrac, University Microfilms, Homework Helper. Our Website URL: http://www.emagazine.com.

E is the only independent (i.e. not published by an advocacy organization) consumer environmental magazine on the market today. *E* covers a wide range of environmental issues and concerns, "from recycling to rainforests," and "from the personal to the political." Full-length feature articles explore major topics such as global warming, plastics recycling, consumerism, population impacts, water quality issues and many others. Regular departments present interviews with leading thinkers and activists, environmental news, product and book briefs, "ecohome" topics, ecotourism, "green business" trends, personal and environmental health issues, and a readers' question and answer page. Of *E, Library Journal* said: "each issue is as imaginative as it is professional; in regard to both subject and point of view, the articles vary enough to appeal to a wide range of readers; and the investigative reporting is fascinating and informative . . . Considering the integration of quality and mass appeal, this bimonthly deserves support."

Games

New in Chess. 1984. 8/yr. $86. Supplements: New in Chess Yearbook. 4/yr. with disks $183; without disks $129; Chess Combination Inc., PO Box 2423, Bridgeport, CT 06608-0423. Email: 70244.1532@compuserve.com.

In-depth interviews with chess superstars, game analysis, tournament reports separate *NIC* from other chess magazines. Quarterly supplement concentrates on computer-assisted surveys of openings with authoritative analysis by the world's leading players.

General Interest

Imagine: Opportunities and Resources for Academically Talented Youth. 1993. 5x/yr. $30.00/yr. The Johns Hopkins University Press, P.O. Box 19966, Baltimore, MD

21211-0966. ISSN 1071-695X. Back issues available.
Aud: EIH, HS, GA

Imagine is a newsletter for academically talented students who want to take an active role in their own education. Directed at students in grades 7-12, *Imagine* identifies opportunities at home, in school, and in the larger community that will satisfy students' intellectual curiosity and need for greater academic challenge. *Imagine* is also a valuable source of information for parents, teachers, administrators, counselors, and librarians.

Girls

New Moon. 1993. bi-m. $29. New Moon Publishing, P.O. Box 3587, Duluth, MN 55803. illus. index. no-adv. Circ: 30,000. Vol. ends: July/Aug. New Moon: the Magazine For Girls and Their Dreams, for every girl age 8-14 who wants their voice heard and their dreams taken seriously.

New Moon is an imaginative, girl-centered, ad-free, international publication that celebrates girls, explores the passage from girl to woman, and helps build healthy resistance to gender inequities. Winner of the 1997 Parent's Choice Gold Award. Subject matter includes fiction, poetry, stories by girls around the world, science experiments, women's work, history, and more. Edited by and for girls 8–14. Will diversify your children's periodical offerings. 1-800-381-4743.

New Moon Network. 1993. Bi-monthly. $25. New Moon Publishing, P.O. Box 3587, Duluth, MN 55803. illus. index. Circ: 5,000. Vol. ends: July/Aug. New Moon Network: For Adults Who Care About Girls.

New Moon Network is the premier place for adults sharing strategies, concerns and successes with other adults working with and raising girls. *New Moon Network* includes reviews, personal essays, descriptions of programs and strategies, as well as thought-provoking questions about gender equity and raising girls. An important resource for parents, educators, coaches, counselors and others who care about girls. 1-800-371-4743.

blue jean magazine. 1996. Bi-m. $29. blue jean magazine, P.O. Box 507, Victor, NY 14564. illus. index. no-adv. Circ. 10,000. sample. Vol. ends Nov/Dec. blue jean magazine: The Only Magazine Written and Produced by Young Women From Around the World.
Aud: Ages 12–19 yrs

blue jean magazine is an alternative to the fashion and beauty magazines targeting young women. *blue jean* is advertising-free so you will find no beauty tips, fashion spreads or supermodels on our pages. Our diverse coalition of teen editors and correspondents are dedicated to publishing what young women are thinking, saying and doing. *blue jean* profiles girls and women who are changing the world! Website: www.bluejeanmag.com.

History

CALLIOPE: World History for Youth. 1990. 9/yr. $26.95. Eds.: Rosalie F. and Charles F. Baker, Cobblestone Publishing Company, 30 Grove Street, Peterborough, NH 03458. Illus. index. Sample. Circ: 10,000. Vol. ends: May/June. Indexed: CMG.
Aud: 9-14 yrs

Now in full color! "I have never seen anything like *CALLIOPE,* from its intelligent and accessible layout and illustrations to its well-written and useful articles." (Prof. Michael Gleason, Millsap College) A passport to exciting and provocative world history themes! Topics chosen cover framework-mandated subjects in a way no textbook can! Maps and time lines, original illustrations and relevant art from major museums complement the text. Regular departments discuss word origins and recent archaeology discoveries. Back issues available. Now published nine times a year!

COBBLESTONE. The History Magazine for Young People. 1980. 9/yr. $26.95. Ed.: Meg Chorlian. Cobblestone Publishing Company, 30 Grove Street, Peterborough, NH 03458. Illus. Sample. Circ: 33,000. Vol. ends: Dec. Indexed: CMG.
Aud: 8-14 yrs

"A very special, highly recommended magazine ... rich in ideas, challenging the students to think ... respectful of young people, their intelligence and their need for thoughtful discussion." (*OAH Magazine of History*) We want our readers' reaction to be, "Wow! I didn't know that!" Every colorful 48-page issue is packed with interesting, lively, and historically accurate articles. Primary documents, historical photographs, original illustrations, maps, activities, and occasional contests.

FOOTSTEPS, African-American History for Kids. 1998. 5/yr. $23.95. Ed. Linda Ekblad. Cobblestone Publishing Company, 30 Grove Street, Peterborough, NH 03458. Illus. Sample. Circ: begins publication September 1998. Vol. ends: May.

FOOTSTEPS is a unique collaboration between Cobblestone Publishing and Curriculum Concept. This new and dynamic magazine is for readers 9–14. With each themed issue, *FOOTSTEPS* illustrates and honors the history and achievements of people of African descent. The subject matter is brought to life by rich and accurate nonfiction, wonderful photography, art, contests, crafts, recipes, maps, time lines, and more.

CALIFORNIA COBBLESTONE. 1998. 5/yr. $23.95. Ed. Ashley Chase. Cobblestone Publishing Company, 30 Grove Street, Peterborough, NH 03458. Illus. Sample. Circ: begins publication September 1998. Vol. ends: May.

The colorful magazine that makes Californian History come alive for readers 9-14! Edited in California, it provides a guided tour of the most exciting moment in California's history. Each themed issue is filled with great nonfiction articles and sidebars, with all the geography, literature, art, and science you need to tell stories of this great state. Included are games, puzzles, activities, and the opportunity to have California-related questions answered by the State's own Dr. History!

Journal of Mississippi History. 1939: q. Ed.: Kenneth McCarty. Mississippi Historical Society, PO Box 571, Jackson, MS 39205-0571. Illus. index. adv. Circ. 1,500 Microform: UMI. Reprint: UMI Indexed: America: History & Life, Historical Abstracts, Bk. rev.: 10-15, 2–3 pages.
Aud: Ac, SA

Scholars, amateur historians, and graduate students contribute to this quarterly scholarly periodical. The focus is on the history of Mississippi, the lower Mississippi Valley, and the South, prehistory through 20th century. Bibliographies of books related to Mississippi history, dissertations, and new manuscript contributions to state libraries and colleges, as well as book reviews and news and notices are regular features. Issues average 100 pages each. The annual index is mailed in May.

International Affairs

The Bulletin of the Atomic Sciences. 1945. 6 issues. Indiv. US/$36.00; Foreign/$46.00. Library Rate. US/$55.00. Foreign/$65.00. Editor: Mike Moore. 6042 S. Kimbark, Chicago, IL 60637. (773) 702-2555. Circ.: 10,000. Back issues available. Advertising Accepted. ISSN 0096-3402. Web Site: http://www.bullatomsci.org/.

The Bulletin. Since 1945, *The Bulletin* has been a leading voice on the threat of nuclear weapons and a range of international security issues. This award-winning magazine is written in a clear, lively style, for nonspecialists, students, academics, and public officials. With a prestige well beyond its circulation, it is frequently cited and an indispensable reference tool.

Internet

Web Feet: The Internet Traveler's Desk Reference. 1998. Rock Hill Press, 14 Rock Hill Rd., Bala Cynwyd, PA 19004. Illus. Monthly. (12 issues a year). $66.50. 1-888-ROCK-HILL, 1-610-667-2040; Web Site: www.rockhillpress.com; info@rockhillpress.com. Bulk rates available. Samples and back issues available. ISSN 1097-4210.

A monthly subject guide to the Web, *Web Feet* brings you "print bookmarks" to the best sites in all fields, annotated by experts. The 3-ring binder is divided into sections that correspond to topics studied in school and to subjects of general interest. The Calendar Connections section allows you to prepare for forthcoming events and observances. Color-coded, dated sheets make it easy to keep information organized and current. Snapshots show what the sites look like and the annotations describe the content. The subject index is updated each month. *Web Feet* is suitable for use in middle and high school libraries, as well as the public library.

Library

Online-Offline. Themes and Resources K-8. 1996. Rock Hill Press, 14 Rock Hill Rd., Bala Cynwyd, PA 19004. Illus. Monthly (9 issues a year). $66.50. 1-888-ROCK-HILL. 1-610-667-2040. Web site: www.rockhillpress.com. Samples and back issues available. ISSN 1090-1930.
Aud: EJH Hs, Ga, Ac

Online-Offline, the first resource guide linking themes with Web sites and other media, each month explores a theme from all angles, seeking new and exciting ways to handle key topics in the curriculum. Experts pose key questions, suggest activities, and compile well-annotated lists of resources to use in the classroom or in independent research. Resources include Web sites, CD-ROM, videos, books, audios, and magazines.

Library Journal. 1876. 20/yr. $99.50: Canada, $129; foreign, $179. Cahners Business Information, Subs to: Library Journal, PO Box 59690, Boulder, CO 80322-9690. 800-667-6694. Web Site: www.ljdigital.com.
Aud: SA

The full service magazine tailored to the information needs of librarians and managers in public, academic, and corporate libraries.

School Library Journal. 1954. 12/yr. $87.50; Canada $129, foreign, $149. Cahners Business Information. Subs to: Library Journal, PO Box 59690, Boulder, CO 80322-7559. 800-456-9409. Web Site: www.slj.com
Aud: SA

The most complete provider of news, information and reviews for librarians and media specialists who serve children and young adults in school and public libraries.

Library Hotline. 50/yr. $87.00; Canada $117, foreign, $127. Cahners Business Information. Subs to: PO Box 6457, Torrance, CA 90504-0457. 800-456-9409.

The leading newsletter written for librarians.

Literary

DoubleTake. 1995. q. $32yr. Center for Documentary Studies at Duke University, 1317 W. Pettigraw St., Durham, NC 27705. illus. adv. Sample. Back Issues available.
Aud: GA, SA, Ac

The award winning magazine edited by Robert Coles, *DoubleTake* was selected "One of the Top-Ten new magazines" by *Library Journal* for its fine writing and photography. Here is fiction and non-fiction, poetry and reportage, reviews and photography which reveal the extraordinary lives of ordinary people. Contributors include Ian Frazier, Mary Gordon, Joyce Carol Oates, Edward Hirsch, Lee Friedlander, Thomas Roma, Tess Gallagher, Phillip Levine; Susan Faludi, Bill McKibben, Alfred Kazin, and others.

Mathematics

Journal for Research in Mathematics Education. 1970. 5/yr. $62 (individuals $57). National Council of Teachers of Mathematics, 1906 Association Dr., Reston, VA 20191-1593. Illus. index. Circ. 10,700. Vol. ends: No. 5 Refereed. Microfilm: UMI. Contents Pages in Education, Current Index to Journals in Education, Education Index, Psychological Abstracts, and Zentralblatt Fur Didaktik Der Mathematik.
Aud: EJH, HS, Ac, Sa

Devoted to the interests of teachers of mathematics and mathematics education at all levels—preschool through adult. The *JRME* is a forum for disciplined inquiry into the teaching and learning of mathematics. It features reports of research, including experiments, case studies, surveys, and historical studies; articles about research; and commentaries on issues pertaining to research.

Mathematics Teacher. 1908. M. (September-May). Membership, $62 (individuals $57). National Council of Teachers of Mathematics, 1906 Association Dr., Reston, VA 20191-1593. Illus. index. Circ. 54,400. Refereed. Microfilm: UMI. Indexed: Biography Index, Contents Pages in Education, Current Index to Journals in Education, Education Index, Exceptional Child Education Resources, Literature Analysis of Microcomputer Publications, Mathematics Reviews, Media Review Digests, and Zentralblatt Fur Didaktik Der Mathematik. Bk. rev.: 4-10, 350-800 words. signed.
Aud: SA, Ac

Mathematics Teacher is devoted to the improvement of math instruction in the junior and senior high schools, two-year colleges, and teacher-education colleges. It contains articles on the teaching and learning of math. The main emphasis is on practical ways of helping teachers teach math more effectively. Features include Activities; letters to the editor; the Monthly Calendar; Connecting Research to Teaching; Implementing the NCTM Standards; Media Clips; Sharing Teaching Ideas; Soundoff; Tech Tips; and four sections that evaluate new technology, projects, products, and publications.

Mathematics Teaching in the Middle School. 1994. 8/yr. (Sept.; Oct; Nov/Dec; Jan., Feb.; March; April; May). Membership, $62 (individuals $57). National Council of Teachers of Mathematics, 1906 Association Dr., Reston, VA 20191-1593. Circ. 34,900. Indexed: Contents Pages in Education, Current Index to Journals in Education, Media Review Digest.
Aud: SA, Ac

Mathematics Teaching in the Middle School addresses the learning needs of all middle school students, the demand these needs place on their teachers, and the issues that capture the vitality of math and characteristics of the middle-grades student. This journal focuses on intuitive-exploratory investigations that help students develop a strong, conceptual mathematical base. Regular features include Assessment, Power On! The Thinking of Students, Mathematics Detective, Teacher to Teacher, On My Mind, and A Window on Resources. Also features three students sections: Menu of Problems, Now and Then, and Cartoon Corner.

Teaching Children Mathematics. (formerly Arithmetic Teacher) 1994. M. (Sept.-May) Membership, $62 (individuals $57). National Council of Teachers of Mathematics, 1906 Association Dr., Reston, VA 20191-1593. Circ. 38,200. Refereed, Microfilm: B&H, UMI. Indexed Academic Index, Biography Index, Contents Pages in Education, Current Index to Journals in Education, Education Index, Exceptional Child Education Resources, Literature Analysis of Microcomputer Publications, Media Review Digest, and Zentralblatt Fur Didaktik Der Mathematik.
Aud: EJH, HS, Ac, SA

Teaching Children Mathematics is the answer to the needs of teachers and children Pre-K–6, as well as parents who want to give support at home. Each issue contains many articles on how to improve the teaching and learning of math by young children. It also contains tear-out activities that are ready for classroom use, opinions on timely issues, a math calendar, information on promising projects and research, and more. Some of the features are Early Childhood Corner, In My Opinion, Investigations, Math by the Month, Reviewing and Viewing, Tech Time, and others.

Military

Naval History. 1987. 6/yr. $20. Ed.: Fred Schultz. U.S. Naval Institute, 118 Maryland Ave., Annapolis, MD 21402-5035. illus. Index. Adv. Circ.: 35,000. Sample. Vol. ends: Nov/Dec. Bk. rev.: Various.
Aud: GA

Naval History is the only magazine published solely on the subject of naval history. Each bi-monthly issue contains full-color photos, historical essays, book reviews, and reminiscences from people who participated in history's great naval moments. *Naval History* covers our nation's maritime heritage with the authority and style typical of all U.S. Naval Institute publications.

Proceedings. 1873. m. $35. Ed.: Fred H. Rainbow. U.S. Naval Institute, 118 Maryland Ave., Annapolis, MD 21402-5035. illus. index. adv. Circ.: 100,000.
Aud: GA

Proceedings is the widely respected magazine for naval officers and others interested in naval affairs. This monthly magazine features articles by military experts and strategists on current naval issues, interviews with naval leaders, full-color pictorials, insights into the U.S. Navy, Marine Corps, and Coast Guard, updates on foreign navies, and information on ships, aircraft, and submarines.

Multicultural

MultiCultural Review. 1992. q. $59. Greenwood Publishing Group, Inc., 88 Post Road West, P.O. Box 5007, Westport, CT 06881-5007. Circ. 5,000. Sample. Vol. ends: Dec.
Aud: EJH, HS, Ac, SA, GA

MultiCultural Review is a quarterly journal for public and school librarians, and educators and administrators at all levels. Each issue includes dozens of reviews of new multicultural materials: books, audio, video, software, and instructional resources. Articles explore current issues in cultural diversity in the United States and describe successful library and classroom programs.

Skipping Stones: A Multicultural Children's Magazine. 1988. Bi-monthly during school year (5 issues/yr.). Subscription: $35. (2-copy) subscription: $50; 5-copy sub: $100/yr. Single Issue: $5. Set of 40 back issues: $165. (low-income discount: 50%) Editor: Arun Narayan Toke. Publisher: Skipping Stones, Inc., P.O. Box 3939, Eugene, OR 97403. Email: skipping @efn.org Tel. (541) 342-4956. illus. Vol. ends: Nov/Dec.
Aud: Ages 8–15, and their teachers/parents

Award-winning, international, nonprofit magazine to expand your students' multicultural and global horizons. Celebrates cultural diversity and ecological richness. Publishes folktales, original writings (sometimes, multilingual with English translations), art and photos by youth and adults. Also contains: International Penpals, Bookshelf, Taking Action and Parent/Teacher Guide. 36 pages. No Ads. Recent themes: Challenging Disability, African, Native, and Latin American Cultures, Life in 2025. Living in the City, World Religions and Celebrations, Changing Families, Living Abroad. Annual *Skipping Stones* Book Awards and Youth Honor Award programs. Now celebrating 10th year! A *must* for any school library! Winner: 1997 NAME Award and 1995 EdPress GOLDEN SHOESTRING Award.

Music

Opera News. 1936. bi-w. (Dec.-April). m. (May-Nov.). $30. Ed.: Patrick J. Smith. 70 Lincoln Center Plaza, New York, NY 10023. Illus. index. adv. Circ. 125,000. Sample. Vol. ends: June. Microform: IAC, UMI. Indexed: music, Readers Guide. Bk. rev.: 3 250-300 words, signed.
Aud: EJH, HS, GA, Ac

The world's largest circulation opera magazine, *Opera News* features profiles of today's leading artists and rising young stars, news and reviews from around the world, and articles on all aspects of opera with special emphasis given to weekly radio broadcasts from New York's Metropolitan Opera and to national opera telecasts. Also included are reviews of opera recordings, books, and video releases. Beautifully illustrated and intelligently written, *Opera News* belongs in most libraries.

Nature

Orion and Orion Afield. 1982, 1997. Two quarterlies, one subscription. $25/yr., $35 Can., $45 intn'l. The Orion Society, 195 Main Street, Great Barrington, MA 01230. Illustr. Circ: 17,000. Back issues available. Orion ISSN 1058-3130/Afield ISSN 1096-9144. (413) 528-4422. web site: www.orionsociety.org; e-mail: orion@orionsociety.org. Indexed: Reader's Guide to Periodical Literature, Environmental Conservation and Outdoor Recreation Bibliography.
Aud: GA, Ac, HS

With fine writing and provocative images, *Orion* is today's leading forum for intellectually sound discourse on humans and the environment. Upholding the highest standards for literary content, analysis, and visual presentation, *Orion* combines diverse perspectives to creatively investigate how humans may build sustainable relationships with the natural world. Articles, fiction, poetry, reviews, and photoessays. No advertising. Contributors include: Wendell Berry, Terry Tempest Williams, Rick Bass, Barry Lopez, Mary Oliver, Ann Zwinger, Gary Snyder, Frans Lanting, Galen Rowell.

Orion Afield balances the philosophical approach of *Orion* with stories of people striving to create a sustainable and equitable future through community-based efforts in conservation, restoration, and education. Profiles of organizations, activists, fundraising tips, reviews, and educational programs and resources. An excellent grassroots networking and educational tool. *Orion* explores a vision for how we may live sanely while *Orion Afield* documents the grassroots efforts that make this vision possible.

Professional

Teaching K-8. (formerly Early Years) is published monthly, except June, July, August and December for $23.97 per year ($28.97 foreign) by Early Years, Inc. a wholly owned subsidiary of Highlights for Children, Inc., 40 Richards Avenue, Norwalk, CT 06854. ISSN 0891-4508.

Teaching K-8. For the elementary classroom teacher presents proven teaching techniques, ideas and activities in all curriculum areas with a heavy emphasis on language arts and children's literature. Also included are monthly ideas for school librarians. Editorial IS CURRENT, CONTEMPORARY MATERIAL FOR PROFESSIONAL TEACHER.

Education Week. 1981. wkly. 43 issues $69.94; foreign $136.94. Editorial Projects in Education, Inc., Suite 100, 6935 Arlington Road, Bethesda, MD 20814. (301) 280-3100. illus. Adv. Circ.: 51,000. ISSN 0277-4232. Back issues available on Microfilm from University Microfilms.

Education Week, American Education's newspaper of record, provides timely objective & comprehensive reports on the trends and developments shaping education. In addition to the weekly reporting of education news, special issues like Quality Counts, the annual state-by-state report on education policy and

Technology Counts, the report on the condition of technology in education make a subscription to *Education Week* a valuable resource in your library's collection.

Teacher Magazine. 1991. mnthly. 8 issues $17.94; foreign $28.20. Editorial Projects in Education, Inc., Suite 100, 6935 Arlington Road, Bethesda, MD 20814. (301) 280-3100. illus. Adv. Circ.: 131,000. ISSN 1046-6193.

Teacher Magazine is the only magazine for teachers to focus exclusively on issues in education. Readers look forward to coverage of major events and trends affecting schools; reports on developments in the disciplines, research, and classroom technology; and the opportunity to exchange ideas and opinion and debate education issues in the Comment section. Teachers and parents will find *Teacher Magazine* a useful addition to your library.

Science

Dragonfly. ISSN: 1089-9006. **Dragonfly Teacher's Companion.** ISSN 1089-9014. 1996. 5 issues (September-May). Library/ Teacher rate (Dragonfly and Dragonfly Teacher's Companion) $21.95; foreign $31.95. National Science Teacher's Association, 1840 Wilson Boulevard, Arlington, VA 22201-3000. Circ.: 5,000. Back issues available. (800) 722-NSTA (6782). Web Site: http://www.muohio.edu/dragon-fly/.

Dragonfly. Explore the creative power of science investigation with this theme-based magazine for young investigators ages 8-12. With each issue both children and scientists share in the excitement of discovery, inspiration, and curiosity of the natural world.

Library/Teacher subscription includes *Dragonfly* magazine and *Dragonfly Teacher's Companion,* a guide exploring related teaching applications. *Dragonfly* has received a 1997 Parent's Choice Award and a 1997 EdPress Distinguished Achievement Award. Advertising in *Dragonfly Teacher's Companion* only.

Science and Children. 1963. 8 issues (September-May). Membership, $70 (individuals $60). Foreign $80 (individuals $70). National Science Teacher's Association, 1840 Wilson Boulevard, Arlington, VA 22201-3000. Circ.: 22,000. Back issues available. ISSN 0036-8148. (800) 722-NSTA (6782). Web Site: http://www.nsta.org/. E-mail membership @nsta.org Available in Microfiche and/or reprinted editions from Xerox University Microfilms, Ann Arbor, MI. Indexed: Current Index to Journals in Education, Education Index, Exceptional Child Education Resources, Media Review Digest, and Women's Studies Abstracts.

Science and Children is a valuable resource for preschool through middle school (grades K–8) science teaching. This journal provides useful hands-on articles, helpful hints, software and book reviews, colorful posters and inserts, think pieces, and on-the-scene reports from classroom teachers. Features the annual Children's Book Council Outstanding Science Trade Books for Children list. Advertising available.

Science Scope. 1983. 8 issues. (September-May). Membership, $70 (individuals $60). Foreign $80 (individuals $70). National Science Teacher's Association, 1840 Wilson Boulevard, Arlington, VA 22201-3000. Circ.: 15,000. Back issues available. ISSN 0887-2376. (800) 722-NSTA (6782). Web Site: http://www.nsta.org/. E-mail: membership@ nsta.org.

Science Scope addresses the needs of both new and veteran educators of middle level (grades 5-9) science. The journal includes practical activities, posters, and teaching tips, along with educational theory focusing on the different ways that adolescents learn. Advertising available.

The Science Teacher. 1963. 9 issues. (September-May). Membership, $70 (individuals $60). Foreign $80 (individuals $70). National Science Teacher's Association, 1840

Wilson Boulevard, Arlington, VA 22201-3000. Circ.: 26,000. Back issues available. ISSN: 00368555. (800) 722-NSTA (6782). Web Site: http://www.nsta org/. E-mail: membership@nsta.org. Available in Microform from University Microfilms International. Indexed: Current Index to Journals in Education, Education Index, International Index to Multi-Media Information, Media Review Digest.

The Science Teacher is a professional journal for junior and senior high-school (grades 5–9) science educators that offers articles on a wide range of scientific topics, innovative teaching ideas and experiments, and current research news. This publication also features reviews, posters, and information on free or inexpensive materials. Advertising available.

Quantum. 1990. 6 issues. Available through membership, $70 (individuals $60). Foreign $80 (individuals $70). Also available through subscription, Library/Institutional rate $45. Please inquire for foreign rate. National Science Teacher's Association, 1840 Wilson Boulevard, Arlington, VA 22201-3000. Circ.: 8,000. Limited back issues available. (800) 722-NSTA (6782). Web Site: http://www.nsta.org/quantum/.

Quantum: The Magazine of Math and Science is a lavishly illustrated publication containing material translated from the Russian magazine Kvant as well as original material specifically targeted to American students. In addition to feature articles and departmental pieces, *Quantum* offers Olympiad-style problems and brainteasers along with an answer section. Available by subscription as well as through membership. Advertising available.

Science News. 1922. weekly. $49.50. Ed.: Julie Ann Miller, Science Service, 1719 N. Street, NW, Washington, DC 20036; Tel: 202-785-2255. Illus. Index. at vol. ends June/Dec. Adv. Circ: 205,000. Sample. Microform: UMI. For Subs call: 1-800-552-4412.

Science News is a 16-page weekly news publication providing up to the minute coverage in all areas of science, including biomedicine, behavioral sciences, chemistry, earth sciences, life sciences, and policy. Listings of newly released science-related books are featured in every issue as an addition to *Science News*'s award-winning editorial content.

Atom (for middle-readers). Established 1997; 6 issues; $25/yr. New World Publishers, 600 West 28th, Suite 205, Austin, TX 78705. To subscribe call 1-888-397-5264; Fax: 512-495-9667. Visit our Web Site www.atom-cogniz.com.

Atom. Imagination in Motion (for middle readers) nurtures the reader's interest in science and math with imaginative, interactive articles. The bi-monthly magazine goes beyond a hands-on approach by actively encouraging readers to ponder, understand, and apply scientific and mathematical concepts. Contains colorful and lively graphics and photos.

Cogniz (for teens). Established 1997; 6 issues; $25/yr. New World Publishers, 600 West 28th, Suite 205, Austin, TX 78705. To subscribe call 1-888-397-5264; Fax: 512-495-9667. Visit our Web Site www.atom-cogniz.com.

Challenging the reader's imagination with articles about nature, science and math, *Cogniz* (for teens) highlights the creative and imaginative elements of the scientific method. *Cogniz* goes beyond a hands-on approach by actively encouraging readers to ponder, understand, and apply scientific and mathematical concepts. With colorful and lively graphics and photos, the magazine delves deep into exciting topics in physics, chemistry, astronomy, and other areas including recent news events in science.

Odyssey. 1991. 9/yr. $26.95. Ed.: Beth Lindstrom, Cobblestone Publishing Company, 30 Grove Street, Peterborough, NH 03458. Illus. Sample. Circ.: 24,000. Vol. ends: Dec. Indexed CMG and VFI HH Wilson.
Aud: 9–14 yrs

"A beautiful, informative science magazine for grades four through nine." (New York Academy Sciences) Each issue shows readers that science is SENSATIONAL. *ODYSSEY* readers "do" science! Each 48 page issue is packed with feature articles, sidebars, interviews with scientists, spectacular photographs and original illustrations, classroom and home activities, frequent contests. Future Forum questions in each issue stimulate thinking and writing skills. A magazine readers refer to again and again!

Creation Research Society Quarterly. 1963. 4/yr. $30. Ed.: Dr. E. Chaffin. Bluefield College, Bluefield, VA 24605. Subs P.O. Box 8263, St. Joseph, MO 64508-8263. Circ.: 2,000. Peer-reviewed papers; panorama of science; book reviews; letters to editor; annual index. For Subs: Call 816-279-2626.
Aud: Ac, GA, SA

CRSQ has been published for 33 years and is the world's foremost and scholarly creationist journal. It has contained field and laboratory research papers on virtually every scientific subject of relevance to the creation/evolution discussion. The editorial staff consists of scientists concerned about understanding nature utilizing a creationist framework. Authors probe past and current science and project hypothesis and theories for the future.

Short Stories

Glimmer Train Stories. 1991. q. $32. Glimmer Train Press, 710 SW Madison Street #504, Portland, OR 97205. Phone: 503/221-0836. Fax: 503/221-0837. Web Site: www.glimmertrain.com No advertising. Circ. 13,000. Sample. ISSN 1055-7520. 160 pages of short stories and interviews with writers and other artists. Illustrated. Full color cover.

"Quite simply, in presentation as well as in content, the pieces are unpretentious and inviting as anything an old-fashioned storyteller would be proud to give voice to.... This will be a fine addition to public libraries where the short story is still regarded as a popular form of fiction and not just an academic exercise." —*Library Journal. Glimmer Train Stories* is a feast of fiction.

Social Studies

APPLESEEDS. 1998 9/yr. 26.95. Ed. Susan Buckley/Barbara Burt, Cobblestone Publishing Company, 30 Grove Street, Peterborough, NH 03458. Illus. Sample. Circ: begins publication September 1998. Vol. ends: May.

Finally, a *Cobblestone*-quality magazine for the younger set! The first issue of this colorful magazine for 7-9 year olds mails September, 1998. Each themed issue is filled with articles, interviews, and stories. Readers will delight in the fascinating photographs and original illustrations. Included are activities and games that develop skills and interest in, geography, history, vocabulary, math, and science in a fun way. Plant the seed of a love for reading with *APPLESEEDS*!

Spirituality

Christian Science Sentinel. 1898. Weekly. Special Library Rate—$45.50. The Christian Science Publishing Society, One Norway Street, Boston, MA 02115-3122. To Subscribe, call (800) 456-4851. Ed.: William E. Moody. illus., Circ.: 55,000. ISSN 0009-563X. Email: sentinel@csps.com.
Aud: GA, EJH, Ac, HS

Christian Science Sentinel is a weekly magazine offering a spiritual perspective on world events and the associated underlying trends in human thought. Inspirational, encouraging and thought provoking, the *Sentinel* is for people of all ages and faiths interested in nurturing their spirituality and using it to foster personal growth, self-improvement, healing, and insight into the world around us. Articles, interviews, news items of interest, commentary, verified firsthand accounts of spiritual healing.

Dramatics. 1929. Monthly 9x/year (Sept-May) $18.00/yr; foreign $28.00/yr. Educational Theatre Association, 3368 Central Parkway, Cincinnati, OH 45225. (513) 559-1996. Illus., contains advertising. Free sample to libraries. Circulation 40,000. Microform: UMI. ISSN 0012-5989. Indexed: American Humanities Index.
Aud: High School students and teachers.

The only magazine edited for high school theatre students and teachers, *Dramatics* features new playscripts, interviews with theatre professionals, practical articles on acting, directing, design, and other aspects of theatre production, and college and career information. Annual special issues offer comprehensive directories of college theatre programs and summer theatre work and study opportunities.

Teaching Theatre. 1989. Quarterly January, April, July, October. Educational Theatre Association, 3368 Central Parkway, Cincinnati, OH 45225. illus. No Advertising. Circ: 1,100. Sample on request. Microform: UMI. Teaching Theatre is a journal for teachers of theatre, primarily at the middle secondary school level.

Teaching Theatre is dedicated to providing K–12 theatre educators with practical innovative information that will make them better teachers and directors; serving [as] an advocacy tool that will help them educate students, fellow teachers, administrators, and parents about value of theatre in the school curriculum; serving as a journal of record for K–12 educational theatre; and providing a forum for the exchange of ideas, opinions, and research on K–12 theatre pedagogy. A typical issue contains an article on curriculum development or a profile of an exemplary program for students or teachers; a practical article on aspects of theatre, such as directing students or selecting plays; and news about current issues, trends, and events that are pertinent to theatre educators.

Video

Video Librarian. 1986. bi-m. $47. Video Librarian, P.O. Box 2725, Bremerton, WA 98310. Tel: 800-692-2270. Illus. index. Sample. Vol. ends: Nov/Dec. Web Site www.videolibrarian. com; E-mail vidlib@videolibrarian.com.
Aud: SA, GA, EJH, HS, Ac

Reviewing some 200 videos per issue in several areas including children's, Multicultural, the arts, business, and how-to's, *Video Librarian* is the "best single all-around source of video information" (Joseph Palmer, SUNY Buffalo). *VL* addresses issues of pricing, public performance, and changing technology; scans the Internet for video news; and keeps readers informed of special bargains. Called "a winner . . . too good to miss" *(Library Hotline)* "the place to turn"—*Library Journal.* ▲

ANNOTATED JOURNAL ARTICLES

Fine, Jana R. "Magazines and Webzines for the Way Cool Set," *School Library Journal* (November 1996): 61–65.
    A survey was given to teens in 10 states to discover which magazines they read. *Seventeen* was the most popular. Teens also gave input on what they look for in magazines and what changes they would like to see. Webzines, magazines on the Internet, were also discussed and rated.

Stoll, Donald R. "Using Magazines with Kids: Tips for Parents," *Reading Today* (April/May 1997): 18.
    The author lists 12 tips for getting kids involved with magazines. The tips include such activities as reading and discussing advice columns and then writing your own; entering a magazine-sponsored essay contest; gluing an animal picture from a nature magazine onto a piece of cardboard and cutting it into a puzzle; and creating a collage of pictures relating to a specific subject.

WEB SITES

CyberKids Home
http://www.cyberkids.com

MidLink Magazine
http://longwood.cs.ucf.edu/~MidLink/

Mom's Magazines
http://sanfords.net/MomDear/Magazines.html

OWLkids
http://www.owl.on.ca/index.html

Ranger Rick
http://www.igc.apc.org/nwf/lib/rr

Sports Illustrated for Kids
http://pathfinder.com/SIFK/

Stone Soup
http://www.stonesoup.com

World
http://www.nationalgeographic.com/ngs/mags/world/world1.html

YES Science Magazine for Kids
http://www.islandnet.com/~yesmag/

Chapter 9

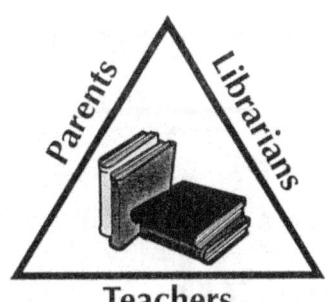

The Fine Art of Picture Books

OVERVIEW

Picture books are a form of visual art. Illustrations contribute to the meaning of a picture book. Unlike an artist who deals with only a single two-dimensional surface, the illustrator of a picture book must extend these choices to the design of the entire book. In addition, the illustrator must consider factors unique to picture book production and make choices about what will appear on the endpapers and what typeface will be used for the words. By using line, shape, color, value, and texture—the elements of art—the illustrator can arouse emotion and convey mood and meaning in a picture book. Some picture book art has been displayed in galleries as "hang-on-the-wall art." But in the best picture books, the pictures depend on one another to relate the story and do not have the same power when isolated.

GUIDED READING QUESTIONS

1. Do you feel that your picture book illustrations could be shown in an art gallery?
2. Do the illustrations describe the story effectively?
3. Are the style of the illustrations and the medium used to create them appropriate to the mood of the text?
4. Do the illustrations convey any special mood or emotion?
5. How would you describe the illustrations?
6. Is the design of the entire book effective?

From *More Reading Connections.* © 1999. Knowles/Smith. Libraries Unlimited. (800) 237-6124.

JOURNAL ARTICLE

Every Picture Tells a Story: The Magic of Wordless Books

These seemingly simple books vary a great deal in terms of style and sophistication . . .

Within the world of children's literature, there are some special titles that can literally be called picture books since their stories are conveyed without words. These seemingly simple books vary a great deal in terms of style and sophistication, and encompass the genres of fantasy, folklore, adventure, animal stories, travel, historical and realistic fiction, and humor. They can be effectively used to stimulate young readers' natural curiosity and to aid in the development of imagination, language skills, and creativity. Most importantly, they can facilitate interactive experiences for youngsters and their reading partners.

Stories without words offer exercises in observation and visual discrimination since they require close attention to detail. Also, since they are not bound by texts, which tend to impose mood, feelings, and meaning, their illustrations stand as poetic literary expressions left to individual taste, interpretation, and cultural orientation. Needless to say, the quality of the artwork in such books is of paramount importance.

In addition to basic cognitive exercises in sequencing and language development, wordless books are ideal tools for introducing older children to creative writing. They can gain from them an understanding of the literary elements of character, plot, setting, style, and theme.

Yet, all too often, these titles are dismissed by adults and older youngsters as being ephemeral, unimportant, and inappropriate "reading" material. How many times have you heard parents say, "Let's choose another book to take home. This one doesn't have any words."

The titles discussed below have been successful in my library programs. The first group works best with preschool and primary-grade audiences. For the most part, they feature basic line drawings with splashes of color and clean, crisp formats. Plots are clear and straightforward with story titles setting the theme.

Shirley Hughes's *Up and Up* (Lothrop, 1979) relates a young girl's fascination with flight. This tenacious child continues her single-minded pursuit of becoming airborne. The "if at first you don't succeed" theme is aided by a bit of magic in the form of a chocolate egg and a "be careful what you wish for" ending, in which she must be rescued by an elderly man in a hot-air balloon.

Fernando Krahn has created numerous tales of adventure, suspense, and intrigue. In *Amanda and the Mysterious Carpet* (Clarion, 1985), a magic carpet becomes a vehicle for a girl's fanciful journey as it floats through the doorway and takes her for a ride. She ends up on the roof of her house and is rescued by her extremely cross mother.

By Barbara Osborne-Harris. Reprinted with permission of *School Library Journal* (August 1994), pages 38–39. Barbara Osborne-Harris is Manager of Youth Services at the Central Library of the Queens Borough Public Library, Jamaica, NY.

In *The Mystery of the Giant's Footprints* (Dutton, 1977; o.p.), two children, their parents, and finally the entire community follow strange tracks through the woods, over rooftops, across a frozen lake, over a cliff, around a mountain, and into a cave. The search culminates in a surprising and amusing discovery.

Nick Butterworth's *Amanda's Butterfly* (Delacorte, 1991) features a bright, spirited girl who explores her yard in search of butterflies. When it starts to rain, she takes shelter in the tool shed and discovers a tiny fairy with a broken wing and nurses her back to health. It's a sensitive and thoughtful fantasy.

Mercer Mayer's *A Boy, a Dog, a Frog and a Friend* (1978), *Frog, Where Are You?* (1969), and *Frog on His Own* (1973, all Dial) weave humorous tales about a young boy and his pets who have all sorts of believable encounters with the world around them.

In Ed Young's *Up a Tree* (HarperCollins, 1983), a curious cat is enchanted with a butterfly, making him easy prey for a nearby dog. From his perch atop a tree, he ignores rescue attempts and comes down only when he is ready. All of the characters in this lively romp remain true to their respective animal natures.

Alexandra Day paints an enchanting fantasy in *Carl Goes Shopping* (Farrar, 1989). Here, the protective Rottweiler takes his young charge to a department store, where infant and dog enjoy a good book, watch television, relax on an oriental rug, have a snack, and visit the pet shop.

Emily Arnold McCully expertly combines real-life occurrences and an element of fantasy to create her heartwarming stories: *Picnic* (1984), *First Snow* (1985), *School* (1987), and *New Baby* (1988, all HarperCollins). All of these titles feature the same endearing family of mice whose exploits mirror those of their human counterparts and offer insight into familiar experiences and feelings.

John S. Goodall's skillful paintings that employ a "turn the flap" technique are used to great effect in *Paddy to the Rescue* (McElderry, 1986; o.p.). The porcine hero innocently enters a building, finds a robbery in progress, and races to the aid of a maiden in distress. The villain escapes through an open window with a bag of jewels and the pursuit is on. Each scene evokes excitement and intriguing suspense. The same excellent quality can be found in other "Paddy" adventures.

Goodall's renditions of *Little Red Riding Hood* (1988) and *Puss in Boots* (both McElderry, 1990) bring folklore to the world of wordless books. In them, the artist follows the traditional sequence of events; however, his Red Riding Hood is a mouse, and all of the other characters are also animals. The illustrations and character representation in *Puss in Boots* are in keeping with the original.

Brinton Turkle's *Deep in the Forest* (Dutton, 1976) gives a creative twist to the tale of "Goldilocks and the Three Bears" by reversing the characters' roles. The friendly intruder is a young bear, who explores the home of some unsuspecting humans.

Children are drawn to these books because of their visual orientation. By learning to "read" pictures, youngsters develop their language and observation skills, patterning, and other essential elements in reading readiness.

The next group of titles features intricately detailed artwork and more complex and highly developed themes. All have multidimensional plots with the titles offering only a hint of what is in store. While younger audiences can enjoy these books, they are best used with children in elementary grades, who come to them with a stronger sense of story.

David Wiesner's Caldecott Award-winning *Tuesday* (Clarion, 1991) is an engaging fantasy in which a group of frogs takes to the skies one evening. This unusual occurrence and its hilarious results open readers' minds and imaginations to limitless possibilities that certainly do not end on Tuesday. The fanciful and humorous presentation understates the more sophisticated "expect the unexpected" theme.

Jeannie Baker's *Window* (Greenwillow, 1991) allows readers to examine and think about change. The artist cleverly uses a window through which readers watch, with a young mother and her son, the physical changes that occur around them as the boy grows. The story ends with the child as a young man holding his own son gazing through a window, which reveals an environment on the brink of full urbanization.

Japanese-born Mitsumasa Anno has emerged as one of the masters of wordless picture books. His 1970 edition of *Topsy-Turvies,* first published in Japan in 1968, is an outstanding, innovative title designed to stretch the imagination.

His meticulous paintings provide a realistic picture of the countryside and town life of Europe *(Anno's Journey* [1981]), Britain *(Anno's Britain* [1982, o.p.]), and Italy *(Anno's Italy* [1984; o.p. all Philomel]). Readers are drawn into the lifestyles of the people, their art, architecture, folklore, and fairy tales. Fine-line drawings capture detail and inserts of national monuments and cultural points of interest add visual challenge. *Anno's U.S.A.* (Philomel, 1992) is particularly fascinating in that the artist weaves together a tapestry of American life. He includes events like the Macy's Thanksgiving Day parade in a setting of skyscrapers and the Indians selling Manhattan Island. He begins his journey with early America, builds to current-day views, and then shows his trademark, blue-suited journey man sailing off in a rowboat in view of a sailing vessel, a log cabin, and Native Americans. Youngsters intrigued with Waldo can find greater artistic expression and depth in these books.

John S. Goodall shows his diverse talent as he combines the elements of travel and historical fiction. *An Edwardian Christmas* (1978; o.p.) captures in detail the beauty of an early 1900s English celebration—combing the woods for fresh holly, decorating the church, and trimming the tree. *The Story of the Seashore* (1990) traces the changing shoreline from the early 1800s with George III's visit to Weymouth, to the Costa del Sol, Spain in the 1990s. *The Story of a Farm* (1989: all McElderry) begins with the early Middle Ages and culminates with a present-day view of a farm. Each illustration captures fine details of the periods.

These stories can be used to encourage children to write their own texts to parallel the illustrations or to stretch their imaginations as they search for deeper meanings. Groups can participate in a read-aloud with individuals interpreting single illustrations or story lines. It is interesting to see the similarities and differences in language and description that emerge. Even reluctant readers are eager to ponder the artwork and trace plot development and outcomes. The discovery of layers of meaning and subplots builds confidence and interest that can be transferred to written works.

Stories without words offer unique and varied creative opportunities for children and the adults in their lives. Parents, librarians, teachers, and caregivers can take part in sharing these singularly satisfying gems with the children they know, and all will be richer for the experience. ▲

ANNOTATED JOURNAL ARTICLES

Evans, Dilys. "Picture Book, Picture Book, on the Wall . . . ," *Horn Book Magazine* (March/April 1998): 258–62.
   Many illustrators of children's books do not consider their work as important as fine art. In the late 1970s, an art gallery in New York City had an exhibition of children's book illustrations. From that time on, there has been a slow emergence of art galleries that show children's book illustrations. Illustrators are finally being taken more seriously—and this attitude has also been financially advantageous for them.

Scheps, Susan. "Books 101: Art Appreciation in Five Easy Steps," *Youth Services in Libraries* (Fall 1997): 71–74.
   This article tells about a project used with first-grade students that could be used with students of any age. The author found that most people view artwork in picture books as "a decorative addition rather than a carefully crafted expression of the story that is an integral part of the book's essence." The project has five easy steps, a long list of picture book titles, samples of different styles and media, and final evaluative questions.

Scieszka, Jon. "Design Matters," *Horn Book Magazine* (March/April 1998): 196–208.
   The design of a picture book is as important to the framework as the text and illustration. It is the "subtle weave of words and pictures that allows both to tell one seamless tale." The job of a book designer is to pick the style, size, and color of type; kind of paper; and size of book, and then to arrange the illustrations and text on the pages. This article is written in Jon Scieszka's comical style, but it certainly does clarify the importance of design in picture books.

ANNOTATED BIBLIOGRAPHY

Brett, Jan. *The Hat*. G. P. Putnam's Sons, 1997.
   Lisa hangs her woolen clothes on a line to air them out. One of the stockings blows off the line. A curious hedgehog finds it and wears it as a hat. Several animals meet Hedgie and each runs off to see what else is hanging on the line. In the borders, this book shows what Lisa was doing, the clothes on the line, and the animals Hedgie will meet next. Lisa finds Hedgie with her stocking and tells him, "Don't you know that animals don't wear clothes!" When Lisa heads back home, she sees all her missing woolens on the various animals. A companion to *The Mitten*.

Crew, Gary. *The Watertower*. Crocodile Books, 1998.
   This book has an interesting design: it is rotated 90 degrees from a normal position. It then changes to a normal position and finally 180 degrees from the starting position. Two boys decide to climb the watertower and then go for a swim in the murky waters inside. When Bubba climbs out of the watertower, his shorts are missing. His friend offers to get another pair of shorts and return shortly. In the meantime, Bubba waits as the watertower takes on a menacing appearance. Winner of the Australian Children's Picture Book of the Year.

From *More Reading Connections*. © 1999. Knowles/Smith. Libraries Unlimited. (800) 237-6124.

Ehlert, Lois. *Hands*. Harcourt Brace, 1997.
>This book is shaped like a work glove and many of the pages are uniquely shaped. Each page is a different color or pattern. It shows what the father and mother do with their hands and the type of tools they use. The daughter helps but knows she will use her hands to be an artist.

Johnson, Stephen T. *Alphabet City*. Viking, 1995.
>The author uses the urban setting in his paintings to show the letters of the alphabet. For example, the letter *E* is a side view of a traffic signal light. This wordless book can be enjoyed over and over by all ages. A Caldecott Honor book.

Taback, Simms. *There Was an Old Lady Who Swallowed a Fly*. Viking, 1987.
>This favorite American folk poem was first heard in the United States in the 1940s. This version was a Caldecott Honor book. The author explains what was going on in the old woman's stomach by using a die-cut hole. The hole and woman increase in size as she swallows larger and larger animals. The moral of the story? Never swallow a horse; you'll die, of course.

Zelinsky, Paul O. *Rapunzel*. Dutton Children's Books, 1997.
>Each page is resplendent with beautifully detailed oil paintings. A sorceress takes Rapunzel at birth. When Rapunzel turns 12, the sorceress takes her to the forest to live in a high tower with no doors. When the sorceress wishes to visit, Rapunzel lets down her long hair and the sorceress climbs up to the top of the tower. One day a prince happens to pass by and hear Rapunzel singing. The prince falls deeply in love. Not even blindness stops his wanderings to find his beloved Rapunzel. A Caldecott Medal winner.

BIBLIOGRAPHY

Alexander, Lloyd. *The Fortune-Tellers*. Illustrated by Trina Schart Hyman. Dutton Children's Books, 1992.

Banks, Kate. *Baboon*. Illustrated by George Hallensleben. Farrar, Straus & Giroux, 1997.

Bannerman, Helen. *The Story of Little Babaji*. Illustrated by Fred Marcellino. HarperCollins, 1996.

Base, Graeme. *Animalia*. Harry N. Abrams, 1986.

Brett, Jan. *Berlioz the Bear*. G. P. Putnam's Sons, 1991.

Buehner, Caralyn. *Fanny's Dream*. Illustrated by Mark Buehner. Dial Books for Young Readers, 1996.

Bunting, Eve. *Train to Somewhere*. Illustrated by Ronald Himler. Clarion Books, 1996.

Burleigh, Robert. *Hoops*. Illustrated by Stephen T. Johnson. Harcourt Brace, 1997.

Carle, Eric. *The Very Hungry Caterpillar*. Philomel, 1981.

Cooney, Barbara. *Miss Rumphius*. Viking, 1982.

Cowan, Catherine. *My Life with the Wave.* Illustrated by Mark Buehner. Lothrop, Lee & Shepard, 1997.

Cummings, Pat. *Talking with Artists.* Bradbury Press, 1992.

———. *Talking with Artists, Volume Two.* Simon & Schuster, 1995.

Davol, Marguerite W. *The Paper Dragon.* Illustrated by Robert Sabuda. Atheneum, 1997.

Demi. *The Firebird.* Henry Holt, 1994.

———. *One Grain of Rice: A Mathematical Folktale.* Scholastic, 1997.

Dorros, Arthur. *Abuela.* Dutton Children's Books, 1991.

Egan, Tim. *Burnt Toast on Davenport Street.* Houghton Mifflin, 1997.

Ehlert, Lois. *Hands.* Harcourt Brace, 1997.

Feelings, Tom. *The Middle Passage: White Ships/Black Cargo.* Dial Books for Young Readers, 1995.

Fleming, Candace. *Gabriella's Song.* Illustrated by Giselle Potter. Simon & Schuster, 1997.

Foreman, Michael. *Seal Surfer.* Harcourt Brace, 1997.

Garay, Luis. *Pedrito's Day.* Orchard, 1997.

Geisert, Arthur. *The Etcher's Studio.* Houghton Mifflin, 1997.

Giblin, James Cross. *Charles A. Lindbergh: A Human Hero.* Houghton Mifflin, 1997.

Haas, Irene. *A Summertime Song.* Simon & Schuster, 1997.

Hamilton, Virginia. *A Ring of Tricksters.* Illustrated by Barry Moser. Scholastic, 1997.

Harper, Isabelle. *Our New Puppy.* Illustrated by Barry Moser. Scholastic, 1996.

Harrison, David. L. *When Cows Came Home.* Illustrated by Chris L. Demarest. Boyds Mills Press, 1994.

Henkes, Kevin. *Lilly's Purple Plastic Purse.* Greenwillow Books, 1996.

Hest, Amy. *Baby Duck and the Bad Eyeglasses.* Illustrated by Jill Barton. Candlewick Press, 1996.

Ho, Minfong. *Brother Rabbit: A Cambodian Tale.* Illustrated by Jean Tseng and Jou-sien Tseng. Lothrop, Lee & Shepard, 1997.

———. *Hush! A Thai Lullaby.* Illustrated by Holly Meade. Orchard, 1996.

Hoberman, Mary Ann. *One of Each.* Illustrated by Marjorie Priceman. Little, Brown, 1997.

Jaffe, Nina. *The Mysterious Visitor: Stories of the Prophet Elijah.* Illustrated by Elivia Savadier. Scholastic, 1997.

Janisch, Heinz, adapter. *Noah's Ark.* Illustrated by Lisbeth Zwerger. North-South Books, 1997.

Jenkins, Steve. *What Do You Do When Something Wants to Eat You?* Houghton Mifflin, 1997.

Kipling, Rudyard. *Rikki-Tikki-Tavi.* Illustrated by Jerry Pinkney. William Morrow, 1997.

Kleven, Elisa. *Hooray, a Piñata!* Dutton Children's Books, 1996.

———. *The Puddle Pail.* Dutton Children's Books, 1997.

Koller, Jackie French. *No Such Thing.* Illustrated by Betsy Lewin. Boyds Mills Press, 1997.

From *More Reading Connections.* © 1999. Knowles/Smith. Libraries Unlimited. (800) 237-6124.

Krull, Kathleen. *Wilma Unlimited: How Wilma Rudolph Became the World's Fastest Woman.* Illustrated by David Diaz. Harcourt Brace, 1996.

Lasky, Kathryn. *The Most Beautiful Roof in the World: Exploring the Rainforest Canopy.* Illustrated by Christopher G. Knight. Harcourt Brace, 1997.

Lester, Julius. *Sam and the Tiger: A New Telling of Little Black Sambo.* Illustrated by Jerry Pinkney. Dial Books for Young Readers, 1996.

Levitin, Sonia. *The Man Who Kept His Heart in a Bucket.* Pictures by Jerry Pinkney. Dial Books for Young Readers, 1991.

Lindbergh, Reeve. *Benjamin's Barn.* Paintings by Susan Jeffers. Dial Books for Young Readers, 1990.

Lionni, Leo. *Swimmy.* Pantheon Books, 1968.

Lobel, Anita. *Alison's Zinnia.* Greenwillow Books, 1990.

London, Jonathan. *Red Wolf Country.* Illustrated by Daniel San Souci. Dutton Children's Books, 1996.

Lowell, Susan. *The Bootmaker and the Elves.* Illustrated by Tom Curry. Orchard, 1997.

Macaulay, David. *Rome Antics.* Houghton Mifflin, 1997.

Mahy, Margaret. *17 Kings and 42 Elephants.* Pictures by Patricia MacCarthy. Dial Books for Young Readers, 1972.

Marshall, James. *Red Riding Hood.* Dial Books for Young Readers, 1987.

McBratney, Sam. *The Dark at the Top of the Stairs.* Illustrated by Ivan Bates. Candlewick Press, 1996.

McCloskey, Robert. *One Morning in Maine.* Viking, 1952.

McPhail, David. *Pigs Aplenty, Pigs Galore!* Dutton Children's Books, 1993.

Melville, Herman. *Catskill Eagle.* Paintings by Thomas Locker. Philomel, 1991.

Miranda, Anne. *To Market, To Market.* Illustrated by Janet Stevens. Harcourt Brace, 1997.

Nikola-Lisa, W. *Til Year's Good End: A Calendar of Medieval Labors.* Illustrated by Christopher Manson. Atheneum, 1997.

Norman, Howard. *The Girl Who Dreamed Only Geese and Other Tales of the Far North.* Harcourt Brace, 1997.

Opie, Iona. *My Very First Mother Goose.* Illustrated by Rosemary Wells. Candlewick Press, 1996.

Otten, Charlotte F. *January Rides the Wind: A Book of Months.* Illustrated by Todd L. W. Doney. Lothrop, Lee & Shepard, 1997.

Pelletier, David. *Graphic Alphabet.* Orchard, 1996.

Perkins, Lynne Rae. *Clouds for Dinner.* Greenwillow Books, 1997.

Philip, Neil. *The Adventures of Odysseus.* Illustrated by Peter Mallone. Orchard, 1997.

Pilkey, Dav. *The Paperboy.* Orchard, 1996.

Pinkney, Brian. *The Adventures of Sparrowboy.* Simon & Schuster, 1997.

Prelutsky, Jack. *The Beauty and the Beast: Poems from the Animal Kingdom.* Illustrated by Meilo So. Alfred A. Knopf, 1997.

Pyle, Howard, adapter. *Bearskin.* Illustrated by Trina Schart Hyman. William Morrow, 1997.

Raschka, Christopher. *The Blushful Hippopotamus.* Orchard, 1996.

Riley, Linnea. *Mouse Mess.* Scholastic, 1997.

Ringgold, Faith. *Aunt Harriet's Underground Railroad in the Sky.* Crown, 1992.

Rodda, Emily. *Power and Glory.* Illustrated by Geoff Kelly. Greenwillow Books, 1996.

Sabuda, Robert. *The Twelve Days of Christmas: A Pop-Up Celebration.* Simon & Schuster, 1996.

Say, Allen. *Grandfather's Journey.* Houghton Mifflin, 1993.

Schroeder, Alan. *Minty: A Story of Young Harriet Tubman.* Illustrated by Jerry Pinkney. Dial Books for Young Readers, 1996.

Scieszka, Jon. *Math Curse.* Illustrated by Lane Smith. Viking, 1995.

Shannon, George. *Tomorrow's Alphabet.* Illustrated by Donald Crews. Greenwillow Books, 1996.

Shapiro, Arnold L. *Mice Squeak, We Speak.* Illustrated by Tomie dePaola. Putnam, 1997.

Shepard, Aaron, reteller. *The Sea King's Daughter: A Russian Legend.* Illustrated by Gennady Spirin. Simon & Schuster, 1997.

Sierra, Judy. *Nursery Tales Around the World.* Illustrated by Sefano Vitale. Houghton Mifflin, 1996.

Sís, Peter. *Starry Messenger: A Book Depicting the Life of a Famous Scientist, Mathematician, Astronomer, Philosopher, Physicist, Galileo Galilei.* Farrar, Straus & Giroux, 1996.

———. *The Three Golden Keys.* Doubleday, 1994.

Sisulu, Elinor Batezat. *The Day Gogo Went to Vote: South Africa, April 1994.* Little, Brown, 1996.

Smith, Lane. *The Happy Hocky Family.* Viking, 1991.

Soto, Gary. *Snapshots from the Wedding.* Illustrated by Stephanie Garcia. Putnam, 1997.

Stadler, John. *The Cats of Mrs. Calamari.* Orchard, 1997.

Stanley, Diane. *Leonardo da Vinci.* William Morrow, 1996.

Steger, Will, and Jon Bowermaster. *Over the Top of the World: Explorer Will Steger's Trek Across the Arctic.* Scholastic, 1997.

Steig, William. *Brave Irene.* Farrar, Straus & Giroux, 1986.

Steptoe, John. *The Story of Jumping Mouse: A Native American Legend.* Lothrop, Lee & Shepard, 1984.

Stevens, Janet. *Tops and Bottoms.* Harcourt Brace, 1995.

Stevenson, James. *That Terrible Halloween Night.* Mulberry Press, 1990.

Stewart, Sarah. *The Gardener.* Illustrated by David Small. Farrar, Straus & Giroux, 1997.

Taback, Simms. *There Was an Old Lady Who Swallowed a Fly.* Viking, 1997.

Thomson, Peggy, and Barbara Moore. *The Nine-Ton Cat: Behind the Scenes at an Art Museum.* Houghton Mifflin, 1997.

Van Allsburg, Chris. *The Mysteries of Harris Burdick.* Houghton Mifflin, 1984.

Voake, Charlotte. *Ginger.* Candlewick Press, 1997.

Wells, Rosemary. *McDuff Comes Home.* Illustrated by Susan Jeffers. Hyperion Books, 1997.

Wisniewski, David. *Golem.* Clarion Books, 1996.

Wood, Audrey. *The Rainbow Bridge.* Paintings by Robert Florczak. Harcourt Brace, 1995.

Yep, Laurence. *The Khan's Daughter.* Illustrated by Jean Tseng and Mou-Sien Tseng. Scholastic, 1997.

Yorinks, Arthur. *Hey Al.* Illustrated by Richard Egielski. Farrar, Straus & Giroux, 1986.

Young, Ed. *Mouse Match: A Chinese Folktale.* Harcourt Brace, 1997.

Zelinsky, Paul O. *Rapunzel.* Dutton Children's Books, 1997.

WEB SITES

Jan Brett
http://www.janbrett.com

Eric Carle
http://www.eric-carle.com

Lynne Cherry
http://www.friend.ly.net/scoop/biographies/lcherry.html

David Diaz
http://www.friend.ly.net/scoop/biographies/ddiaz.html

Leo and Diane Dillon
http://www.best.com/~libros/dillon

Lois Ehlert
http://www.friend.ly.net/scoop/biographies/lehlert.html

Denise Fleming
http://www.friend.ly.net/scoop/biographies/dfleming.html

Michael Hague
http://www.friend.ly.net/scoop/biographies/mhague.html

Susan Jeffers
http://www.friend.ly.net/scoop/biographies/sjeffers.html

Ezra Jack Keats
http://www.lib.usm.edu/~degrum/keats/main.html
http://ocean.st.usm.edu/~dajones/EJKeats.htm

Steven Kellogg
http://www.friend.ly.net/scoop/biographies/skellogg.html

Emily Arnold McCully
http://www.bdd.com/teachers/mccu.html

Dav Pilkey
http://www.pilkey.com

Beatrix Potter
http://www.peterrabbit.co.uk/index2.html

Arthur Ransome
http://humboldt1.com/ar/

Allen Say
http://www.eduplace.com/rdg/author/say/index.html

Janet Stevens
http://www.janetstevens.com

Chris Van Allsburg
http://www.wondersociety.com/rws/art/illusbk/

Audrey Wood
http://www.audreywood.com

Chapter 10

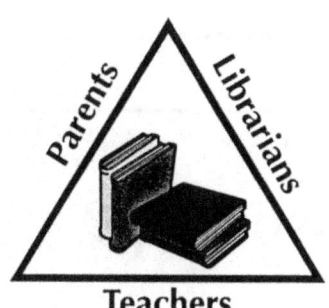

Selection or Censorship?

OVERVIEW

Sometimes the books that teachers and librarians choose to use in classrooms provoke adverse reactions from parents or other members of the community. A parent may simply request that his or her child not read a particular book, or the parent may demand that *no* child be allowed to read a particular book. Suppressing reading material is called censorship and often causes more problems than it solves. We should be selecting reading material that is appropriate for the particular student population. *Censorship* is the attempt to deny others the right to read something the censor thinks is offensive. *Selection* is the process of choosing appropriate material for readers according to literary and educational judgments.

GUIDED READING QUESTIONS

1. What do you think about censorship?
2. Do you think it is appropriate to leave the choice of school reading materials up to the teachers and librarian?
3. Do you censor what your child reads? If so, what are your criteria for censoring?
4. Have you ever had anyone censor what you read?

From *More Reading Connections*. © 1999. Knowles/Smith. Libraries Unlimited. (800) 237-6124.

JOURNAL ARTICLE

Better Libraries Through Censorship?

It took a fevered book challenge to
firm up support for intellectual freedom.

Censorship and positive change. An oxymoron? During a major censorship controversy in our school two years ago, I would have thought so, but examining a problem at hand is like looking through a microscope. Minuscule details stand out in perfect focus while the big picture remains blurry. Now, I can step back and see how censorship changed our district... for the better.

In September 1994, after being a school librarian for a month, I received the first of three book challenges. The initial request for reconsideration sparked nine difficult months of meetings, discussions, and decisions. Newspaper headlines and letters to the editor, television broadcasts, and pressure during school board hearings were all daunting. The issue pervaded our community for months.

The school board voted to remove the first challenged title despite the fact that the campus reconsideration committee supported it. A few months later, after a thorough examination of the selection process and consideration of public opinion, the board overturned its decision and voted unanimously to return the book.

Not all censorship conflicts end as positively as ours did. When the decision came to reinstate the book, I felt more shell-shocked than elated. The experience was my worst nightmare and my best teacher. Censorship changed our district for the better because it prompted us to examine current practices and policies, and provided impetus for us to do the following:

1. Strengthen Selection Policy

Although revised shortly before the first challenge, our selection policy remained untested, like a new car gleaming on the showroom floor. It looked great, but how did it drive? The first challenge highlighted three areas that needed to be changed. First, we added parents to the reconsideration committee. Second, we created a district-level review committee so appeals would not jump directly to the school board. Finally, we added a time frame with specific deadlines for responses to the reconsideration process.

To revise our policy, we examined reconsideration documents from exemplary schools in Texas and consulted with leaders in the profession. The result: a thoughtful document tailored to our district. "While the issue polarized the community," said our assistant superintendent, "it highlighted a critical issue for our teachers and allowed us to put into place a policy that was both structured and reassuring for teachers as well as parents."

2. Broaden Library Support

When the school board—at the urging of about 20 people—voted to remove the challenged book from the middle school library,

---

By Leigh Ann Jones. Reprinted with permission of *School Library Journal* (October 1996), page 54. Leigh Ann Jones is Librarian, Carroll Middle School, Southlake, TX.

newspaper headlines captured the attention of our suburban community. Concerned parents obtained more than 300 signatures on a petition calling for it to be returned to the library. Attendance at later hearings soared, and the same informally organized group of parents distributed green ribbons to overflow crowds symbolizing their opposition to censorship. Over 40 people spoke passionately about the freedom to read at three separate board meetings. Positive letters to the editor began to outnumber negative ones, and censorship became an issue in the local school board election. While we were fortunate that parents mobilized themselves, it's clear that Friends groups and other supportive organizations are worthwhile—*before* a title is challenged.

3. Affirm Intellectual Freedom

As the saying goes, you don't know what you have until you lose it. Or almost lose it, in this case. When challenged, the right to read became more dear to those who supported the book. Shelly Cook, a high school English teacher, drew applause at a board hearing when she said, "It's not about a word. It goes beyond that. It extends to an idea, then to life—and life can be pretty messy."

4. Empower Librarians

When the board reinstated the book, each member spoke of the importance of placing the selection of materials firmly in the hands of professional personnel, a change that I attribute to the group's newfound awareness of the media specialist's role. That reaffirmation of trust, along with a tested selection policy, empowered librarians and teachers to select materials more thoughtfully, but not more cautiously.

5. Enhance Library Role

Fortunately, the right to read in our school district prevailed because the best interests of students overrode other concerns. Because librarians are central to the educational goals of our district, the issue became larger than one word, larger than one book. The issue became access to all library materials. This near-miss reinforced our belief that academic excellence cannot exist without intellectual freedom. ▲

ANNOTATED JOURNAL ARTICLES

Peck, Richard. "From Strawberry Statements to Censorship," *School Library Journal* (January 1997): 28–29.

    Parents, who in their youth marched against authority, are now censoring what young people read. In a very powerful way, Peck writes about the types of young adult books that are currently being attacked. He claims that censorship is only a symptom of a vast problem. The authority of American families has collapsed and now the teacher is to assume a parental role. He says teachers can't teach reading to students who are more politically empowered than they are.

West, Mark I. "Speaking of Censorship: An Interview with Phyllis Reynolds Naylor," *Youth Services in Libraries* (Winter 1997): 177–82.

    Phyllis Reynolds Naylor is the author of more than 60 books for children and young adults. *Shiloh* is the most frequently attacked of her books. Naylor was both perplexed and angry over the attacks, which centered on the language used by the villain in the book. She is well known for her six books about witches and she was not surprised when they were attacked. Naylor states that the books do not promote witchcraft and were only written because as a child she liked scary stories. She says she does not let the censors influence the way she writes.

ANNOTATED BIBLIOGRAPHY

Blume, Judy. *Blubber*. Dell, 1974.

    Jill Brenner is in the fifth grade and her mother and friends warn her that she can be pretty tough on others. When Jill becomes the negative focus of her class, she learns how it feels to be on the outside. This intermediate novel shows how different personalities react to student pressures.

Cormier, Robert. *The Chocolate War*. Pantheon Books, 1974.

    Jerry has a poster of a solitary man standing upright on the beach, mounted inside his locker. Inscribed on the poster is the slogan: "Do I Dare Disturb the Universe." Jerry comes to understand the poster when he defies a teacher; the Vigils, an underground organization; and ultimately the entire school. He sadly learns that people only let you do your own thing when it happens to be their own thing.

Coville, Bruce. *My Teacher Is an Alien*. Pocket Books, 1989.

    Susan is upset to learn that her teacher, Ms. Schwartz, is not returning after spring break. Mr. Smith, the substitute, has no plans to do the customary class play. Susan forms an unlikely friendship with Peter Thompson, the class brain, and Duncan, the class bully, to find out what happened to Ms. Schwartz and why Mr. Smith is so strange.

Dahl, Roald. *James and the Giant Peach*. Alfred A. Knopf, 1961.

    Orphaned at four years of age, James Henry Trotter goes to live with his two mean aunts. He has a horrible life with them until he meets an old man who gives him a bag of tiny, green things. In his haste to follow the old man's instructions, James trips and falls, spilling the green things at the base of the peach tree in the yard. The tree suddenly produces a huge peach and the aunts charge admission to see the peach. After James crawls down a hole in the peach, it rolls away, flattens the aunts, and takes James on an exciting adventure.

Salinger, J. D. *The Catcher in the Rye*. Little, Brown, 1945.

Pency Private School has dismissed Holden Caulfield. Holden reminisces about people and incidents that took place four or five days before Christmas vacation. Holden becomes more and more depressed no matter what he does. His world is full of phonies and stupid people.

Holden's parents do not know about his expulsion from school yet, so Holden leaves school and goes to New York. Within a few days, he goes through his money, hires a prostitute, and gets drunk. He decides to travel out West, but he wants to see his little sister Phoebe first. Phoebe understands Holden when she states, "You don't like anything that's happening." She asks Holden what he would like to become. Holden would like to catch little children if they were running toward a cliff, a catcher in the rye. Phoebe persuades Holden to come home, get help, and face the future.

BIBLIOGRAPHY

Following each bibliographic entry is the reason behind the challenge.

American Heritage Dictionary. Houghton Mifflin, 1969. Objectionable language.

Angelou, Maya. *I Know Why the Caged Bird Sings*. Random House, 1970. Explicit sexual scenes.

Banks, Lynne Reid. *The Indian in the Cupboard*. Doubleday, 1980. Subtle stereotypes.

Barth, Edna. *Witches, Pumpkins, and Grinning Ghosts: The Story of the Halloween Symbols*. Clarion Books, 1972. Promotes witchcraft.

Bauer, Dane Marion. *On My Honor*. Clarion Books, 1986. Vulgar and profane language.

Bellairs, John. *The Figure in the Shadows*. Dial Books for Young Readers, 1975. Promotes witchcraft.

Blume, Judy. *Blubber*. Bradbury Press, 1974. Inappropriate language.

———. *Forever*. Bradbury Press, 1975. Sexually explicit.

———. *Then Again, Maybe I Won't*. Bradbury Press, 1971. Promotes profanity and voyeurism.

Chaucer, Geoffrey. *Canterbury Tales*. Oxford University Press, 1986. Sexual content.

Cohen, Daniel. *Curses, Hexes, and Spells*. J. B. Lippincott, 1974. Promotes the occult.

Collier, James Lincoln, and Christopher Collier. *My Brother Sam Is Dead*. Four Winds Press, 1974. Language and violent passages.

Cormier, Robert. *The Chocolate War*. Pantheon Books, 1974. Sexually explicit and disrespectful of religion.

Coville, Bruce. *My Teacher Is an Alien*. Pocket Books, 1989. Portrayal of adults.

Dahl, Roald. *George's Marvelous Medicine*. Alfred A. Knopf, 1981. Promotes inappropriate safety conditions.

———. *James and the Giant Peach*. Alfred A. Knopf, 1961. Promotes tobacco, alcohol, and witchcraft.

———. *Revolting Rhymes*. Puffin Books, 1995. Violence.

Dictionary of American Slang. Thomas Y. Crowell, 1975. Objectionable language.

Faulkner, William. *As I Lay Dying*. Random House, 1930. Language.

Feelings, Muriel. *Jambo Means Hello: The Swahili Alphabet*. Dial Press, 1974. Promotes racial separation.

Fritz, Jean. *Around the World in a Hundred Years: Henry the Navigator Magellan*. G. P. Putnam, 1994. Anti-Christian.

Garden, Nancy. *Annie on My Mind*. Farrar, Straus & Giroux, 1982. Promotes homosexuality.

Golding, William. *Lord of the Flies*. Coward-McCann, 1962. Racist language and profanity.

Grimm, Jacob, and Wilhelm Grimm. *The Complete Fairy Tales of the Brothers Grimm*. Bantam Books, 1987. Promotes violence and negative portrayal of female characters.

———. *Little Red Riding Hood*. Harcourt Brace, 1968. Inappropriate for first-graders.

Huxley, Aldous. *Brave New World*. Harper & Row, 1946. Negative behavior.

King, Stephen. *Christine*. Viking, 1983. Violence and profanity.

———. *Cujo*. Viking, 1981. Profanity and sexual content.

Koontz, Dean. *Night Chills*. Atheneum, 1976. Sexual imagery.

L'Engle, Madeleine. *A Wrinkle in Time*. Farrar, Straus & Giroux, 1962. Anti-Christian values.

Merriam, Eve. *Halloween ABC*. Macmillan, 1987. Promotes Satanism.

Myers, Walter Dean. *Fallen Angels*. Scholastic, 1988. Profane language.

Newman, Leslea. *Heather Has Two Mommies*. Alyson, 1991. Promotes homosexuality.

Parks, Gordon. *The Learning Tree*. Harper & Row, 1963. Profanity and sexual references.

Paterson, Katherine. *Bridge to Terabithia*. Thomas Y. Crowell, 1977. Vulgar language and disrespectful of religion.

———. *The Great Gilly Hopkins*. Thomas Y. Crowell, 1978. Profanity and blasphemy.

Peck, Robert. *A Day No Pigs Would Die*. Alfred A. Knopf, 1972. Profanity and explicit language.

Rockwell, Thomas. *How to Eat Fried Worms*. Franklin Watts, 1973. Language and family values.

Salinger, J. D. *Catcher in the Rye*. Little, Brown, 1951. Objectionable language and vulgarity.

Schwartz, Alvin. *More Scary Stories in the Dark*. J. B. Lippincott, 1984.

———. *Scary Stories in the Dark*. J. B. Lippincott, 1981.

———. *Scary Stories 3: More Tales to Chill Your Bones*. J. B. Lippincott, 1991. Promotes Satanism and occult, aberrant behavior.

Sendak, Maurice. *In the Night Kitchen*. Harper & Row, 1970. Promotes nudity and child abuse.

Silverstein, Shel. *A Light in the Attic*. Harper & Row, 1974. Promotes disrespect, horror, and violence.

Snyder, Zilpha. *The Headless Cupid*. Atheneum, 1971. Occult and witchcraft.

———. *The Witches of Worm*. Atheneum, 1972. Promotes Satanism and witchcraft.

Steig, William. *Sylvester and the Magic Pebble*. Simon & Schuster, 1969. Police portrayed as pigs.

Steinbeck, John. *The Grapes of Wrath*. Viking, 1939. Profanity and sexual innuendo.

———. *Of Mice and Men*. Viking, 1965. Objectionable language.

Stine, R. L. "Goosebumps" series. Frightening situations.

Twain, Mark. *The Complete Adventures of Tom Sawyer and Huckleberry Finn*. Harper & Row, 1978. Racist language.

Walker, Alice. *The Color Purple*. Washington Square Press, 1982. Sexual content.

Wright, Richard. *Native Son*. Harper & Row, 1940. Profanity, violence, and sexuality.

X, Malcolm, and Alex Haley. *The Autobiography of Malcolm X*. Ballantine Books, 1992. Racist viewpoint and criminal behavior.

Zindel, Paul. *The Pigman*. Harper & Row, 1968. Disrespectful and destructive behavior.

WEB SITES

The American Library Association's Banned Book Week Web Site
http://www.ala.org/bbooks/

Banned Books and Censorship Information and Resources
http://www.luc.edu/libraries/banned/

Banned Books on the Internet
http://www.lhup.edu/~rparker/acvcomp/papers/bressle.htm
http://www.banned-books.com/read

Banned Books Online
http://www.cs.cmu.edu/Web/People/spok/banned-books.html

Judy Blume
http://www.judyblume.com
http://www.bdd.com/bin/forums/teachers/blum.html

Robert Cormier
http://www.bdd.com/bin/forums/teachers/corm.html

Chapter 11

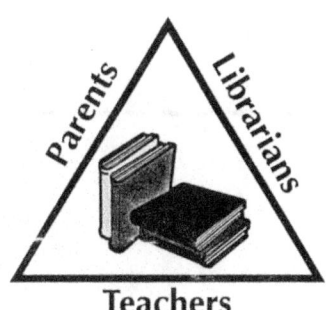

Link to the Internet

OVERVIEW

The World Wide Web was first created in 1992. Of the 50 million users today, more than 1 million are kids. You can do many things on the Internet: communicate, explore, find, learn, and play. The URL (uniform resource locator) is the address of the Web site; URLs begin with http:// (hypertext transfer protocol). You can tell the type of domain from the URL:

edu = educational	org = nonprofit organization
com = commercial or business	gov = government

To find information on the Internet, you must know the URL of the site you want. If you do not, you can use a search engine such as Lycos, Alta Vista, Yahoo, InfoSeek, or Excite. Type in the subject and you will be rewarded with many "hits" or addresses. There are software programs available that serve as filters so that your students/kids don't get into areas on the Net where they shouldn't be. It is important to caution students/kids that they should not give out personal information on the Net, that they should be brief and not harass anyone, and that they should be careful of how they use copyrighted material.

There is so much available on the Internet! Once you explore one site, you will find a list of *hyperlinks* (or connections) to other Web sites that might be of interest to you. You must realize that Web sites can change from one day to the next or disappear altogether. What you thought was a safe and appropriate site might one day have a banner or hyperlink to a questionable site. It is important to check Web sites regularly and monitor your students and children often when they use the Internet.

GUIDED SURFING QUESTIONS

1. Do you know how to locate information on the Internet?
2. Do you know how to "bookmark" favorite Web sites?
3. Do you know how to organize your favorite places?
4. Do you know how to use a search engine effectively?

From *More Reading Connections*. © 1999. Knowles/Smith. Libraries Unlimited. (800) 237-6124.

JOURNAL ARTICLE

The Littlest Surfers

Check out these educational and activity sites
for toddlers and preschoolers.

Help! I can't find enough web sites that are simple enough for my toddler.

Help! I can't find enough web sites with activities for preschoolers.

You've probably heard pleas like these from frustrated parents, babysitters, or preschool staff. The good news is that there are many great web sites out there for toddlers and pre-schoolers, as well as for their parents. The bad news is that there are not a lot of "tot central" sites to help you locate them easily.

Here, then, are some of my favorite sites, each brimming with age-appropriate resources and educational content that parents and librarians can start using today.

"T" Is for Tots

Rolando Merino, a parent, created three wonderfully simple web sites for his young son, Rollie, and put them on the Internet for toddlers worldwide to enjoy.

Merino's *These Are the Letters of the Alphabet* page contains brightly colored letters, animated illustrations, and simple descriptions kids will understand. His page called *The Farm Animals* contains delightful animal pictures and simple descriptions that children or their caregivers can read. *The Zoo Animals* page not only contains animated zoo animals and amusing descriptions, but sound links to go along with them. These pages are appropriate for the very youngest surfers, either alone or with an adult.

It's no surprise that the *Sesame Street* web site contains great material for toddlers and preschoolers. Some of the very best resources on *Sesame Street Central* are links to the simple online storybooks: "Elmo Minds the Farm," "High Noon," and Forgetful Jones in "Thanks for the Memories." These stories are colorful and fun to read, so consider using an LCD projector or panel and featuring them at an "online story time." *Sesame Street Central* also has lots of web pages especially designed to print out and color. The alphabet, numbers, and shapes pages also include pictures of all the *Sesame Street* characters.

Connect the Dots

Besides offering previews of its CD-ROM products, *Enchanted Learning* Software's web site has lots of free, online educational activities for toddlers, preschoolers, and your youngest students.

"Connect-the-Dots" and "Make-a-Truck" are simple, interactive activities that can help toddlers learn to use a mouse and relate to a computer screen image. "Rebus Rhymes: Mother Goose and Others" can help preschoolers learn to associate words with pictures and build their reading skills. "Dinosaur and Bird Jokes" offers wholesome fun for preschoolers and

---

By Gail Junion-Metz. Reprinted with permission of *School Library Journal* (December 1997), page 45. Gail Junion-Metz (gail@iage.com) *SLJ*'s Surf For columnist, is a librarian and President of Information Age Consultants.

kindergartners. Elsewhere on the site, young children of various ages can use the "Little Explorers Picture Dictionary."

You can find additional toddler and preschooler activities at some sites geared for a wider age range. I listed a number of these sites in two previous columns ("It's Elementary," March 1997, p. 117; and "When Kids Come for Fun," July 1997, p. 38; or www.slj.com/surf-for.articles).

Run Out of Ideas?

Never fear. Connect to *World Village's Idea Box* and look no further. Updated weekly, it features both a site and idea of the week, along with news of interest to parents, teachers, and librarians.

You'll also find links to lots of printable learning, activity, and coloring pages, as well as recipes, projects, games, crafts, and seasonal activities.

KidSource Online is the place for parents, caregivers, and librarians to go for information about young children. The site's extraordinarily wide range of topics includes education, health, parenting skills, child safety, product recalls, nutrition, child development, toys, and fun.

You'll also find valuable, hard-to-find information in sections called "What's New," "Recent Recalls," and "New Products."

Web Addresses

For past "Surf For" links, visit SW Online at www.slj.com/surf-for.articles.

Letters of the Alphabet
www.pacificnet.net/~cmoore/alphabet/index.htm

The Farm Animals
www.magickeys.com/books/farm/index.html

The Zoo Animals
www.pacificnet.net/~cmoore/zoo/index.htm

Sesame Street Central
www.ctw.org/sscentral

Enchanted Learning
www.EnchantedLearning.com

World Village's Idea Box
www.worldvillage.com/ideabox/index.html

KidSource Online
www.kidsource.com/kidsource/pages/toddlers.html
www.kidsource.com/kidsource/pages/preschoolers.html ▲

ANNOTATED JOURNAL ARTICLES

Dresang, Eliza T. "Developing Student Voices on the Internet," *Book Links* (September 1997): 10–15.

    The fact that students have the unprecedented opportunity to speak for themselves online is discussed. Sites created by and for young people encourage public expression of private thoughts, preferences, and opinions. The article lists Internet sites and annotated book connections in three areas: discovering self and others, exploring issues and events, and creating and critiquing a story.

Leu, Donald J., Jr. "Caity's Question: Literacy as Deixis on the Internet," *Reading Teacher* (September 1997): 62–66.

    Deixis is a linguistic term used to capture the special qualities of words such as *today*, *tomorrow*, and *here*, whose meanings are dependent on the time or space in which they are uttered. This article indicates that *literacy* has become a deictic term—its meaning constantly changing as we travel the Internet where one text links to millions of others. The article lists areas where the Internet has been successfully used in the classroom to enhance the literacy of students. Literacy is now essential to enable individuals and societies to get the best information in the shortest time, in order to solve problems and make important decisions.

Rosen, Judith. "Children's Books Make Strong Internet Showing," *Publishers Weekly* (January 13, 1997): 32–35.

    A growing number of publishers of children's books have Web sites. Publicity on the Web is cheaper, because e-mail is cheaper than mailings and putting information on the Web is cheaper than producing and mailing catalogues. Larger companies with recognizable names have an advantage over smaller companies. The larger publishers can provide links to each of their best-selling series, where children can learn about their favorite books and characters and even read sample chapters. Random House was first to release a new book online before putting it out in print. This article lists all sorts of "firsts" as well as the largest and best publishers' Web site addresses.

BIBLIOGRAPHY

Frazier, D., B. Kurshan, and S. Armstrong. *The Internet for Your Kids.* Sybex, Inc., 1998.

Haag, T. *Internet for Kids.* Teacher Created Materials, 1996.

Harris, Judi. *Design Tools for the Internet-Supported Classroom.* Association for Supervision and Curriculum Development, 1998.

———. *Virtual Architecture.* International Society for Technology in Education, 1996.

Leininger, L., and C. Rowan. *The Kid-Friendly Web Guide.* Monday Morning Books, Inc., 1997.

Lifter, M., and M. E. Adams. *Make and Take Technology: Using Technology to Create Teaching Materials the Easy Way.* Visions Technology in Education, 1997.

Pederson, T., and F. Moss. *Internet for Kids: A Beginner's Guide for Surfing the Net.* Putnam & Grosset, 1997.

Robin, B., E. Keeler, and R. Miller. *Educators' Guide to the Web.* Henry Holt, 1997.

Sharp, V., M. Levine, and R. Sharp. *The Best Web Sites for Teachers.* International Society for Technology in Education, 1996.

Thorson, B. *Integrating Technology into the Classroom.* Teacher Created Materials, 1998.

Vega, D. *Learning the Internet for Kids.* DDC Publishing, 1998.

Williams, B. *The Internet for Teachers.* IDG Books Worldwide, 1995.

WEB SITES

Professional Organizations for Educators

American Association of School Administrators
http://www.aasa.org

American Federation of Teachers
http://www.aft.org

American Library Association
http://www.ala.org

The Association for Supervision and Curriculum Development
http://www.ascd.org

Association for the Advancement of Computers in Education
http://www.aace.org

Global SchoolNet Foundation
http://www.gsn.org

The International Reading Association
http://ira.org

International Society for Technology in Education
http://www.iste.org

National Art Education Association
http://www.naea-reston.org

National Association of State Boards of Education
http://www.nasbe.org

National Council for Geographic Education
http://www.ncge.org

National Council for Teachers of Math
http://www.nctm.org

National Council of Teachers of English
http://www.ncte.org

National Education Association
http://nea.org

National Middle School Association
http://www.nmsa.org

The National PTA
http://www.pta.org

National School Boards Association
http://www.nsba.org

National Science Teachers Association
http://www.nsta.org

Principals Online
http://www.naesp.org (elementary)
http://www.nassp.org (secondary)

United Federation of Teachers
http://www.uft.org

Homework/References

Bartlett's Familiar Quotations
http://www.columbia.edu/acis/bartleby/bartlett

Digital Library for Schoolkids
http://www.npac.syr.edu/textbook/kidsweb/

Education World
http://www.education-world.com

Encyclopedia
http://www.encyclopedia.com

Homework Helper
http://www.homeworkhelper.com

Information Please
http://www.infoplease.com

Internet Public Library Reference Center
http://www.ipl.org/ref/

Knowledge Adventure Encyclopedia
http://www.adventure.com/encyclopedia/

OneLook Dictionaries
http://www.onelook.com

Research-It!—One Stop Reference Desk
http://www.itools.com/research-it/

From *More Reading Connections.* © 1999. Knowles/Smith. Libraries Unlimited. (800) 237-6124.

Roget's Internet Thesaurus
http://www.thesaurus.com

Study Web
http://www.studyweb.com

Search Engines

Alta Vista
http://altavista.digital.com

Excite
http://excite.com

InfoSeek
http://infoseek.com

Lycos
http://lycos.com

Magellan
http://www.mckinley.com

WebCrawler
http://webcrawler.com

Yahoo
http://yahoo.com

Yahooligans (Yahoo for Young Students)
http://www.yahooligans.com

Internet Filters

Cyber Patrol
http://www.cyberpatrol.com

CYBERsitter
http://www.solidoak.com

Net Nanny
http://netnanny.com

Net Sheperd
http://www.sheperd.net

Safe Surf
http://www.safesurf.com/index.html

The United Federation of Child-Safe Web Sites
http://www.childsafe.com

For Teachers

American Library Association's 700+ Best Sites for Kids, Parents, and Teachers
http://www.ala.org/parentspage/greatsites/amazing.html

Book Nook
http://i-site.on.ca/booknook.html

Carol Hurst's Children's Literature Site
http://www.carolhurst.com

Children's Book Council
http://www.cbcbooks.org

Children's Literature
http://www.rci.rutgers.edu/~mjoseph/childlit/about.html

Children's Literature: Beyond Basals
http://www.beyondbasals.com

The Children's Literature Web Guide
http://www.acs.ucalgary/~dkbrown/

Classroom Connect
http://www.classroom.net

Education World
http://www.education-world.com

Fairrosa Cyber Library
http://www.users.interport.net/~fairrosa

4 Teachers
http://4teachers.org

Global Schoolhouse
http://www.gsh.org

Kathy Schrock's Guide for Educators
http://www.capecod.net/schrockguide

KidLit Children's Literature Home Page
http://mgfx.com/kidlit/

New Teacher Page
http://www.geocities.com/Athens/Delphi/7862/

The Scoop
http://www.Friend.ly.Net/scoop/

Teacher's Edition Online—Tools for Teachers
http://www.teachnet.com/lesson.html

Teachers Helping Teachers
http://www.pacificnet.net/~mandel

Vandergrift's Children's Literature Page
http://www.scils.rutgers.edu/special/kay/Childlit.html

Chapter 12

Middle School Challenge

OVERVIEW

Do you realize that there are many children who do not like to read? These children are able to read but do not enjoy reading. They think that "pleasure reading" is an oxymoron. They read what is required at school but choose other activities for their free time.

Statistics show that avid readers have better vocabularies, are improved and more creative writers, and have more general knowledge. Somehow we lose many enthusiastic readers in the upper elementary and middle school grades, where it is often found that liking to read is not cool. How does this happen?

Video games, computer games, the Internet, chat rooms, and MTV are some of the free-time activities that children are selecting. In schools, the change from basals to literature has discouraged some children. The practice of using novels as teaching tools, where a delightful story like *The Indian in the Cupboard* is reduced to vocabulary lists, comprehension questions, and chapter quizzes and tests, has now become the norm in many classrooms. This often takes the pleasure out of reading novels.

What can we do to keep children reading? One thing would be to read aloud to children long after picture books. Parents should encourage pleasure reading for children in the upper elementary grades by reading with their children. Help to expand your child's personal library as well as the classroom and school libraries. Have a family reading time when all family members spend just 20 minutes reading for pleasure.

Being comfortable with reading will help your child in all areas of school. If your children are turned off to reading, you can begin to turn things around by reading to them and with them and by introducing them to some wonderful books to read for fun!

GUIDED READING QUESTIONS

1. Is your middle school child a reader?
2. Do you have a family reading time?
3. Would a middle school student enjoy your book?
4. Was there anything unusual about your book?
5. Do you feel that the author provided a good plot and well-developed characters?
6. Would you be comfortable reading your book along with your middle school student?
7. Did you find anything objectionable in your book?

From *More Reading Connections*. © 1999. Knowles/Smith. Libraries Unlimited. (800) 237-6124.

The Betrayal of Teenagers: How Book Awards Fail America's Most Important Readers

With no top award, we're sending a subtle message that YA literature is second-rate.

The American Library Association's last Midwinter Meeting was a satisfying and educational one for me, but it was also devastating. What I learned there reminded me for the thousandth time that we systematically ignore teenagers and the literature written for them.

After Elizabeth Crawford's translation of Lutz Van Dijk's *Damned Strong Love* garnered enthusiastic support from reviewers, I arrived in San Antonio hopeful that it would be a candidate for the Batchelder Award for best children's book in translation. But, at the last moment I realized there was a serious problem, and it is that problem that exposes our utter betrayal of teenage readers. The Batchelder, like the Newbery, is an award given by the Association for Library Service to Children (ALSC). By rule, only books for readers age 14 and under are eligible, and this book is mainly for older teens. Fortunately committee members thought the book would appeal to younger readers and named *Damned Strong Love* a Batchelder honor book. But the ALSC awards necessarily exclude the fastest growing cohort of young readers.

Think of what this implies: there is no way to honor the single best book in translation aimed directly at teenagers, nor the best book by a Latino (the new Pura Belpre Award from REFORMA is cosponsored by ALSC), nor the best YA novel by *any*one, nor the best artwork (which in the days of graphic novels is not a trivial issue). None. Zero. Zilch.

This intolerable silence is not limited to ALA. There is no older YA category in the *Boston Globe/Horn Book* Award, nor any in the *New York Times*. Even *VOYA* and the *ALAN Review* avoid selecting single titles as the year's best. The only magazine to come close is the *Hungry Mind Review* with its three YA "books of distinction." Why is everyone unwilling to honor singular achievements in one entire branch of literature? And even more interesting, why hasn't anyone noticed?

A Tough Balancing Act

In its March 1995 ALA conference report (p. 133), *SLJ* reported that the Young Adult Library Services Association (YALSA) accepted a bequest to create a kind of older Newbery, but the terms of this award make it a bizarro inverse of a true honor. According to the rules of the donation, the judges of the

---

By Mark Aronson. Reprinted with permission of *School Library Journal* (May 1996), pages 23–25. Mark Aronson is a senior editor at Henry Holt where he is responsible for the Edge imprint. He recently won the 1995 Literary Market Place Award for excellence in children's book publishing and his article in the January 1995 issue of *SLJ*, "The YA Novel Is Dead, and Other Fairly Stupid Tales," won a Distinguished Achievement Award from the Educational Press Association of America.

Amelia Walden award *must* give equal weight to popularity and quality, they are required to choose books that promote "positive values," and they have to consider both original novels and paperback reprints.

Clearly an award encumbered with these rules is nothing like an older Newbery. Instead of rewarding the "most distinguished contribution to American literature" for an older age group, it honors some amalgam of good marketing, knock-out jacket art, able writing, and perhaps the odd clever plot device or telling image.

How could an award with these rules possibly be administered? While astute librarians would surely be able to circumvent the pernicious "positive values" rule easily enough—reading is a "positive value," so any book qualifies—how could they weigh popularity against quality? How many thousands of books sold equals one great character? How many tens or hundreds of thousands override formulaic or didactic writing? Finally, waiting for paperback sales to determine popularity would impose at least a two-year delay on each book, making this a kind of way station on the road to the Margaret Edwards award, which requires a five-year cooling-off period for each book it considers. If such an award were to have an effect on the industry, it would only be to confirm prevailing beliefs about the weakness of YA writing.

The Attention They Deserve

Until recently, children's publishers have not seen any great need to challenge the award system. And you can guess how booksellers feel when you realize that the large chains have no distinct YA sections, only shelving units attached to those for children's books. There is no better way to exclude older teenagers than to put books in the children's section. While parents and younger children enjoy shopping in a family-friendly area decorated with pink rabbits and stage-set castles, and adults like browsing through quiet bookstore aisles on their own, teenagers are most often in peer packs. Until stores make spaces designed to be used that way—or create special nights or events where a section of the store is turned over to adolescents—they will never sell significant numbers of books to teenagers. And until they do, they won't pay much attention to the literature.

Writers and agents (to whom "YA" has long been a term meaning poor quality, inferior status, and lousy sales) fight desperately to avoid having their work consigned to this category. Some fearless and dedicated authors follow their muses wherever they lead—which is why we do have books that deserve to be honored with awards. (See Wall of Shame for a list of the best books ignored because they're for older teens.) Unfortunately, when talk at writer's colonies like Yaddo or MacDowell turns to writing for young adults, their peers treat YA writers as if they had some socially unacceptable Victorian disease. Yet when any of those certifiably adult writers deals with coming of age, reviewers across the land hail their books as the first such title since *Huckleberry Finn* or *The Catcher in the Rye*.

Shattering the Myths

Historical and structural forces like these explain a lot about why we ignore books for older teenagers. But logic goes only so far. There is also a layer of myth and prejudice that has prevented us from noticing the absurdity that we accept as normal. Time and again discussions of books for older teenagers turn to the same "truths": they don't read, they only read adult books, they have too much to read for school. Everyone should be suspicious of shopworn "truths" like these. The last one to hold sway in publishing was "blacks don't buy books." There is a haunting similarity between prejudice by race and by age.

Both views reduce individuals to stereotypes, and neither is supported by real evidence. Worse, there is plenty of counterevidence. The more you talk with librarians who work with teenagers every day, the more you are struck by the young adults' eagerness to read books that challenge them.

Audra Caplan was chair of YALSA's Best Books for Young Adults (BBYA) committee in 1994. The following year she began working in a new Columbia, MD, library and wanted to set up a teenage advisory group. She was not sure if she could get enough kids interested. Fifty joined right away, 25 of whom showed up on a day's notice to record their opinions for ALA. Why the loyalty? According to Audra, it is because "we told them we needed them. No one takes teenagers seriously. When they learned that their opinions mattered, they could not wait to give them."

Reports from groups like Audra's, and Ann Sparanese's in Englewood, NJ, show more than teenagers' eagerness to be heard. "You shouldn't underestimate their sophistication," Audra cautions. Real teenagers, unlike the ones in our biased myths, often respond avidly to difficult, provocative books. Their insights can be probing, serious, intelligent, and revealing. And yet the entire world of publishers, librarians, and critics has managed to avoid granting the best books aimed at these readers the singular honors they deserve.

To be more accurate, *almost* the entire publishing world. There are two exceptions, and they underline the insanity of our award structure. The Coretta Scott King Medal is not granted by either ALSC or YALSA, but by ALA's Social Responsibilities Round Table. Thus it is not constrained by artificial age limitations and specifically includes a category for high school readers through 12th grade. The National Book Foundation has recently decided to reinstate an award for literary excellence in children's books. It, too, encompasses all grade levels, K-12. What can we make of the disparity between the age criteria for these awards and that employed by every other award committee?

The only books for older teenagers that can be singled out by the library world must be by African-American authors. This is doubly unfair. It ghettoizes a great book like Walter Dean Myers'[s] *Fallen Angels* as exceptional because it is by a black author, rather than as the best book published in a particular year. And it makes it impossible for any non-African-American author of books for older teens to be honored at all.

With this latest award from the National Book Foundation, we have turned over judging the merit of the entire field of non-adult publishing to an outside group, which must somehow find a best book without any consideration of age. Who will judge this award? Certainly it should not be the very authors and critics who populate writers' colonies and treat YA literature with such contempt. True, there are a few reviewers and teachers who can evaluate the entire field of children's literature, but I certainly don't envy them the task. This award is a significant step forward, and it may well—from time to time—honor a book for older teenagers. But it dissolves such books into the general soup of children's books, rather than highlighting them as a distinct branch of literature.

Only an award for older YA books granted by reviewers, teachers, and librarians who concentrate on such books can possibly give the books, and their readers, the attention they deserve.

Soul Searching

What is to be done? Here are three suggestions and one great question.

1. At ALA's Annual Conference this July in New York City, Michael Cart is hosting a panel that will consider how adult and young adult categories blur together. It takes place on Sunday, July 7, from noon to 1:30 p.m. and will include myself, the author Francesca Lia Block, the literary agent George Nicholson, and Carla Parker, senior buyer for Barnes & Noble. Perhaps it is time to redefine older YA as part of the larger spectrum of the literature of coming-of-age that stretches well into adult.

2. This year for the first time, the BBYA committee chose the top ten books from its

long list of winners, though the choices weren't well publicized. The problem here is the way the top titles are selected—by the most votes cast during the regular balloting. For example, a book read by 15 members and recommended with a 14–1 vote wins out over one approved unanimously by only nine readers. If the committee truly wants to pick the year's top ten books, it needs to do so on a separate ballot.

3. At that same conference, the BBYA committee is again scheduled to have a session in which teenage readers give their views. There is also talk of having a national teleconference of teenage advisory groups at a future ALA. Perhaps only these voices will finally convince librarians, publishers, and booksellers that teenagers exist, that they read, that they think, and that they value literature that speaks to them.

And that leads to a final question: Isn't adolescence itself the real problem? In ignoring literature for teenagers and the intense reading done by teenagers, are we not also wishing teenagers themselves out of sight? In the end, I believe we have been content with our patently unfair award structure because we do not want to think about teenage life.

Perhaps, as Elizabeth Devereaux of *Publishers Weekly* astutely puts it, most of us don't want to remember with all that much clarity who we were as teenagers. Perhaps we don't want to look all that closely at those brilliant tacticians of emotional mayhem—the teenagers around us. Perhaps as a society, we sense that the growing cohort that is beginning to hold protests over hair length rules, school club policies, and religious teaching is likely to upset all of our carefully created applecarts, be they "family values" or half-hearted multiculturalism.

No one has minded ignoring YA fiction because no one has cared enough about YAs. It is time for that to stop. The best YA books are too good, and the growing army of YA readers are too important. Wake up America, before our consistent marginalizing of teenagers marginalizes us.

Wall of Shame

Some of the most remarkable novels for youth have been for older teens and, thus, ineligible for our most prestigious awards. Although the titles below were disqualified from the medal races, the starred books were later recognized when their authors won the Margaret A. Edwards Award.

Classic:

Lipsyte, Robert. *The Contender*. HarperCollins, 1967.

Hinton, S. E. *The Outsiders*.* Viking, 1967.

Zindel, Paul. *The Pigman*. HarperCollins, 1968.

Cormier, Robert. *The Chocolate War*.* Pantheon, 1974.

Klein, Norma. *Mom, the Wolf Man, and Me*. Avon, 1972, o.p.

Blume, Judy. *Forever*.* Simon & Schuster, 1975.

Contemporary:

Myers, Walter Dean. *Fallen Angels*. Scholastic, 1988.

Block, Francesca Lia. *Weetzie Bat*. HarperCollins, 1989.

Johnson, Angela. *Toning the Sweep*. Orchard, 1993.

Mori, Kyoko. *Schizuko's Daughter*. Henry Holt, 1993.

Wolff, Virginia Euwer. *Make Lemonade*. Henry Holt, 1993.

Kerr, M. E. *Deliver Us from Evie*. HarperCollins, 1994.

Cofer, Judith Ortiz. *An Island Like You: Stories from the Barrio*. Orchard, 1995. ▲

ANNOTATED JOURNAL ARTICLES

Beers, G. Kylena. "No Time, No Interest, No Way! Part I," *School Library Journal* (February 1996): 30–33.

    The term *aliteracy* includes middle-school-aged readers through adults who know how to read but choose not to. There are many ideas as to how this happens—from reading programs that overemphasize skills to parents' failure to model positive reading habits. The nonreaders are classified into three categories: dormant, uncommitted, and unmotivated. The dormant person likes to read but is too busy to do so. An uncommitted person does not like to read because reading is a skill, but cannot decide whether reading could become an activity of the future. Unmotivated persons do not like to read and do not see themselves reading in the future. The article includes a reference list of books for adults who are concerned about aliteracy.

Beers, G. Kylena. "No Time, No Interest, No Way! Part II," *School Library Journal* (March 1996): 110–13.

    This is the second of two articles on teen aliteracy. Tips and techniques for motivating reluctant readers are included. It first reviews the three categories of aliterate students. Then the article deals with motivating reluctant readers by giving them choices, offering nonfiction and books with illustrations, reading aloud to them, allowing them to illustrate the story elements, and giving them magazines to read.

Cope, Jim. "Beyond Voices of Readers: Students on School's Effects on Reading," *English Journal* (March 1997): 18–23.

    The author of the article surveyed almost 300 seniors in 5 high schools and found that their school reading experiences were negative. Two authors came under fire the most: Shakespeare and Dickens. The article states that Shakespeare's plays were never meant to be read as books, but were meant to be heard and seen as plays. Other complaints from students included spending too much time on a particular work or until "all the juice of literature was sucked out" through overanalysis. Students devised coping strategies to get through it, which is far from the goal of embracing quality literature. Many resort to dishonesty to get by—by using Cliff Notes, old book reports, or borrowed book reports. Students reported that the most intense personal negative experience was being forced to read aloud. All liked being able to make their own book choices and being read to by their teachers.

Hipple, Ted. "It's the THAT, Teacher," *English Journal* (March 1997): 15–17.

    The "that" of teenagers' reading is much more important than the "what." The author worries about the preoccupation with classics for most teen literature classes. Today's secondary students spend more time reading Cliff Notes than the classics. Young adult literature should be what teens are reading in class because it focuses on their problems and interests, and uses their language. You can still find theme, plot, and characters to analyze in YA literature, which should be the central focus of the curriculum. We want to excite teens about reading when they are in school so that they will become adults who read and pass on a love for reading to their children. The article also includes the Reader's Bill of Rights, which every middle and secondary level literature teacher should see!

From *More Reading Connections*. © 1999. Knowles/Smith. Libraries Unlimited. (800) 237-6124.

ANNOTATED BIBLIOGRAPHY

Avi. *What Do Fish Have to Do with Anything and Other Stories.* Candlewick Press, 1997.
This book has seven unusual stories about kids. The first story is about a boy whose father has left and whose mother is upset. The boy continuously asks questions about happiness, which no one can answer. Another story depicts an overwhelming change in a bad boy when he listens to the life story of a dying man. Another is about a girl haunted by the ghosts of her two dead cats. All stories are about turning points in middle school students' lives.

Farmer, Nancy. *The Ear, the Eye, and the Arm.* Crestwood House, 1992.
This story takes place in Zimbabwe in the year 2194. Siblings Tendai, Rita, and Kuda, children of General Amadeus Matsika, the country's Chief of Security, embark on an adventure. (African Shona mythology inspired the story. The Shona were the most powerful political group—80 percent of the population—when Zimbabwe became independent in 1980.) When the three overprotected siblings start out on their first excursion by themselves, they are kidnapped by the She-elephant who rules the once-toxic waste dump where they mined plastic. The mother and father hire a detective agency—the Ear, the Eye, and the Arm—whose agents are always one-step behind the children. This is a long and unusual story.

Hesse, Karen. *Out of the Dust.* Scholastic, 1997.
This is one year in the life of 14-year-old Billy Jo. She lives on a farm in the midst of the Great Depression in the Oklahoma dust bowl. After 14 years, her Ma is pregnant. Ma copes with the dust and accepts a position in life less than what she had hoped. On a day in July, Daddy puts a pail of kerosene next to the stove. Ma, thinking it is water, begins to pour it to make coffee, but instead, "Ma made a rope of fire." Ma runs outside screaming for Daddy. Billy Jo grabs the kerosene pail and throws it out the door. Unbeknownst to Billy Jo, Ma is returning to the kitchen, and the burning kerosene goes all over her. Ma is burned all down the front of her and Billy Jo, who has had a promising career as a pianist, burns her hands. Ma and the baby brother both die a month later in childbirth. There is no one to raise and comfort Billy Jo. Her father barely talks because he is so involved in his own grief and maintaining the farm during the drought. Billy Jo is so desperate to leave that she catches a freight train west. She arrives in Arizona and realizes that getting away isn't any better. She decides to return home. At last, she forgives Daddy for leaving the kerosene pail and forgives herself for all that happened later. A 1997 Newbery Award winner.

Myers, Walter Dean. *Harlem.* Scholastic, 1997.
Many interesting facts about the art, music, people, and everyday life in Harlem are expressed in this poem. It is a Caldecott Honor Book and the winner of the Coretta Scott King Award. Bright, bold pictures contribute to the reader's understanding of life in Harlem.

From *More Reading Connections.* © 1999. Knowles/Smith. Libraries Unlimited. (800) 237-6124.

Sleator, William. *The Beasties.* Dutton Children's Books, 1997.

>Doug and Colette have been warned about the Beasties who live in the woods behind old houses. Soon after their family moves to the woods, Colette becomes involved with the Beasties, or "family" as they like to be called. Doug tries to protect Colette and goes on a mission to collect information about the logging camp and the location of the men and machinery within. The Beasties' horror is real and Doug is ready to sacrifice his eye to help perpetuate the colony of Beasties.

Spinelli, Jerry. *Wringer.* HarperCollins, 1977.

>Palmer LaRue receives the treatment when he is nine. It consists of nine hard ones by a knuckle on his left arm along with a new name, Snots. The treatment is part of the town's tradition, along with Family Fest in August. The festival is a week of bumper cars, music, and cotton candy. It culminates on Saturday with Pigeon Day. On Pigeon Day, many crates of pigeons are brought into town. As the pigeons are released, the shooters take aim and fire. Any pigeons that are wounded or flopping around are put out of their misery by wringers. Palmer dreads his 10th birthday because then he too can be a wringer. Will he have the courage to oppose tradition and his friend's expectations?

BIBLIOGRAPHY

Alexander, Lloyd. *The Black Cauldron.* Dell, 1965.

———. *The Book of Three.* Holt, Rinehart & Winston, 1964.

———. *The Castle of Lllyr.* Dell, 1966.

Atkin, S. Beth. *Voices from the Streets: Young Former Gang Members Tell Their Stories.* Little, Brown, 1996.

Avi. *Beyond the Western Sea: The Escape from Home.* Orchard, 1996.

———. *Nothing But the Truth: A Documentary Novel.* Orchard, 1991.

———. *The True Confessions of Charlotte Doyle.* Orchard, 1990.

Blumberg, Rhonda. *Admiral Perry in the Land of Shogun.* Lothrop, Lee & Shepard, 1985.

———. *The Incredible Journey of Lewis and Clark.* Lothrop, Lee & Shepard, 1987.

Brooks, Bruce. *The Moves Make the Man.* Harper & Row, 1987.

Burleigh, Robert. *Hoops.* Harcourt Brace, 1997.

Cooney, Caroline. *The Voice on the Radio.* Delacorte Press, 1996.

Creech, Sharon. *Walk Two Moons.* HarperCollins, 1994.

Crew, Linda. *Children of the River.* Delacorte Press, 1989.

Curtis, Christopher. *The Watsons Go to Birmingham—1963.* Delacorte Press, 1995.

Cushman, Karen. *Catherine, Called Birdy.* Houghton Mifflin, 1994.

———. *The Midwife's Apprentice.* Houghton Mifflin, 1995.

Dahl, Roald. *Boy: Tales of a Childhood.* Farrar, Straus & Giroux, 1984.

Deuker, Carl. *On the Devil's Court.* Little, Brown, 1989.

Dickinson, Peter. *A Bone from a Dry Sea.* Delacorte Press, 1993.

———. *Eva.* Delacorte Press, 1989.

Doherty, Berlie. *Dear Nobody.* Orchard, 1992.

Duncan, Lois. *Killing Mr. Duncan.* Little, Brown, 1978.

Farmer, Nancy. *A Girl Named Disaster.* Orchard, 1996.

Fine, Anne. *The Tulip Touch.* Little, Brown, 1997.

Fleischman, Sid. *The Abracadabra Kid: A Writer's Life.* Greenwillow Books, 1996.

———. *The Borning Room.* HarperCollins, 1991.

Fox, Paula. *The Moonlight Man.* Bradbury Press, 1986.

———. *One-Eyed Cat.* Macmillan, 1984.

Freedman, Russell. *Children of the Wild West.* Houghton Mifflin, 1983.

———. *Eleanor Roosevelt.* Houghton Mifflin, 1993.

———. *The Life and Death of Crazy Horse.* Holiday House, 1996.

Freeman, Suzanne. *The Cuckoo's Child.* Greenwillow Books, 1996.

George, Jean Craighead. *Julie's Wolf Pack.* HarperCollins, 1997.

Giblin, James Cross. *Charles A. Lindbergh: A Human Hero.* Clarion Books, 1997.

Giff, Patricia Reilly. *Lily's Crossing.* Delacorte Press, 1997.

Glenn, Mel. *Who Killed Mr. Chippendale? A Mystery in Poems.* Lodestar, 1996.

Haddix, Margaret Peterson. *Running Out of Time.* Simon & Schuster Books for Young Adults, 1995.

Hamilton, Virginia. *Her Stories: African American Folktales, Fairy Tales and True Tales.* Scholastic, 1995.

Hesse, Karen. *Letters from Rifka.* Henry Holt, 1992.

———. *The Music of Dolphins.* Scholastic, 1996.

———. *Out of the Dust.* Scholastic, 1997.

Hinton, S. E. *The Outsiders.* Viking, 1967.

Hobbs, Will. *Far North.* Morrow Junior Books, 1996.

Jacques, Brian. *Redwall.* Putnam, 1987.

Jiang, Ji-Li. *Red Scarf Girl: A Memoir of the Cultural Revolution.* HarperCollins, 1997.

Kipling, Rudyard. *Rikki-Tikki-Tavi.* Morrow Junior Books, 1997.

Le Guin, Ursula K. *The Farthest Shore.* Atheneum, 1972.

———. *The Tombs of Atuan.* Atheneum, 1971.

———. *A Wizard of Earthsea.* Parnassus, 1968.

From *More Reading Connections.* © 1999. Knowles/Smith. Libraries Unlimited. (800) 237-6124.

Levine, Gail Carson. *Ella Enchanted*. HarperCollins, 1997.

Lowry, Lois. *The Giver*. Houghton Mifflin, 1993.

McKinley, Robin. *Beauty*. Harper & Row, 1993.

———. *The Hero and the Crown*. Greenwillow Books, 1984.

McKissack, Patricia C., and Frederick L. McKissack. *Rebels Against Slavery: American Slave Revolts*. Scholastic, 1996.

Myers, Walter Dean. *Harlem*. Scholastic, 1997.

———. *Scorpions*. Harper & Row, 1989.

Napoli, Donna Jo. *Zel*. Dutton, 1996.

Nix, Garth. *Sabriel*. HarperCollins, 1995.

Nolan, Han. *Dancing on the Edge*. Harcourt Brace, 1997.

O'Dell, Scott. *The King's Fifth*. Houghton Mifflin, 1966.

Paterson, Katherine. *Bridge to Terabithia*. Thomas Y. Crowell, 1977.

———. *Jacob Have I Loved*. Thomas Y. Crowell, 1980.

———. *Jip, His Story*. Lodestar, 1996.

Paulsen, Gary. *Hatchet*. Bradbury Press, 1987.

———. *Puppies, Dogs, and Blue Northers: Reflections on Being Raised by a Pack of Sled Dogs*. Harcourt Brace, 1996.

Philbrick, Rodman. *Freak the Mighty*. Blue Sky Press, 1993.

Pullman, Philip. *The Golden Compass*. Alfred A. Knopf, 1996.

———. *The Subtle Knife*. Alfred A. Knopf, 1997.

Rinaldi, Ann. *Wolf by the Ears*. Scholastic, 1991.

Rogasky, Barbara. *Smoke and Ashes: The Story of the Holocaust*. Holiday House, 1988.

Smith, Roland. *Thunder Cave*. Hyperion Books, 1995.

Spinelli, Jerry. *Crash*. Alfred A. Knopf, 1996.

Stanley, Jerry. *Children of the Dustbowl: The True Story of the School at Weedpatch Camp*. Random House, 1993.

Taylor, Mildred. *Roll of Thunder, Hear My Cry*. Dial Press, 1976.

Taylor, Theodore. *The Bomb*. Harcourt Brace, 1995.

Temple, Frances. *The Ramsay Scallop*. Orchard, 1994.

Turner, Megan Whalen. *The Thief*. Greenwillow Books, 1996.

Voigt, Cynthia. *Bad, Badder, Baddest*. Scholastic, 1997.

———. *Dicey's Song*. Simon & Schuster, 1982.

———. *Homecoming*. Fawcett, 1981.

———. *Izzy, Willy-Nilly*. Atheneum, 1986.

White, Ruth. *Belle Prater's Boy*. Farrar, Straus & Giroux, 1996.

Wick, Walter. *A Drop of Water*. Scholastic, 1997.

Wolff, Virginia Euwer. *The Mozart Season*. Henry Holt, 1991.

Wood, June Rae. *When Pigs Fly*. Putnam, 1995.

WEB SITES

Avi
http://www.avi-writer.com

Caroline B. Cooney
http://www.bdd.com/bin/forums/teachers/caro.html

Lois Duncan
http://www.iag.nat/~barq/lois.html

Jean Craighead George
http://www.jeancraigheadgeorge.com

S. E. Hinton
http://www.bdd.com/bin/forums/teachers/sehi.html

Lois Lowry
http://www.bdd.com/bin/forums/teachers/lowr.html
http://www.scils.rutgers.edu/special/kay/lowry.html

Donna Jo Napoli
http://www.friend.ly.net/scoop/biographies/dnapoli.html

Jean Lowery Nixon
http://www.bdd.com/bin/forums/teachers/nixo.html

Scott O'Dell
http://www.bdd.com/bin/forums/teachers/odel.html

Katherine Paterson
http://www.terabithia.com
http://www.childrensbookguild.org/Kpaterson.html

William Sleator
http://www.friend.ly.net/scoop/biographies/wsleator.html

Theodore Taylor
http://www.friend.ly.net/scoop/biographies/ttaylor.html

Paul Zindel
http://www.bdd.com/bin/forums/teachers/zind.html

Chapter 13

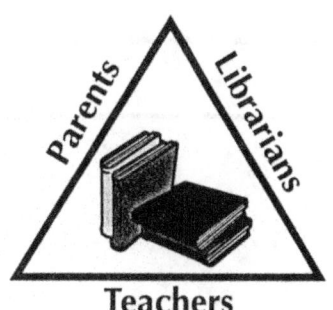

Is There Gender Equity in Children's Literature?

OVERVIEW

Contemporary literature should provide innumerable occasions for young people to experience strong female characters in a variety of roles and settings. Literature should be gender-fair, multicultural, and represent all diversities, including race, age, and class. It is important that we promote literature in which females exhibit independent selves—separate from fathers, brothers, husbands, or boyfriends. Unfortunately, the dominant male–weaker female pattern is still frequently found in children's literature. Boys, in turn, are expected to hide and stifle emotions such as fear, unhappiness, and affection. Movies, television, advertisements, and video games feature men who are violent, greedy, and disrespectful to women. It is important to find books that give contemporary as well as fair representations of both male and female characters.

GUIDED READING QUESTIONS

1. How are girls treated in the book? How are boys treated?
2. Are any stereotyped traits assigned to boys or girls?
3. Do female characters have control of their destinies?
4. How are adults portrayed?

JOURNAL ARTICLE

Bonding Through Books

A librarian finds that mothers and their pre-teen daughters
have a lot to talk about over books.

I brushed the sand off the bottom of my feet and curled up in the beach house with a pile of books. Sighing with contentment—it's so nice to have the time to read on vacation—I opened the top book on the pile: *Little Girls in Pretty Boxes* by Joan Ryan (Doubleday, 1995). The title intrigued me. It apparently intrigued my 13-year-old daughter as well. "Look at that skinny girl on the cover," Kate said. "Is she one of those famous gymnasts?" As soon as I finished reading, she rushed over and picked up the book.

I smiled at our similar reading tastes. And I remembered a summer vacation in England more than 25 years ago, when my mom and I wildly guessed "whodunit" as we made our way through the Agatha Christie mysteries.

Flash forward to fall 1996 and a library meeting room crowded with moms and their pre-teen daughters. As they munched M&Ms, the girls loudly interrupted each other, barely able to wait to share opinions on the novel they'd just read. The comments from the girls and moms led the group through many issues. And the mother-daughter book discussion group soon became one of the hottest things to hit the Chappaqua (NY) Public Library.

My idea for the group sprang from experiences with my own daughter, as well as the frequent questions I answered in the library. Many parents would ask for books for their children, commenting how much they'd enjoyed some book or another at the same age.

In planning the program, I first wondered what ages the girls should be. I was concerned that girls in their later teens would be too heavily involved with sports, jobs, homework, and boys to participate. After talking to Teresa Bueti, our Children's Librarian, I decided to make the program a bridge from juvenile to young adult services by designing it for fifth- through seventh-grade girls.

High Quality, High Appeal

When I chose titles, I started with the assumption that all the books should have as a central theme the relationship between mothers and daughters. I also wanted to incorporate both contemporary titles and classics. But I decided the most important criteria were high quality and high appeal. With help from librarians on PUBYAC, Teresa and I settled on books we felt most of the girls and their moms would enjoy and that were all available in paperback. We arranged the schedule to allow more reading time for "fatter" books and to alternate between more mature books and those that are easier to read. We would meet one Thursday evening a month for six months. Though scheduled to last an hour, the sessions ran an hour-and-a-half.

I knew it was critical to start the program with a sure-fire winner, a really exceptional book. Angela Johnson's *Toning the Sweep* (Orchard, 1993) seemed just right. It's beautifully written, has characters from different generations,

---

By Susan R. Farber. Reprinted with permission of *School Library Journal* (April 1997), page 57. Susan Farber is Director of the Ardsley (NY) Public Library. She won the Econ-o-Clad Award for this program.

deals lightly with serious issues, and appeared on several "best" lists. The book is also short enough not to intimidate less confident readers. As a grand finale, Teresa invited Jean Van Leeuwen to the final meeting, when we would discuss her very funny book, *Dear Mom, You're Ruining My Life* (Dial, 1989).

Girls Sprawled on the Floor

Within days of distributing flyers, we had filed our registration with 20 mother-daughter teams. I re-read the books and planned questions to spark conversation.

The first night, my initial nervousness vanished quickly as the girls sprawled on the floor looking like a group of half-grown puppies. Their comments ranged from innocent to surprisingly mature, and they spurred each other on as they jumped from one idea to the next. Some mothers watched quietly; others dove into the conversation. We talked about what would happen after *Toning the Sweep* ends—could Ola, a main character, possibly be happy in Ohio, far from her beloved desert? We talked about whether the book would appeal to boys, about the meaning of a "sweep" (a type of plow), and about the characters' ethnicity: the main characters are African American, but interestingly, the author never states the race of their friends. Mothers and daughters sometimes reacted very differently to books, but they were always respectful.

The mother-daughter group demonstrated for me the power of writing to create bonds between generations. It reinforced my belief that a talented author can help us face our concerns and learn from the experiences of others. Currently, I'm searching for titles on the immigrant experience for a program tentatively scheduled for the fall. Oprah Winfrey, move over.

More Mother-Daughter Books

Bauer, Marion Dane. *A Dream of Queens and Castles* (Clarion, 1990).

Smith, Betty. *A Tree Grows in Brooklyn* (Harper, 1943).

Hermes, Patricia. *Mama, Let's Dance* (Little, Brown, 1991).

Sullivan, Faith. *The Cape Ann.* (Crown, 1988). ▲

ANNOTATED JOURNAL ARTICLES

Troisi, Andrea. "Gender Equity in the Elementary School Library Media Center," *Library Talk* (January/February 1997): 14–15.

    According to the article, a national study by the American Association of University Women showed that gender bias in our schools prevents girls from fulfilling their potential. It was discovered that during the middle school years, gender becomes a barrier to both aspirations and achievement for girls. The article lists 21 ways to help your school library become more gender-equitable.

Walter, Virginia A. "Girl Power: Multimedia and More," *Book Links* (May 1998): 37–42.

    This article deals with the gender issue in regard to computer use and software. Some software companies are beginning to specialize in and market software for girls; the author reviews some of these software products. After each review is a book connection, listing books about the same topic.

ANNOTATED BIBLIOGRAPHY

Avi. *The Fighting Ground.* Harper Trophy, 1984.

    When Jonathan is thirteen, he answers the call of the bell at the tavern. He can barely carry a gun, but he joins the small band and begins walking. Jonathan learns about the fear he has seen in his father's eyes ever since his father was wounded in the Revolutionary War. The book is broken into short vignettes by the minutes of the hours.

Bradbury, Marie. *More Than Anything Else.* Orchard, 1995.

    Booker T. Washington is nine years old and works from sunup to sundown packing salt in barrels at the saltworks. More than anything else, he wants to learn how to read. His Mama hands him a blue book, purchased with the little money she makes washing and ironing clothes. Booker tries to figure out what the alphabet means on his own, but he fears his dreams of reading are slipping away.

Christiansen, Candace. *Calico and Tin Horns.* Dial Books for Young Readers, 1992.

    Wealthy landowners along the Hudson promised land to the returning American Revolutionary War veterans. Sixty-five years later, the landowners reneged on their promises yet demanded a share of the descendents' harvest and livestock. In 1844, the farmers banded together and formed the Calico Indians.

    Hannah knows something is happening, because of the leather masks and calico shirts and pants her mother and father are making. Her family thinks she is too young to understand that the farmers will not pay rent anymore. Even if the sheriff comes to the farms, the Calico Indians will drive him from the mountains. One day Hannah is picking berries on a high hill and sees the sheriff and a small army headed toward their farm. It is up to Hannah to alert the other farmers and save her farm.

Henkes, Kevin. *Chrysanthemum.* Greenwillow Books, 1991.

    Chrysanthemum thinks her name is perfect until she starts school. Victoria, Rita, and Jo tease Chrysanthemum that her name is too long—why, it scarcely fits on her nametag! She is named after a flower, so why not smell her and pick her? Chrysanthemum begins to think her name is absolutely dreadful until she meets Mrs. Twinkle, the music teacher, who changes everything.

Hopkinson, Deborah. *Sweet Clara and the Freedom Quilt.* Alfred A. Knopf, 1993.

Sweet Clara is taken from her mother and sent to Home Plantation because they need another field hand. Aunt Rachel takes care of Clara and teaches her to be a seamstress. They work together in the Big House, and it is there that Clara first hears about the Underground Railroad. Clara sews a quilt in the form of a map, which shows the way to freedom.

Warren, Andrea. *Orphan Train Rider.* Houghton Mifflin, 1996.

Lee Nailing rode the orphan train to Texas with his two brothers in 1926. In alternating chapters, the author relates Lee's life and the history of orphan trains. More than 200,000 children rode the orphan trains west between 1854 and 1930.

Lee, seven years old, is the middle child of seven children. His mother dies from complications after the birth of his youngest brother. Thereafter, his father tells the two oldest brothers and sister to leave home. The two youngest brothers are given away, while Lee and Leo are taken to Jefferson County Orphan Asylum in Watertown, New York. Lee does not understand why he is considered an orphan, because he still has a father. Life in the orphanage is difficult. Food is scarce and Lee is often punished for getting into fights. Lee takes care of Leo as best as he can. Two years after their arrival at the orphanage, Leo and Lee are selected for the orphan train. The selected children are given new clothes to wear. Lee has never had anything new before. It is all very confusing—and just before they board, his father shows up and gives Lee his three-year-old brother to take with him on the train. Lee begs his father to take all three boys back home. Finally, Lee is pulled away, and he never sees his father again.

Not all of the orphans were placed in loving families. Some were abused and many were treated as servants. Lee was the last selected, but at the age of nine he was a bitter, lonely boy. He was fortunate; the Nailings were good, loving parents. Sixty years later, he shares his story with school children and imparts the message that "their attitude toward what happens to them is the key to their lives."

BIBLIOGRAPHY

Books for Boys

Primary

Alexander, Lloyd. *The Fortune-Tellers.* Dutton Children's Books, 1992.

Bang, Molly. *The Paper Crane.* Greenwillow Books, 1985.

Bannerman, Helen. *The Story of Little Babaji.* Harper & Row, 1996.

Borden, Louise. *The Little Ships: The Heroic Rescue at Dunkirk in World War II.* Margaret K. McElderry, 1997.

From *More Reading Connections.* © 1999. Knowles/Smith. Libraries Unlimited. (800) 237-6124.

Bradbury, Marie. *More Than Anything Else*. Orchard, 1995.

Brown, Marc. *Arthur's Eyes*. Little, Brown, 1979.

Brusca, Maria Cristina. *On the Pampas*. Henry Holt, 1991.

Bunting, Eve. *Smoky Night*. Harcourt Brace, 1994.

———. *The Wall*. Clarion Books, 1990.

Byars, Betsy. *My Brother, Ant*. Viking, 1996.

Carrick, Carol. *Patrick's Dinosaurs*. Clarion Books, 1983.

Cohen, Miriam. *Will I Have a Friend?* Macmillan, 1967.

Coy, John. *Night Driving*. Henry Holt, 1996.

dePaola, Tomie. *The Art Lesson*. G. P. Putnam, 1994.

Emberley, Ed. *Go Away, Big Green Monster!* Little, Brown, 1992.

Erdrich, Louise. *Grandmother's Pigeon*. Hyperion Books, 1996.

Fox, Mem. *Tough Boris*. Harcourt Brace, 1994.

Freeman, Don. *Corduroy*. Viking, 1968.

Giff, Patricia Reilly. *The Beast in Ms. Rooney's Room*. Dell, 1984.

Heide, Florence Parry, and Judith Heide Gilliland. *The Day of Ahmed's Secret*. Lothrop, Lee & Shepard, 1990.

Henkes, Kevin. *Owen*. Greenwillow Books, 1991.

Howe, James. *Pinky and Rex*. Atheneum, 1990.

Hurd, Thacher. *Mama Don't Allow*. Harper & Row, 1984.

Hurwitz, Joanna. *The Adventures of Ali Baba Bernstein*. William Morrow, 1985.

Hutchins, Pat. *The Very Worst Monster*. Greenwillow Books, 1985.

Johnson, Stephen T. *Alphabet City*. Viking, 1995.

Joyce, William. *Bently and Egg*. Harper & Row, 1992.

Keats, Ezra Jack. *The Snowy Day*. Viking, 1962.

Keller, Holly. *Island Baby*. Greenwillow Books, 1992.

Kellogg, Steven. *The Mysterious Tadpole*. Viking, 1977.

Kimmel, Eric. *Hershel and the Hanukkah Goblins*. Holiday House, 1989.

Krauss, Ruth. *The Carrot Seed*. Harper & Row, 1945.

Leaf, Munro. *The Story of Ferdinand*. Viking, 1936.

Locker, Thomas. *The Mare on the Hill*. Dial Books for Young Readers, 1985.

Maccarone, Grace. *Soccer Game*. Scholastic Paper, 1994.

Mahy, Margaret. *The Boy Who Was Followed Home*. Franklin Watts, 1975.

Marshall, James. *George and Martha*. Houghton Mifflin, 1972.

Martin, Rafe. *Mammoth*. Putnam, 1989.

Mayer, Mercer. *There's an Alligator Under My Bed*. Dial Books for Young Readers, 1987.
Meddaugh, Susan. *Hog-Eye*. Houghton Mifflin, 1995.
Numeroff, Laura Joffe. *If You Give a Mouse a Cookie*. Harper & Row, 1985.
Pinkney, Brian. *The Adventures of Sparrowboy*. Simon & Schuster, 1997.
Raschka, Chris. *Charlie Parker Played Be Bop*. Orchard, 1992.
———. *Yo! Yes!* Orchard, 1993.
Rathman, Peggy. *Officer Buckle and Gloria*. Putnam, 1995.
Rounds, Glen. *Cowboys*. Holiday House, 1991.
Rylant, Cynthia. *Mr. Putter and Tabby Pour the Tea*. Harcourt Brace, 1994.
Sachar, Louis. *Marvin Redpost: Kidnapped at Birth?* Random House, 1992.
Say, Allen. *The Lost Lake*. Houghton Mifflin, 1989.
Schlein, Miriam. *The Year of the Panda*. Thomas Y. Crowell, 1990.
Scieszka, Jon, and Lane Smith. *Knights of the Kitchen Table*. Viking, 1991.
———. *Math Curse*. Viking, 1995.
Sendak, Maurice. *Where the Wild Things Are*. Harper & Row, 1963.
Sharmat, Marjorie Weinman. *Nate the Great*. Dell, 1972.
Sís, Peter. *Komodo!* Greenwillow Books, 1993.
Soto, Gary. *Chato's Kitchen*. Putnam, 1995.
Steig, William. *Amos and Boris*. Farrar, Straus & Giroux, 1971.
———. *Doctor De Soto*. Farrar, Straus & Giroux, 1982.
Stevenson, James. *Could Be Worse*. Greenwillow Books, 1977.
Sutcliff, Rosemary. *The Minstrel and the Dragon Pup*. Candlewick Press, 1993.
Van Allsburg, Chris. *The Garden of Abdul Gasazi*. Houghton Mifflin, 1979.
———. *The Polar Express*. Houghton Mifflin, 1985.
Viorst, Judith. *The Tenth Good Thing About Barney*. Atheneum, 1971.
Waber, Bernard. *Ira Sleeps Over*. Houghton Mifflin, 1972.
Wells, Rosemary. *Max's Dragon Shirt*. Dial Books for Young Readers, 1991.
Wood, Audrey. *King Bidgood's in the Bathtub*. Harcourt Brace, 1985.
Yashima, Taro. *Crow Boy*. Viking, 1955.

General

Alexander, Lloyd. *The Book of Three*. Henry Holt, 1964.
———. *Westmark*. E. P. Dutton, 1981.
Avi. *Something Upstairs*. Orchard, 1988.
Babbitt, Natalie. *The Search for Delicious*. Farrar, Straus & Giroux, 1969.

Brooks, Bruce. *Everywhere.* Harper & Row, 1990.

———. *The Moves Make the Man.* Harper & Row, 1984.

Byars, Betsy. *The Burning Questions of Bingo Brown.* Viking, 1988.

Clements, Andrew. *Frindle.* Simon & Schuster, 1996.

Coman, Carolyn. *What Jamie Saw.* Front Street, 1995.

Cooper, Susan. *The Boggart.* Margaret K. McElderry, 1993.

Dahl, Roald. *James and the Giant Peach.* Alfred A. Knopf, 1961.

Douglass, Frederick. *Escape from Slavery: The Boyhood of Frederick Douglass in His Own Words.* Alfred A. Knopf, 1994.

Fine, Anne. *Flour Babies.* Little, Brown, 1994.

———. *Step by Wicked Step.* Little, Brown, 1996.

Fisher, Leonard Everett. *Gutenberg.* Macmillan, 1993.

Fleischman, Sid. *Jim Ugly.* Greenwillow Books, 1992.

Freedman, Russell. *Out of Darkness: The Story of Louis Braille.* Clarion Books, 1997.

Fritz, Jean. *Bully for You, Teddy Roosevelt!* Putnam, 1991.

———. *The Great Little Madison.* Putnam, 1989.

Gardiner, John Reynolds. *Stone Fox.* Harper & Row, 1980.

Haskins, Jim. *I Have a Dream: The Life and Words of Martin Luther King, Jr.* Millbrook Press, 1992.

Henkes, Kevin. *Words of Stone.* Greenwillow Books, 1992.

Hobbs, Will. *Bearstone.* Atheneum, 1989.

Huynh, Quang Nhuong. *The Land I Lost.* Peter Smith, 1982.

Juster, Norton. *The Phantom Tollbooth.* Alfred A. Knopf, 1961.

King-Smith, Dick. *Martin's Mice.* Crown, 1989.

Konigsburg, E. L. *The View from Saturday.* Simon & Schuster, 1996.

L'Engle, Madeleine. *A Wrinkle in Time.* Farrar, Straus & Giroux, 1962.

Lowry, Lois. *All About Sam.* Houghton Mifflin, 1988.

———. *Switcharound.* Houghton Mifflin, 1988.

MacLachlan, Patricia. *Arthur, for the Very First Time.* Harper & Row, 1980.

McKay, Hilary. *Dog Friday.* Margaret K. McElderry, 1995.

Myers, Walter Dean. *Me, Mop, and the Moondance Kid.* Dell Paper, 1988.

Namioka, Lensey. *Yang the Youngest and His Terrible Ear.* Little, Brown, 1992.

Paterson, Katherine. *Bridge to Terabithia.* Harper & Row, 1977.

———. *Come Sing, Jimmy Jo.* E. P. Dutton, 1985.

Paulsen, Gary. *Canyons.* Peter Smith, 1990.

———. *Nightjohn.* Delacorte Press, 1993.

Pinkwater, Daniel. *The Snarkout Boys and the Avocado of Death*. Lothrop, Lee & Shepard, 1982.

Sachar, Louis. *There's a Boy in the Girls' Bathroom*. Alfred A. Knopf, 1987.

Sobol, Donald J. *Encyclopedia Brown: Boy Detective*. Dutton Children's Books, 1963.

Soto, Gary. *The Pool Party*. Delacorte Press, 1993.

Spinelli, Jerry. *Maniac Magee*. Little, Brown, 1990.

Stanley, Diane. *Bard of Avon: The Story of William Shakespeare*. William Morrow, 1992.

———. *Leonardo da Vinci*. William Morrow, 1996.

Winterfield, Henry. *Detectives in Togas*. Harcourt Brace, 1956.

Books for Girls

Primary

Bemelmans, Ludwig. *Madeline's Rescue*. Viking, 1953.

Brett, Jan. *Annie and the Wild Animals*. Houghton Mifflin, 1985.

Brown, Marc. *D.W. Flips*. Little, Brown, 1987.

Carlson, Nancy. *I Like Me!* Viking, 1988.

Cole, Babette. *Princess Smartypants*. Putnam, 1987.

Cole, Joanna. *The Magic School Bus in the Time of the Dinosaurs*. Scholastic, 1994.

Cooney, Barbara. *Miss Rumphius*. Viking, 1982.

Cristaldi, Kathryn. *Baseball Ballerina*. Random House, 1992.

dePaola, Tomie. *Strega Nona*. Simon & Schuster, 1975.

Dorros, Arthur. *Abuela*. Dutton Children's Books, 1991.

Henkes, Kevin. *Chester's Way*. Greenwillow Books, 1988.

———. *Julius, the Baby of the World*. Greenwillow Books, 1990.

———. *Sheila Rae, the Brave*. Greenwillow Books, 1987.

Hoffman, Mary. *Amazing Grace*. Dial Books for Young Readers, 1991.

Hopkinson, Deborah. *Sweet Clara and the Freedom Quilt*. Alfred A. Knopf, 1993.

Keller, Holly. *Geraldine's Blanket*. Greenwillow Books, 1984.

Levinson, Nancy Smiler. *Clara and the Bookwagon*. Harper & Row, 1988.

Lionni, Leo. *Tillie and the Wall*. Alfred A. Knopf, 1989.

Marshall, James. *The Cut-Ups*. Viking, 1984.

Mayer, Mercer. *There's Something in My Attic*. Dial Books for Young Readers, 1988.

McCully, Emily Arnold. *Mirette on the High Wire*. Putnam, 1992.

McKissack, Patricia C. *Flossie and the Fox*. Dial Books for Young Readers, 1986.

———. *Mirandy and Brother Wind*. Alfred A. Knopf, 1988.

Meddaugh, Susan. *Hog-Eye*. Houghton Mifflin, 1995.

———. *Martha Calling*. Houghton Mifflin, 1994.

Newman, Leslea. *Heather Has Two Mommies*. Alyson, 1989.

O'Connor, Jane. *Molly the Brave and Me*. Random House, 1990.

Pinkney, Brian. *JoJo's Flying Side Kick*. Simon & Schuster, 1995.

Pinkwater, Daniel. *Aunt Lulu*. Macmillan, 1988.

Pomerantz, Charlotte. *The Piggy in the Puddle*. Macmillan, 1974.

Ringgold, Faith. *Tar Beach*. Crown, 1991.

Roop, Peter, and Connie Roop. *Keep the Lights Burning, Abbie*. Carolrhoda Books, 1985.

Rosenberg, Liz. *The Carousel*. Harcourt Brace, 1995.

Sadler, Marilyn. *Elizabeth and Larry*. Simon & Schuster, 1990.

Schecter, Ellen. *The Warrior Maiden: A Hopi Legend*. Bantam Books, 1992.

Schwartz, Amy. *Bea and Mr. Jones*. Bradbury Press, 1982.

Sisulu, Elinor Batezat. *The Day Gogo Went to Vote: South Africa, April 1994*. Little, Brown, 1996.

Steig, William. *Brave Irene*. Farrar, Straus & Giroux, 1986.

Turkle, Brinton. *Do Not Open*. Dutton Children's Books, 1981.

Van Allsburg, Chris. *The Widow's Broom*. Houghton Mifflin, 1992.

Vaughan, Marcia. *Whistling Dixie*. Harper & Row, 1995.

Westcott, Nadine Bernard, adapter. *The Lady with the Alligator Purse*. Little, Brown, 1988.

Williams, Linda. *The Little Old Lady Who Was Not Afraid of Anything*. Harper & Row, 1986.

Yolen, Jane. *Owl Moon*. Philomel, 1987.

Young, Ed. *Seven Blind Mice*. Philomel, 1992.

General

Ackerman, Karen. *The Night Crossing*. Alfred A. Knopf, 1994.

Adler, David A. *Our Golda: The Story of Golda Meir*. Viking, 1984.

———. *A Picture Book of Florence Nightingale*. Holiday House, 1992.

Avi. *Poppy*. Orchard, 1995.

———. *The True Confessions of Charlotte Doyle*. Orchard, 1990.

Babbitt, Natalie. *Tuck Everlasting*. Farrar, Straus & Giroux, 1975.

Bawden, Nina. *Granny the Pag*. Clarion Books, 1996.

Beatty, Patricia. *Eight Mules from Monterey*. William Morrow, 1992.

Brown, Don. *Ruth Law Thrills a Nation*. Ticknor & Fields, 1993.

Bulla, Clyde Robert. *Shoeshine Girl*. Thomas Y. Crowell, 1975.

Carter, Dorothy Sharp. *His Majesty, Queen Hatshepsut*. J. B. Lippincott, 1987.

Cleary, Beverly. *Ramona the Pest*. William Morrow, 1968.

Coles, Robert. *The Story of Ruby Bridges*. Scholastic, 1995.

Cushman, Karen. *Catherine, Called Birdy*. Clarion Books, 1994.

———. *The Midwife's Apprentice*. Clarion Books, 1995.

Fisher, Leonard Everett. *Marie Curie*. Macmillan, 1994.

Fitzhugh, Louise. *Harriet the Spy*. Harper & Row, 1964.

Garden, Nancy. *Dove and Sword: A Novel of Joan of Arc*. Farrar, Straus & Giroux, 1995.

George, Jean Craighead. *Julie of the Wolves*. Harper & Row, 1972.

———. *The Talking Earth*. Harper & Row, 1983.

Griffin, Peni R. *Switching Well*. Margaret K. McElderry, 1993.

Haddix, Margaret Peterson. *Running Out of Time*. Simon & Schuster, 1995.

Hesse, Karen. *Letters from Rifka*. Henry Holt, 1992.

———. *Sable*. Henry Holt, 1994.

Hyatt, Patricia Rausch. *Coast to Coast with Alice*. Carolrhoda Books, 1995.

Klause, Annette Curtis. *Alien Secrets*. Delacorte Press, 1993.

Konigsburg, E. L. *From the Mixed-up Files of Mrs. Basil E. Frankweiler*. Atheneum, 1967.

Krull, Kathleen. *Wilma Unlimited: How Wilma Rudolph Became the World's Fastest Woman*. Harcourt Brace, 1996.

Lindgren, Astrid. *Pippi Longstocking*. Viking, 1950.

Lowry, Lois. *Number the Stars*. Houghton Mifflin, 1989.

MacLachlan, Patricia. *Sarah, Plain and Tall*. Harper & Row, 1985.

McCully, Emily Arnold. *The Pirate Queen*. Putnam, 1995.

McGovern, Ann. *The Secret Soldier: The Story of Deborah Sampson*. Four Winds Press, 1987.

Mikaelsen, Ben. *Stranded*. Hyperion Books, 1995.

Nabb, Magdalen. *Josie Smith*. Margaret K. McElderry, 1989.

O'Dell, Scott. *Island of the Blue Dolphins*. Houghton Mifflin, 1960.

Oneal, Zibby. *A Long Way to Go*. Puffin Books, 1990.

Paterson, Katherine. *Lyddie*. E. P. Dutton, 1991.

Pullman, Philip. *The Ruby in the Smoke*. Alfred A. Knopf, 1987.

Ringgold, Faith. *Aunt Harriet's Underground Railroad in the Sky*. Crown, 1993.

Schroeder, Alan. *Minty: A Story of Young Harriet Tubman*. Dial Books for Young Readers, 1996.

Speare, Elizabeth George. *The Witch of Blackbird Pond*. Houghton Mifflin, 1958.

Stanley, Diane, and Peter Vennema. *Cleopatra*. William Morrow, 1994.

Staples, Suzanne Fisher. *Shabanu: Daughter of the Wind*. Alfred A. Knopf, 1989.

Taylor, Theodore. *The Trouble with Tuck*. Doubleday, 1981.

From *More Reading Connections*. © 1999. Knowles/Smith. Libraries Unlimited. (800) 237-6124.

Voigt, Cynthia. *Bad Girls*. Scholastic, 1996.

———. *Homecoming*. Atheneum, 1981.

White, E. B. *Charlotte's Web*. Harper & Row, 1952.

Wolff, Virginia Euwer. *The Mozart Season*. Henry Holt, 1991.

Wright, Betty Ren. *The Ghost Witch*. Scholastic, 1993.

Yolen, Jane. *The Ballad of the Pirate Queens*. Harcourt Brace, 1995.

WEB SITES

American Girl Online
http://www.americangirl.com/ag/ag.cgi

Cyber Sisters
http://worldkids.net/clubs/CSIS

Distinguished Women
http://www.netsrq.com/~dbois/

E. L. Konigsburg
http://www.bdd.com/bin/forums/teachers/koni.html

Expect the Best from a Girl
http://www.academic.org

Female Coming-of-Age Stories
http://www.scils.rutgers.edu/special/kay/age.html

FeMiNa
http://www.femina.com/

4000 Years of Women in Science
http://www.astr.ua.edu/4000WS/

Gary Paulsen
http://falcon.jmu.edu/~ramseyil/paulsen.htm
http://www.bdd.com/bin/forums/teachers/paul.html

Gender and Culture in Picture Books
http://www.scils.rutgers.edu/special/kay/culture.html

Go Girl!
http://www.gogirlmag.com/

An Income of Her Own
http://www.aioho.com/

Male Coming-of-Age Stories
http://www.scils.rutgers.edu/special/kay/male.html

Nancy Carlson
http://www.nancycarlson.com

National Women's Hall of Fame
http://www.sbaonline.sba.gov/womeninbusiness/fame.html

New Moon Magazine
http://www.newmoon.org/

PlanetGirl.com
http://www.planetgirl.com

Purple Moon Place
http://www.purple-moon.com/cb/laslink/pm?stat+pm_place

Tomie dePaola
http://falcon.jmu.edu/~ramseyil/depaola.htm

Will Hobbs
http://www.bdd.com/bin/forums/teachers/hobb.html

Women Athlete Profiles
http://www.feminist.org/other/olympic/wap.html

Women of NASA
http://quest.arc.nasa.gov/women/intro.html

WWW Women's Sports Page
http://fiat.gslis.utexas.edu/~lewisa/womsprt.html

Chapter 14

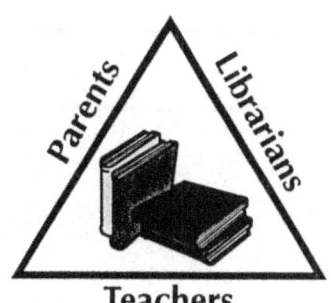

As Long As We're Talking About Books . . .

OVERVIEW

"So many books, so little time," certainly describes a teacher's frustrations about recommending titles to students. Booktalking usually is a librarian's job. The main objective of a booktalk is to recommend a book, tell a little about the story (just enough to "whet the appetite"), and get a child interested enough to want to read the book and find out what happens. Teachers and parents are in perfect positions to help children find something enjoyable to read.

There is no set way to do a booktalk—really, anything goes. The sole purpose is to get children interested in reading books. You can talk about the main character, theme, setting, plot, or style. It is important to be enthusiastic and brief. You could even do a booktalk about an author and then introduce some or all of that author's titles with just a brief word or two. You might also do a booktalk on books with a common theme. Sometimes a booktalk might consist of simply reading an exciting, unusual, or hilarious passage from a book. It is helpful to have an author or book poster to display with the book. It is also good to have at least one copy (better yet, several copies) of the books you are booktalking.

Next, you might incorporate booktalks into your students' book reports. Instead of having them write a book report or do some sort of a project involving their book, request that they prepare and present a booktalk. It could be described as "selling" the book to their classmates. They might bring a prop or two, make a poster, or dress in a certain way to help share the excitement of the book with their classmates.

Today, as reading a book falls lower and lower on the list of good things to do in free time, it is very important to turn kids on to reading. Everyone needs to get involved!

From *More Reading Connections*. © 1999. Knowles/Smith. Libraries Unlimited. (800) 237-6124.

Unbeatable Booktalks

Try booktalking nonfiction; kids (and you) will find it irresistible.

Booktalking. The very word can fill me with dread. Looking at the tomes written on that subject, I quail in horror. Who wants to memorize a long booktalk? For storytelling, I have a bag of tricks that work well for me. Why can't I have the same for booktalks?

A few years ago, while visiting a second grade classroom, I brought along *The Titanic: Lost and Found* by Judy Donnelley (Random, 1987), and a very intelligent, curious little boy asked a lot of questions. His enthusiasm and desire to know more motivated everyone, and in moments I was inundated. Although I was always fascinated by the *Titanic*, I was no expert. I felt inadequate.

Back at the library, I found three adult *Titanic* books. After reading them all, I went, book in hand, to another classroom. Any question asked, I knew the answer. I developed a standard *Titanic* talk. When Robert Ballard's *Exploring the Titanic* (Scholastic, 1988) came out, boys literally would pore over the book, staring at the photos, totally engrossed. They were devastated when I had to take the book when I left. Eventually, several schools I'd visited started teaching units on the *Titanic*. Topics we'd discussed, such as the different treatment for women and children when boarding lifeboats, lent themselves to discussion: e.g., although women got on the lifeboats first, they couldn't vote.

By Kathleen Baxter. Reprinted with permission of *School Library Journal* (March 1997), page 121. Kathleen Baxter is Youth Services Supervisor, Anoka County Library, Blaine, MN.

I started wondering about other topics that interest just about everybody. It hit me that booktalking nonfiction, booktalking subjects might open new realms.

Surefire Subjects

Maritime disasters and their recovery are great. *Treasure Hunt: The Sixteen Year Search for the Lost Treasure Ship Atocha* (Holt, 1987), by George Sullivan, fascinates many a would-be treasure hunter. Loaded with gold, the Spanish ship *Atocha* sank in 1622. A man named Mel Fisher spent years in libraries reading everything he could on the topic; his determination resulted in a multimillion-dollar discovery. I saw some of that gold once, and held a 400-year-old coin—in a store right here in Anoka County. I tell the kids that to make stories personal and real.

It's not surprising that personal hygiene issues have a certain appeal. From time to time in my booktalks, I use color transparencies. One comes from page nine of Fiona Macdonald's *A Medieval Castle* (P. Bedrick, 1990), showing a tiny man defecating in a castle privy: the sewage goes straight into the moat. This appalls children. When someone invariably asks about toilet paper, I tell them there was none. Robin Hood had no toilet paper. Heck, there wasn't even any paper! This is a shocker, a great discussion opener. Once, it got a group of disturbed adolescents in a lock-up ward going like mad, and their counselor later told me that he had never seen the kids so interested and engaged before.

Try science experiments. Vicki Cobb's books, *Bet You Can!* (Avon, 1983) and *Bet You Can't!* (Lothrop, 1980), are loaded with them.

I want children to have fun with me, to associate the librarian with good times and positive experiences. If you are not afraid to sing in public, "Mary Had a Stick of Gum" from *And the Green Grass Grows All Around* (Harper, 1992) by Alvin Schwartz will bring down the house. And it took me two years to figure out which famous songs all of the poems in Jack Prelutsky's *Tyrannosaurus Was a Beast* (Greenwillow, 1988) can be sung to. This exercise is hysterically funny. Teachers tell me that students who hate poems learn them by heart—in order to sing them.

Don't we all love optical illusions? *Picture Puzzler* by Kathleen Westray (Ticknor, 1994) has some particularly fine ones. *You Won't Believe Your Eyes* (National Geographic, 1987) by Catherine O'Neill is yet another tantalizing book. Ask kids if they can figure out what is wrong with the picture of the crazily tilted city scene.

Tell them about historical figures whose lives are still irresistibly interesting. Include books about your own area. My hometown is Walnut Grove, MN, site of *On the Banks of Plum Creek, Searching for Laura Ingalls* (Macmillan, 1993) by Kathryn Lasky, which describes a family who flew into Minneapolis, rented a camper, and drove to sites we take for granted because they're here. Children love hearing that other people think the place they live is neat.

Show them one of the many wonderful books about Frederick Douglass and then compare it to Gary Paulsen's *Nightjohn* (Delacorte, 1993). Nightjohn taught other slaves to read, which was illegal. I let kids know that if they want power, one of the best ways to get it is to read.

When I walk into a classroom to talk about books, I am determined to make a positive impression. I keep moving, use both transparencies and books, and show the children how excited I am about what I have read and am learning. If I'm not excited, why should they be? Approaching booktalking with this attitude has made my job a lot more fun and my talks to children very effective. ▲

ANNOTATED BIBLIOGRAPHY

Bauermeister, Erica, and Holly Smith. *Let's Hear It for the Girls: 375 Great Books for Readers 2–14.* Penguin Books, 1997.

    All the books covered were in print as of February 1996. Fiction and nonfiction books featuring female characters of all nationalities provide girls with good role models. Only one illustrated and one chapter book per author is included. The titles are arranged alphabetically in four sections: Picture Books: Ages 2–5; Storybooks: Ages 3–8; Chapter Books: Ages 6–11; Moving On: Age 10 and up.

Berman, Matt. *What Else Should I Read? Guiding Kids to Good Books, Volume 1.* Libraries Unlimited, 1995.

    This book is meant to be shared. It webs 30 children's books in three different ways. The most detailed is the bookmark, with a topic from the main book and then several related books for grades 3 on up. Each book has a number of topic webs, each of which contains a short summary. Indexes include author, title, and topic.

Bodart, Joni. *Booktalk! Booktalking and School Visiting for Young Adult Audiences.* H. W. Wilson, 1980.

    This book contains the author's "ideas about booktalks: what they are, and how to write them, deliver them, and make them work." It highlights how to do booktalks but includes only a few actual talks.

Bodart, Joni Richards. *Booktalking the Award Winners 1993–1994.* H. W. Wilson, 1995.

    This annual series promotes the best of children's and young adult literature. The subject books have all won awards on a national level. A sampling of award books from Britain, Canada, and Australia are included as well. Purely informational books and most picture books are not included unless they qualify as "picture books for all ages." The booktalks are arranged in alphabetical order by title of the book. It includes a list of awards and award-winning titles, bibliography by author, bibliography by age level, selective bibliography by theme and genre, and index to booktalks and booktalkers.

———. *Booktalking the Award Winners: Young Adult Retrospective Volume.* H. W. Wilson, 1996.

    Books that won awards before 1992 are covered here. They must be relevant and of interest to today's teenager. They must also still be in print. The 500 selected titles are for recreational reading. The books were selected from three annual lists: Best Books for Young Adults, Recommended Books for Reluctant Readers (now known as quick picks), and *School Library Journal*'s Best of the Year. The booktalks are arranged in alphabetical order by title of the book. It includes a list of awards and award-winning titles, bibliography by author, selective bibliography by theme and genre, and index to booktalks and booktalkers.

———. *The New Booktalker*. Libraries Unlimited, 1992.

    This book is divided into two sections, "New Titles (1990–92)" and "Older Titles." The initial part of the book includes five articles written by booktalkers. The extensive indexes include author, title, subject, genre, grade-level, paperbound books, and contributors. There are 175 booktalks arranged alphabetically by title.

Cianciolo, Patricia J. *Picture Books for Children*. American Library Association, 1997.

    The purpose of the book is to provide children with "enjoyable, informative, and discriminating literary experiences, foster the habit of reading and initiate an appreciation for and an understanding of the beautiful and creative in the graphic arts." It is to serve as a reference resource and guide for anyone who works with or is around children. The books are grouped in four chapters: "Me and My Family," "Other People," "The World I Live In," and "The Imaginative World." It includes an index and suggested resources.

Cullinan, Bernice E. *Let's Read About: Books They'll Love to Read*. Scholastic, 1993.

    Find the right book to tempt a reluctant reader, picky reader, or a voracious reader. The first couple of chapters deal with creating the right environment, discovering the child's interests, and how to find suitable books. The remaining chapters are divided into preschoolers, five- and six-year-olds, seven- and eight-year-olds, nine- and ten-year-olds, and eleven- and twelve-year-olds. Books are listed alphabetically in each chapter by interest categories.

Gillespie, John T., and Corinne J. Naden. *Juniorplots 4: A Book Talk Guide for Use with Readers Ages 12–16*. R. R. Bowker, 1993.

    This edition is part of a booktalking series. New editions will appear every five years. *Seniorplots (Ages 15–18)*, *Introducing Bookplots 3 (Ages 8–12)*, and *Primaryplots (Ages 4–8)* are companion books. Eighty-one bookplots are divided by subjects: teenage life and concerns, adventure and mystery, science fiction and fantasy, historical fiction, sports fact and fiction, biography and true adventure, guidance and health, and the world around us. Each detailed title is analyzed under four headings: plot summary, thematic and booktalks materials, related books, and book review sources.

McElmeel, Sharron L. *Educator's Companion to Children's Literature. Volume I*. Libraries Unlimited, 1995.

———. *Educator's Companion to Children's Literature. Volume II*. Libraries Unlimited, 1996.

    These two volumes could be used in a variety of ways. They are arranged by genre with a discussion of the topic, particular books, and representative authors. Included is a list of books with summaries to read aloud and books for children to explore further. Indexes include author, title, and subject entries.

———. *Great New Nonfiction Reads.* Libraries Unlimited, 1995.

> The books are arranged topically in chapter two. Under each topic there is one book to be shared with others and connections to other similar books for further reading. More than 120 topics and 500 suggested reading books are included. Chapter 3 focuses on biographies. Indexes include author, title, illustrator, and subject.

———. *The Latest and Greatest Read-Alouds.* Libraries Unlimited, 1994.

> The intent of this book is to provide a list of quality books published after 1988 for parents and teachers. There are three main chapters: "Reading Early—Reading Often," "The Next Step," and "Going Beyond Reading Aloud." An author, illustrator, title, and subject index is included.

Odean, Kathleen. *Great Books for Boys: More Than 600 Books for Boys.* Ballantine Books, 1998.

> Books were carefully chosen for boys, to show them that reading is fun and that it is okay to like to read. Strong male characters have feelings, compassion, and affection for others. These books will appeal to the interests of boys. This companion book is set up the same way as *Great Books for Girls*.

———. *Great Books for Girls: More Than 600 Books to Inspire Today's Girls and Tomorrow's Women.* Ballantine Books, 1997.

> Included are 600 titles about girls who defy the stereotypes of women. The girls and women solve their own problems and face challenges with bravery, athleticism, and independence. The six main chapters are: "Picture-Story Books," "Folktales," "Books for Beginning Readers," "Books for Middle Readers," "Books for Older Readers," and "Resources for Parents." This annotated reference would be useful for the very young through young adult.

Spirt, Diana L. *Introducing Bookplots 3: A Book Talk Guide for Use with Readers Ages 8–12.* R. R. Bowker, 1988.

> Provides reading guidance, booktalks, and titles of books to read aloud for middle school readers. Plot summaries introduce 81 featured books, followed by thematic analysis, discussion, and related materials. This is not a list of best books but rather books useful in reading guidance and booktalking, based on middle school developmental goals.

Trelease, Jim. *Hey! Listen to This: Stories to Read Aloud.* Viking, 1992.

> These favorite stories are suitable for children in kindergarten through fourth grade. Shorter tales are at the beginning of the book, gradually working toward longer, more complicated tales near the end. Many of the stories are chapters from books and could be used for booktalking. Background information about the author and the story makes for interesting reading and sharing.

———. *The New Read-Aloud Handbook.* Penguin Books, 1989.

    Jim Trelease started reading to his children; he did it because his father had read to him. He knew there was intrinsic value in it but he didn't have the research, at that time, to support his feelings. We can all make a difference, by reading aloud to children and by introducing them to books that will interest them. The handbook for reading aloud is contained in the first nine chapters. The second half of the book consists of 300 annotated titles, with additional books of interest at various listening and reading levels.

WEB SITE

Booktalks—Quick and Simple
http://www.concord.k12.nh.us/schools/rundlett/booktalks

Chapter 15

Conclusion

ODDS AND ENDS

How about varying the meeting format? Ask local experts to make a presentation: public librarian, storyteller, local bookstore owner, or an educator. Invite children to attend a session with their parents to discuss the current topic. Invite a local author, illustrator, or poet to attend. Vary the meeting time, have a "bring-a-friend" meeting—whatever will boost attendance and keep members active.

Can you add materials and canvass your members? Once the club has started, stay aware of possible articles of interest in magazines and newspapers. Ask your club members to watch also. Add articles to this book, so that you keep current and aware of publishing trends. Survey the parents and club members both formally and informally and see what their interests and concerns are. Topics included in this book are a direct response to the needs and concerns of the members of our own book club.

QUESTIONNAIRE

1. Did you find the meetings useful? Do you feel more knowledgeable about the books available for your child?

   _____

   _____

2. Were you satisfied with the format of the meetings?

   _____

   _____

3. Which topic was most interesting?

   _____

4. Were the handouts helpful?

   _____

5. How can we generate more interest within our school community?

   _____

   _____

   _____

6. Were you satisfied with the frequency of the meetings?

   _____

   _____

7. Would you be willing to join us next year?

   _____

8. Please list any topics you would like to see discussed in future meetings.

   _____

   _____

   _____

   _____

9. General comments:

   _____

   _____

   _____

   _____

Thank you!

From *More Reading Connections.* © 1999. Knowles/Smith. Libraries Unlimited. (800) 237-6124.

15 ▲ CONCLUSION

REFERENCE LIST FOR TEACHERS AND PARENTS

Albyn, Carole Lisa, and Lois Sinaiko Webb. *The Multicultural Cookbook for Students*. Oryx Press, 1993.

Barstow, Barbara, and Judith Riggle. *Beyond Picture Books: A Guide to First Readers*. R. R. Bowker, 1995.

Bauer, Caroline Feller. *Celebrations: Read-Aloud Holiday and Theme Book Programs*. H. W. Wilson, 1985.

Benedict, Susan, and Lenore Carlisle. *Beyond Words: Picture Books for Older Readers and Writers*. Heinemann, 1992.

Berman, Matt. *What Else Should I Read? Guiding Kids to Good Books, Volume 1*. Libraries Unlimited, 1995.

Bernhardt, Edythe. *ABC's of Thinking with Caldecott Books*. Book Lures, 1988.

Blass, Rosanne, and Nancy E. Allen Jurenka. *Responding to Literature, Activities for Grades 6, 7, 8*. Teacher Ideas Press, 1991.

Bodart, Joni. *Booktalk! Booktalking and School Visiting for Young Adult Audiences*. H. W. Wilson, 1980.

Borba, Michele, and Dan Ungaro. *Bookends: Activities, Centers, Contracts, and Ideas Galore to Enhance Children's Literature*. Good Apple, 1982.

Buhler, Cheryl, Nolan Fossum, and Paula Spence. *An Annotated Bibliography of Thematic Literature*. Teacher Created Materials, 1993.

Carroll, Joyce Armstrong. *Poetry Book: Reading, Writing, Listening, Speaking, Viewing, and Thinking*. Teacher Ideas Press, 1995.

Cummings, Renee. *Multicultural Literature-Based Reading*. Instructional Fair, 1993.

Devers, William, and James Cipielewski. *Every Teacher's Thematic Booklist*. Scholastic Professional, 1993.

Donavin, Denise Perry, ed. *American Library Association: Best of the Best for Children*. Random House, 1992.

Dreyer, Sharon Spredemann. *The Bookfinder: When Kids Need Books*. American Guidance Service, 1985.

Elkind, David. *The Hurried Child*. Addison-Wesley, 1985.

Foerstel, Herbert N. *Banned in the U.S.A.: A Reference Guide to Book Censorship in Schools and Public Libraries*. Greenwood, 1994.

Fredericks, Anthony D. *Involving Parents Through Children's Literature—Grades 5-6*. Teacher Ideas Press, 1993.

Freeman, Judy. *Books Kids Will Sit Still For: A Guide to Using Children's Literature for Librarians, Teachers, and Parents*. Alleyside Press, 1984.

Gillespie, John T., and Corrine J. Naden. *Best Books for Children Preschool Through Grade 6*. R. R. Bowker, 1994.

———. *Juniorplots 4: A Book Talk Guide for Use with Readers Ages 12–16*. R. R. Bowker, 1992.

Huck, Charlotte S., Susan Hepler, and Janet Hickman. *Children's Literature in the Elementary School*. Harcourt Brace College, 1993.

Huck, Charlotte S., Susan Hepler, Janet Hickman, and B. Z. Kiefer. *Children's Literature in the Elementary School*. Brown and Benchmark, 1997.

Knowles, Elizabeth, and Martha Smith. *The Reading Connection: Bringing Parents, Teachers, and Librarians Together*. Libraries Unlimited, 1997.

Kollar, Judith L. *An Annotated Bibliography of Multicultural Literature*. Teacher Created Materials, 1993.

Lima, Carolyn W., and John A. *A to Zoo: Subject Access to Children's Picture Books*. R. R. Bowker, 1993.

Lipson, Eden Ross. *The New York Times Parent's Guide to the Best Books for Children*. Times Books, 1988.

MacDonald, Margaret Read. *Booksharing: 101 Programs to Use with Preschoolers*. Library Professional Publications, 1988.

McArthur, Janice, and Barbara McGuire. *Using Literature Genres, Grades 4–6*. Frank Schaffer, 1995.

McElmeel, Sharron L. *An Author a Month (for Pennies)*. Libraries Unlimited, 1988.

———. *Bookpeople: A First Album*. Teacher Ideas Press, 1990.

———. *Great New Nonfiction Reads*. Libraries Unlimited, 1995.

———. *The Latest and Greatest Read-Alouds*. Libraries Unlimited, 1994.

———. *McElmeel Booknotes: Literature Across the Curriculum*. Teacher Ideas Press, 1993.

Miller-Lachmann, Lyn. *Our Family, Our Friends, Our World: An Annotated Guide to Significant Multicultural Books for Children and Teenagers*. R. R. Bowker, 1992.

Odean, Kathleen. *Great Books for Boys*. Ballantine Books, 1998.

———. *Great Books for Girls*. Ballantine Books, 1997.

Paulin, Mary Ann. *Creative Uses of Children's Literature*. Library Professional Publications, 1982.

Polette, Nancy. *Teaching Critical Reading with Children's Literature*. Book Lures, 1988.

Polkingharn, Anne T., and Catherine Toohey. *More Creative Encounters: Activities to Expand Children's Responses to Literature*. Libraries Unlimited, 1988.

Price, Anne, and Juliette Yaakov. *Middle and Junior High School Library Catalog*. H. W. Wilson, 1995.

Raines, Shirley C., and Robert J. Candy. *More Story S-T-R-E-T-C-H-E-R-S: More Activities to Expand Children's Favorite Books*. Gryphon House, 1991.

Reuter, Janet. *Creative Teaching Through Picture Books for Middle School Students*. Frank Schaffer, 1993.

Rochman, Hazel. *Against Borders*. American Library Association, 1993.

Ryan, Connie. *Hooked on Books, A Genre-Based Guide for 30 Adolescent Books.* Frank Schaffer, 1993.

Schurr, Sandra, and Imogene Forte. *Using Favorite Picture Books to Stimulate Discussion and Encourage Critical Thinking.* Incentive, 1995.

Sitarz, Paula Gaj. *More Picture Book Story Hours from Parties to Pets.* Libraries Unlimited, 1990.

———. *Picture Book Story Hours from Birthdays to Bears.* Libraries Unlimited, 1987.

Spirt, Diana L. *Introducing Bookplots 3: A Book Talk Guide for Use with Readers Ages 8–12.* R. R. Bowker, 1988.

Stangl, Jean. *Story Sparklers (Starters and Extenders for 66 Noted Children's Picture Books).* T. S. Denison, 1991.

Trelease, Jim. *Hey! Listen to This: Stories to Read-Aloud.* Viking, 1992.

———. *The New Read-Aloud Handbook: Including a Giant Treasury of Great Read-Aloud Books.* Penguin Books, 1989.

———. *Read All About It! Great Read-Aloud Stories, Poems, and Newspaper Pieces for Preteens and Teens.* Penguin Books, 1993.

Vick, Diane. *Favorite Authors of Young Adult Fiction.* Frank Schaffer, 1995.

Wendelin, Karla Hawkins, and M. Jean Greenlaw. *Storybook Classrooms: Using Children's Literature in the Learning Center.* Humanics, 1986.

Woolman, Bertha, and Patricia Litsey. *The Newbery Award Winners: The Books and Their Authors.* T. S. Denison, 1992.

Yaakov, Juliette, ed. *Children's Catalog.* H. W. Wilson, 1991.